CAMBRIDGE SCHOOL

Shakespeare

Hamlet

Edited by Richard Andrews and Rex Gibson

Series Editor: Rex Gibson
Director, Shakespeare and Schools Project

CAMBRIDGE
UNIVERSITY PRESS

PUBLISHED BY THE PRESS SYNDICATE OF THE UNIVERSITY OF CAMBRIDGE
The Pitt Building, Trumpington Street, Cambridge CB2 1RP, United Kingdom

CAMBRIDGE UNIVERSITY PRESS
The Edinburgh Building, Cambridge CB2 2RU, United Kingdom
40 West 20th Street, New York, NY 10011–4211, USA
10 Stamford Road, Oakleigh, Melbourne 3166, Australia

First published 1994
Fifth printing 1998

Printed in the United Kingdom at the University Press, Cambridge

A catalogue record for this book is available from the British Library

Library of Congress Cataloguing in Publication data applied for

ISBN 0 521 43494 7 paperback

Prepared for publication by Stenton Associates
Designed by Richard Morris, Stonesfield Design
Picture research by Callie Kendall
Cover illustration by Sue Windett

Thanks are due to the following for permission to reproduce photographs:

10, 202, Morris Newcombe; 26, 247*tl*, Rex Gibson; 36, 155*b*, 186, Clive Barda/Performing
Arts Library; 42, 172, 236, courtesy of Columbia Tristar Home Video/photo by BFI; 57,
222, Shakespeare Centre Library, Stratford-upon-Avon: Joe Cocks Studio Collection; 58,
99*t*, 118, 138, 155*t*, 162, 199, 230, 247*bl*, 251*br*, 255, 267*b*, Donald Cooper/Photostage; 66,
photograph by Anthony Crickmay/from the collections of the Theatre Museum, by
courtesy of the Trustees of the Victoria & Albert Museum; 84, still from the film 'Hamlet'
by courtesy of the Rank Organisation Plc/photo by BFI; 99*b*, 208, 247*br*, 251*tl*, Shakespeare
Centre Library, Stratford-upon-Avon; 100, courtesy of Columbia Pictures, © 1969
Columbia Pictures Industries Inc. All rights reserved/photo by BFI; 146, 251*tr*, Raymond
Mander & Joe Mitchenson Theatre Collection; 166, 267*t*, Sovexport Film/photo by BFI;
180, Shakespeare Centre Library, Stratford-upon-Avon: Tom Holte Theatre Photographic
Collection; 196, Tate Gallery, London; 247*tr*, Zoë Dominic/Dominic Photography;
251*bl*, Douglas Jeffery; 257, from *The Intaglio Prints of Albrecht Dürer*, ed. Walter L.
Strauss, 1977/by permission of the Syndics of the Cambridge University Library.

Contents

List of characters   1

Hamlet   3

The world of Elsinore   242

The character of Hamlet   246

Revenge Tragedy   252

Madness and melancholia   256

Sin and salvation   258

The language of *Hamlet*   260

Theatre and acting in *Hamlet*   264

William Shakespeare   268

Cambridge School Shakespeare

This edition of *Hamlet* is part of the *Cambridge School Shakespeare* series. Like every other play in the series, it has been specially prepared to help all students in schools and colleges.

This *Hamlet* aims to be different from other editions of the play. It invites you to bring the play to life in your classroom, hall or drama studio through enjoyable activities that will increase your understanding. Actors have created their different interpretations of the play over the centuries. Similarly, you are encouraged to make up your own mind about *Hamlet*, rather than having someone else's interpretation handed down to you.

Cambridge School Shakespeare does not offer you a cut-down or simplified version of the play. This is Shakespeare's language, filled with imaginative possibilities. You will find on every left-hand page: a summary of the action, an explanation of unfamiliar words, a choice of activities on Shakespeare's language, characters and stories.

Between each act and in the pages at the end of the play, you will find notes, illustrations and activities. This will help to increase your understanding of the whole play.

There are a large number of activities to give you the widest choice to suit your own particular needs. Please don't think you have to do every one. Choose the activities that will help you most.

This edition will be of value to you whether you are studying for an examination, reading for pleasure, or thinking of putting on the play to entertain others. You can work on the activities on your own or in groups. Many of the activities suggest a particular group size, but don't be afraid to make up larger or smaller groups to suit your own purposes.

Although you are invited to treat *Hamlet* as a play, you don't need special dramatic or theatrical skills to do the activities. By choosing your activities, and by exploring and experimenting, you can make your own interpretations of Shakespeare's language, characters and stories. Whatever you do, remember that Shakespeare wrote his plays to be acted, watched and enjoyed.

Rex Gibson

This edition of *Hamlet* uses the text of the play established by Philip Edwards in *The New Cambridge Shakespeare*.

List of characters

The Royal House of Denmark

HAMLET Prince of Denmark
CLAUDIUS King of Denmark, Hamlet's uncle
GERTRUDE Queen of Denmark, Hamlet's mother
GHOST of King Hamlet, Hamlet's father

The Court of Denmark

POLONIUS Counsellor to the king
OPHELIA his daughter
LAERTES his son
REYNALDO his servant

OSRIC
LORDS
GENTLEMAN
} Courtiers

MESSENGER and ATTENDANTS

VOLTEMAND
CORNELIUS
} Ambassadors to Norway

MARCELLUS
BARNARDO
FRANCISCO
} Officers of the Watch

SOLDIERS and GUARDS

Former fellow students of Hamlet

HORATIO Hamlet's friend
ROSENCRANTZ
GUILDENSTERN
} Sent for by Claudius to inform on Hamlet

Norway

FORTINBRAS Prince of Norway   CAPTAIN in Fortinbras's army

Other characters in the play

First PLAYER
Other players
} actors visiting Elsinore

English AMBASSADORS
SAILORS

CLOWN gravedigger and sexton
SECOND CLOWN his assistant
PRIEST at Ophelia's funeral

The action of the play is set in and around
the Danish royal palace at Elsinore.

1

Midnight. Francisco is on sentry duty. Barnardo comes to relieve him.
Horatio and Marcellus arrive to join Barnardo.

---

1 Setting the scene (in groups of four)

Every production of *Hamlet* aims to make the opening moments of the play as gripping and dramatic as possible. The actors know they must create a tense, urgent and ominous atmosphere using Shakespeare's words.

Work out how you would stage these opening nineteen lines. Talk together first about the questions below, then prepare and act out a version that will have maximum dramatic effect.

a What will be the first thing the audience sees?

b Would you have Francisco on sentry duty, patrolling the stage, before the first members of the audience enter?

c Why does Barnardo, the newcomer, challenge Francisco, contrary to military practice? (Francisco should challenge him.)

d How would you show the audience that the night is bitterly cold?

e What are the soldiers wearing? Sketch their costumes.

f What accent or speech-style would you advise for each character?

g Francisco never appears again. Would you wish to make him a memorable character? If so, how?

h It is just after midnight, dark but star-lit. How will you ensure the audience sees clearly what you want them to see?

i In Shakespeare's time, the play was staged in broad daylight. Identify all the words or phrases that help create the impression of night and darkness.

---

unfold identify
rivals partners

liegemen to the Dane loyal
followers of the Danish king

Hamlet, Prince of Denmark

ACT 1   SCENE 1
A gun platform on the battlements of Elsinore Castle

Enter BARNARDO *and* FRANCISCO, *two sentinels*

BARNARDO Who's there?

FRANCISCO Nay answer me. Stand and unfold yourself.

BARNARDO Long live the king!

FRANCISCO Barnardo?

BARNARDO He.   5

FRANCISCO You come most carefully upon your hour.

BARNARDO 'Tis now struck twelve, get thee to bed Francisco.

FRANCISCO For this relief much thanks, 'tis bitter cold
      And I am sick at heart.

BARNARDO Have you had quiet guard?

FRANCISCO   Not a mouse stirring.   10

BARNARDO Well, good night.
      If you do meet Horatio and Marcellus,
      The rivals of my watch, bid them make haste.

FRANCISCO I think I hear them.

Enter HORATIO *and* MARCELLUS

                       Stand ho! Who is there?

HORATIO Friends to this ground.

MARCELLUS   And liegemen to the Dane.   15

FRANCISCO Give you good night.

MARCELLUS   Oh farewell honest soldier,
      Who hath relieved you?

FRANCISCO   Barnardo hath my place.
      Give you good night.   *Exit Francisco*

MARCELLUS   Holla, Barnardo!

BARNARDO   Say,
      What, is Horatio there?

HORATIO   A piece of him.

Marcellus reports that he and Barnardo have seen the Ghost twice. Horatio doesn't believe them, but is struck with fear and amazement when the Ghost of Hamlet's father appears.

1 From disbelief to . . .? (in pairs)

Horatio doesn't believe Marcellus's story but then sees the Ghost with his own eyes. He speaks five times on the opposite page. Talk together about the tone of his voice each time he speaks. Try speaking the lines in an appropriate style. What does the range of emotions suggest to you about Horatio's character?

2 'Enter GHOST' (in groups of four)

The entry of the Ghost of Hamlet's father is a thrilling moment in the theatre. Each new production attempts to ensure that the entry is as electrifying and memorable as possible. Choose one or more of the following:

a What does the Ghost look like? Horatio gives a clue in lines 47–9.

b Talk together about how the Ghost should enter. Slowly? Suddenly? From which direction? Decide whether he makes any kind of gesture, and if you would use any accompanying sound effects. How would he leave the stage?

c Sometimes the bell strikes once at the Ghost's appearance. Give reasons why you would or would not have it strike in your production.

d In some productions the Ghost does not physically appear. The audience has to imagine his presence through lighting, sound and the reactions of the other characters. Talk together about how effective you think this style of presenting the Ghost might be.

Touching concerning
approve our eyes believe our story
assail your ears tell you forcefully
pole pole star (North star)
scholar student (ghosts were
  believed to speak Latin)

harrows tortures, tears
usurp'st wrongfully seizes
buried Denmark the dead King
  Hamlet
charge order

BARNARDO Welcome Horatio, welcome good Marcellus.   20
MARCELLUS What, has this thing appeared again tonight?
BARNARDO I have seen nothing.
MARCELLUS Horatio says 'tis but our fantasy,
          And will not let belief take hold of him
          Touching this dreaded sight, twice seen of us.   25
          Therefore I have entreated him along
          With us to watch the minutes of this night,
          That if again this apparition come
          He may approve our eyes, and speak to it.
HORATIO Tush, tush, 'twill not appear.
BARNARDO   Sit down awhile,   30
          And let us once again assail your ears,
          That are so fortified against our story,
          What we two nights have seen.
HORATIO   Well, sit we down,
          And let us hear Barnardo speak of this.
BARNARDO Last night of all,   35
          When yond same star that's westward from the pole
          Had made his course t'illume that part of heaven
          Where now it burns, Marcellus and myself,
          The bell then beating one –

Enter GHOST

MARCELLUS Peace, break thee off. Look where it comes again.   40
BARNARDO In the same figure, like the king that's dead.
MARCELLUS Thou art a scholar, speak to it Horatio.
BARNARDO Looks a not like the king? Mark it Horatio.
HORATIO Most like. It harrows me with fear and wonder.
BARNARDO It would be spoke to.
MARCELLUS   Question it Horatio.   45
HORATIO What art thou that usurp'st this time of night,
          Together with that fair and warlike form
          In which the majesty of buried Denmark
          Did sometimes march? By heaven I charge thee speak.
MARCELLUS It is offended.
BARNARDO   See, it stalks away.   50
HORATIO Stay! Speak, speak, I charge thee speak!

Exit Ghost

Horatio agrees that the Ghost is the exact image of the dead King Hamlet. He thinks it foretells disasters for Denmark. Horatio begins to explain why there are so many preparations for war.

1 Imaginative truth (in small groups)

There is much disagreement about the meaning of lines 62–3. Some believe they tell of Denmark's king defeating the Polish army ('Polacks') in a battle on the ice ('sledded' = on sledges). Others think they mean that the king, in an angry discussion ('parle') with the Norwegians, struck his battle axe (poleaxe) on the ice like a sledge hammer (= 'sledded'). In some editions of the play, the word is printed as 'polax'.

Work out two tableaux (frozen pictures) to show each interpretation. Which version do you think is more imaginative and dramatic?

2 Denmark prepares for war

Marcellus describes Denmark feverishly preparing for war (lines 70–8). Guards are mounted everywhere. Cannons are rolling off the production line daily. Weapons are bought in foreign countries and imported ('foreign mart for implements of war'). Ships are being built by forced labour ('impress'), working night and day.

Make up four further lines listing other war preparations that Marcellus might have described. Write them in the same style as lines 71–8 to catch the frantic military activity as Denmark arms for war.

3 One sentence! (in pairs)

Horatio begins his story with a sentence of sixteen lines (lines 80–95) telling how Hamlet's father killed King Fortinbras of Norway. Such a long sentence might suggest something about Horatio's character. Speak the sentence to your partner in what you feel is an appropriate style for Horatio.

---

sensible and true avouch evidence
jump exactly
martial stalk military stride
In what particular . . . work how to think about it
gross and scope general view

bodes . . . state is ominous for us and Denmark
toward in preparation
emulate jealous
sealed compact treaty
law and heraldy laws of chivalry

MARCELLUS 'Tis gone and will not answer.
BARNARDO How now Horatio? you tremble and look pale.
        Is not this something more than fantasy?
        What think you on't?   55
HORATIO Before my God, I might not this believe
        Without the sensible and true avouch
        Of mine own eyes.
MARCELLUS   Is it not like the king?
HORATIO As thou art to thyself.
        Such was the very armour he had on   60
        When he th'ambitious Norway combated;
        So frowned he once, when in an angry parle
        He smote the sledded Polacks on the ice.
        'Tis strange.
MARCELLUS Thus twice before, and jump at this dead hour,   65
        With martial stalk hath he gone by our watch.
HORATIO In what particular thought to work I know not,
        But in the gross and scope of mine opinion
        This bodes some strange eruption to our state.
MARCELLUS Good now sit down, and tell me he that knows,
        Why this same strict and most observant watch
        So nightly toils the subject of the land,
        And why such daily cast of brazen cannon,
        And foreign mart for implements of war,
        Why such impress of shipwrights, whose sore task   75
        Does not divide the Sunday from the week.
        What might be toward, that this sweaty haste
        Doth make the night joint-labourer with the day?
        Who is't that can inform me?
HORATIO   That can I –
        At least the whisper goes so. Our last king,   80
        Whose image even but now appeared to us,
        Was as you know by Fortinbras of Norway,
        Thereto pricked on by a most emulate pride,
        Dared to the combat; in which our valiant Hamlet –
        For so this side of our known world esteemed him –   85
        Did slay this Fortinbras; who by a sealed compact,
        Well ratified by law and heraldy,
        Did forfeit (with his life) all those his lands
        Which he stood seized of, to the conqueror;

[handwritten marginal note: strange things going on in Denmark]

7

Horatio tells that young Fortinbras intends to regain the lands his father lost when killed by King Hamlet. The Ghost's appearance predicts violence, just as Caesar's death was foretold by ominous events.

1 Horatio's story (in groups of six to eight)

In lines 80–107 Horatio gives his explanation of why Denmark is preparing for war. The King of Norway (old Fortinbras) had dared King Hamlet of Denmark (Hamlet's father) to personal combat. Both men wagered ('gaged') large possessions of land on the outcome of the duel. Hamlet killed Fortinbras and so took over his lands. Now young Fortinbras, with an army of mercenaries ('landless resolutes'), seeks to recover his father's lost lands. The Danes are hastily preparing to defend themselves against the imminent invasion.

Bring Horatio's story vividly to life! One person narrates, the others enact each episode. Lines 80–107 contain over twenty-five separate actions that could be shown. (For example, 'sharked up' is a vivid image of a shark feeding indiscriminately.)

2 Predicting disasters

'A mote it is to trouble the mind's eye' says Horatio (line 112): the appearance of the Ghost is an irritant (mote) to the imagination. It is an omen or augury of disasters that lie ahead. Shakespeare had written *Julius Caesar* shortly before *Hamlet*. The recollection of the ominous signs that preceded the death of Caesar was fresh in his mind. Horatio lists the portents: the living dead; comets; bloody rain; sunspots; an eclipse of the moon ('the moist star').

Is Horatio superstitious? He at first disbelieved the supernatural events that Marcellus had described. Yet now he seems to believe in omens and auguries. Try two ways of speaking the lines. First, straightforwardly as obvious truth. Then sceptically, showing you don't really believe what you say.

---

moiety competent equal amount
comart . . . design treaty
unimprovèd mettle untested
  bravery
a stomach in't courage in it
terms compulsatory forced
  agreement

post-haste and romage frantic
  activity and turmoil
Neptune's empire the sea
precurse forewarning of doom
  (pre-curse)
harbingers messengers
climatures territories

Against the which a moiety competent   90
Was gagèd by our king, which had returned
To the inheritance of Fortinbras
Had he been vanquisher; as by the same comart
And carriage of the article design,
His fell to Hamlet. Now sir, young Fortinbras,   95
Of unimprovèd mettle hot and full,
Hath in the skirts of Norway here and there
Sharked up a list of landless resolutes
For food and diet to some enterprise
That hath a stomach in't; which is no other,   100
As it doth well appear unto our state,
But to recover of us by strong hand
And terms compulsatory those foresaid lands
So by his father lost. And this, I take it,
Is the main motive of our preparations,   105
The source of this our watch, and the chief head
Of this post-haste and romage in the land.
[BARNARDO I think it be no other but e'en so.
Well may it sort that this portentous figure
Comes armèd through our watch so like the king   110
That was and is the question of these wars.
HORATIO A mote it is to trouble the mind's eye.
In the most high and palmy state of Rome,
A little ere the mightiest Julius fell,
The graves stood tenantless and the sheeted dead   115
Did squeak and gibber in the Roman streets;
As stars with trains of fire, and dews of blood,
Disasters in the sun; and the moist star,
Upon whose influence Neptune's empire stands,
Was sick almost to doomsday with eclipse.   120
And even the like precurse of feared events,
As harbingers preceding still the fates
And prologue to the omen coming on,
Have heaven and earth together demonstrated
Unto our climatures and countrymen.]   125

Horatio demands of the reappearing Ghost to say why it comes. The cock crows and the Ghost vanishes without reply. Horatio says it behaved like a criminal summoned to justice.

'Lo where it comes again!' Royal Shakespeare Company, 1993.

1 Questioning the Ghost

Horatio refers to three popular superstitions as reasons for the Ghost's appearance: it seeks someone whose action will enable it to rest in peace (lines 130–1); it knows of a future disaster in store for Denmark (lines 133–4); it seeks buried treasure, unjustly acquired ('extorted') when alive (lines 136–7).

Work out how you would stage Horatio's questioning of the Ghost (lines 126–42). Advise the two actors what they should do, line by line.

privy to knowledgeable about
uphoarded hoarded, hidden
partisan pike, long-handled spear
invulnerable impossible to hurt
vain blows futile attempts to hit
extravagant and erring wandering

hies . . . confine hurries to his prison (cell, place of confinement)
present object apparition (Ghost)
probation proof

Enter GHOST

But soft, behold, lo where it comes again!
I'll cross it though it blast me. Stay, illusion.
It spreads his arms
If thou hast any sound or use of voice,
Speak to me.
If there be any good thing to be done   130
That may to thee do ease, and grace to me,
Speak to me.
If thou art privy to thy country's fate,
Which happily foreknowing may avoid,
Oh speak.   135
Or if thou hast uphoarded in thy life
Extorted treasure in the womb of earth,
For which they say you spirits oft walk in death,   *The cock crows*
Speak of it. Stay and speak! Stop it Marcellus.
MARCELLUS Shall I strike at it with my partisan?   140
HORATIO Do if it will not stand.
BARNARDO   'Tis here.
HORATIO   'Tis here.
MARCELLUS 'Tis gone.
                                                 Exit Ghost
We do it wrong being so majestical
To offer it the show of violence,
For it is as the air invulnerable,   145
And our vain blows malicious mockery.
BARNARDO It was about to speak when the cock crew.
HORATIO And then it started like a guilty thing
Upon a fearful summons. I have heard,
The cock, that is the trumpet to the morn,   150
Doth with his lofty and shrill-sounding throat
Awake the god of day; and at his warning,
Whether in sea or fire, in earth or air,
Th'extravagant and erring spirit hies
To his confine. And of the truth herein   155
This present object made probation.

Marcellus claims that the cockerel crows all night long at Christmas, a time when no harm can be done. Horatio seems to agree. He proposes that they tell Hamlet about the Ghost.

1 Blunt soldier or awe-struck poet? (in pairs)

Marcellus is a soldier. He may be dressed in armour for his night's vigil, but his words are filled with wonderment. They do not seem to be the words of a no-nonsense military man. Experiment with ways of speaking lines 156–64. For example: full of religious awe; bluntly and factually; conspiratorially, as a great secret; or sceptically (showing you disbelieve what you say).

Decide how you think the lines should be spoken, and why you think Shakespeare put this eloquent poetry into the mouth of Marcellus.

2 Daybreak after darkness (in small groups)

Dawn is breaking. The mood of fear, tension and apprehension gives way to a different emotional climate. Talk together about non-verbal ways in which the change of mood could be conveyed in the theatre (perhaps through lighting, sound or posture).

3 Horatio: believer or sceptic?

If you were directing the play, would you advise Horatio to emphasise 'in part' at line 165? Give reasons for your advice.

4 Personification

Horatio likens daybreak to a traveller dressed in a reddish coloured cloak (lines 166–7). This is a personification, describing the red glow that spreads across the horizon at dawn. You will find other personifications as you read through the play.

---

ever 'gainst always before (or, in expectation of)
our Saviour Jesus Christ
strike have an evil influence

takes bewitches, does harm
hallowed holy
russet mantle reddish-coloured cloak

MARCELLUS It faded on the crowing of the cock.
        Some say that ever 'gainst that season comes
        Wherein our Saviour's birth is celebrated,
        This bird of dawning singeth all night long,   160
        And then, they say, no spirit dare stir abroad,
        The nights are wholesome, then no planets strike,
        No fairy takes, nor witch hath power to charm,
        So hallowed and so gracious is that time.
HORATIO So have I heard, and do in part believe it.   165
        But look, the morn in russet mantle clad
        Walks o'er the dew of yon high eastward hill.
        Break we our watch up, and by my advice
        Let us impart what we have seen tonight
        Unto young Hamlet, for upon my life   170
        This spirit, dumb to us, will speak to him.
        Do you consent we shall acquaint him with it,
        As needful in our loves, fitting our duty?
MARCELLUS Let's do't I pray, and I this morning know
        Where we shall find him most conveniently.   175

                                        Exeunt

Claudius announces to the court that, although he grieves for his dead brother, he has, with joy, married Gertrude. He turns his attention to the political situation: Fortinbras is threatening the state.

1 The king enters (in large groups)

King Hamlet has only recently died. Claudius, his brother, has become King of Denmark and has married Gertrude. So Claudius now possesses his dead brother's throne and his wife. Try out different ways of staging the entry of Claudius and his court (for example, have Claudius loved and respected by his court). Then try a version in which Claudius is feared, and his courtiers suspect he may become a tyrant. Stage other possibilities to find a version you prefer.

2 What kind of king? (in small groups)

Claudius explains his marriage to his sister-in-law Gertrude so soon after her first husband's death (lines 1–16). He then turns to political affairs (lines 17–39). Experiment with different styles of speaking Claudius's opening speech to his court:

a in confident control of his personal and public life
b uneasy and insecure, aware that dangerous questions may be asked
c drunk, but trying to be 'kingly', continually prompted by Polonius
d uneasy about his early marriage, fully confident in state affairs
e honest and sincere
f devious and crafty
g some other way.

Work out appropriate gestures, expressions and movements to accompany each different style of speaking. Think particularly about how he behaves towards Gertrude (for example, does he embrace her?). Then decide how you would advise the actor playing Claudius to deliver lines 1–39 to express your view of his character.

---

green young, fresh
us befitted was appropriate
imperial jointress joint ruler of the state
auspicious promising happiness
dirge sad song
dole sadness

barred rejected, disregarded
Holding . . . worth underestimating us
Colleaguèd linked
Importing concerning
bands of law legally binding agreements

ACT 1 SCENE 2
The Great Hall of Elsinore Castle

Trumpet call   Enter CLAUDIUS *King of Denmark,* GERTRUDE *the queen,* HAMLET, POLONIUS, LAERTES, OPHELIA, VOLTEMAND, CORNELIUS, LORDS *attendant*

CLAUDIUS Though yet of Hamlet our dear brother's death
The memory be green, and that it us befitted
To bear our hearts in grief, and our whole kingdom
To be contracted in one brow of woe,
Yet so far hath discretion fought with nature   5
That we with wisest sorrow think on him,
Together with remembrance of ourselves.
Therefore our sometime sister, now our queen,
Th'imperial jointress to this warlike state,
Have we, as 'twere with a defeated joy,   10
With one auspicious and one dropping eye,
With mirth in funeral and with dirge in marriage,
In equal scale weighing delight and dole,
Taken to wife; nor have we herein barred
Your better wisdoms, which have freely gone   15
With this affair along – for all, our thanks.
Now follows that you know: young Fortinbras,
Holding a weak supposal of our worth,
Or thinking by our late dear brother's death
Our state to be disjoint and out of frame,   20
Colleaguèd with this dream of his advantage,
He hath not failed to pester us with message
Importing the surrender of those lands
Lost by his father, with all bands of law,
To our most valiant brother. So much for him.   25
Now for ourself and for this time of meeting
Thus much the business is: we have here writ
To Norway, uncle of young Fortinbras,

15

Claudius sends messengers to the King of Norway to prevent Fortinbras from attacking Denmark. He asks Laertes to state his request. Laertes wishes to return to France. Polonius says he has reluctantly agreed.

1 Is it a sneer?

Claudius describes the King of Norway as 'impotent and bed-rid' (line 29). Suggest ways of speaking the line that might give the audience an insight into Claudius's character (for example, does he smile at Gertrude as he speaks, to stress his own virility and manhood?).

2 'These dilated articles . . .'

Write the 'dilated articles' (clear, full statements) that Claudius sends to 'old Norway'. Start with a formal greeting from one king to another. Set out a list of statements to clarify the political situation. Then make clear your demand: the King of Norway must put an end to Fortinbras's attempt to reclaim Danish territory. Include some Danish place-names in your 'articles'. You may wish to add authenticity to the document that Cornelius and Voltemand take to the King of Norway (for example, by sealing it with wax and tying it with ribbon).

3 Who's who? (in groups of eight)

Work out the relative status of the named characters in this scene (Claudius, Gertrude, Hamlet, Polonius, Laertes, Ophelia, Cornelius and Voltemand). Choose one line from the opposite page and present a tableau (a frozen picture or snapshot) of the group at that moment. Present your tableau to other students and invite them to identify the characters and the line.

---

impotent powerless (in politics and sex)
further gait herein going further
in that because
levies/lists soldiers
full proportions army necessary for this campaign
subject people

suit request
the Dane the King of Denmark
instrumental serviceable
bend again turn again
slow leave reluctant permission
laboursome petition persistent asking
hard consent grudging agreement

Who, impotent and bed-rid, scarcely hears
Of this his nephew's purpose, to suppress   30
His further gait herein, in that the levies,
The lists, and full proportions, are all made
Out of his subject; and we here dispatch
You, good Cornelius, and you, Voltemand,
For bearers of this greeting to old Norway,   35
Giving to you no further personal power
To business with the king, more than the scope
Of these dilated articles allow.
Farewell, and let your haste commend your duty.

CORNELIUS ⎫
VOLTEMAND ⎭ In that and all things will we show our duty.   40

CLAUDIUS We doubt it nothing, heartily farewell.

Exeunt Voltemand and Cornelius

And now Laertes, what's the news with you?
You told us of some suit, what is't Laertes?
You cannot speak of reason to the Dane
And lose your voice. What wouldst thou beg Laertes,   45
That shall not be my offer, not thy asking?
The head is not more native to the heart,
The hand more instrumental to the mouth,
Than is the throne of Denmark to thy father.
What wouldst thou have Laertes?

LAERTES   My dread lord,   50
Your leave and favour to return to France,
From whence though willingly I came to Denmark
To show my duty in your coronation,
Yet now I must confess, that duty done,
My thoughts and wishes bend again toward France,   55
And bow them to your gracious leave and pardon.

CLAUDIUS Have you your father's leave? What says Polonius?

POLONIUS He hath my lord wrung from me my slow leave
By laboursome petition, and at last
Upon his will I sealed my hard consent.   60
I do beseech you give him leave to go.

Claudius grants Laertes's request to return to France. He asks Hamlet why he is so melancholy. Gertrude urges Hamlet to cease grieving for the death of his father. He replies that his mourning is truly felt.

1 Hamlet's first words

Claudius addresses Hamlet as 'son' and 'cousin' (a word that could mean any close relative). Hamlet's first words are an aside. Asides are something not heard by other characters on stage, and they usually reveal what a character is really thinking. So Hamlet's aside suggests his feelings about Claudius ('less than kind' = I'm unlike you, not of your kind).

Hamlet's first words also reveal his alertness to language. He listens carefully to everything that is said to him, and often plays or puns on the words he has heard, giving them different meaning and significance. Hamlet picks up the kinship implications of 'cousin' and 'son', and puns on 'kin' and 'kind' (see page 261).

Advise the actor playing Hamlet how to speak line 65 (to himself? the audience? bitterly? thoughtfully?). Then offer advice on line 67 (for example, which word or words might Hamlet stress to question his kinship to Claudius?).

2 Appearance and reality (in pairs)

Hamlet seizes on Gertrude's 'seems' (line 75) and insists that his appearance really does match the way he feels. His black clothes and mournful behaviour truly reflect his sorrow for his father's death. He is not just playing a part, but is genuinely grief-stricken.

To gain an insight into Hamlet's feelings, try this: one person slowly reads aloud lines 76–86, pausing at each punctuation mark. In each pause, the other partner says 'I know not seems', stressing whichever of the four words seems appropriate to what has just been spoken.

---

thy best graces your good characteristics
nighted dark, gloomy
Denmark the king (Claudius)
vailèd lids downcast eyes
windy suspiration sighs
haviour of the visage facial expression

obsequious dutiful, as required by funeral rites (obsequies)
persever/In obstinate condolement keep up this stubborn mourning
impious unholy

18

CLAUDIUS Take thy fair hour Laertes, time be thine,
　　　　　And thy best graces spend it at thy will.
　　　　　But now my cousin Hamlet, and my son –
HAMLET (*Aside*) A little more than kin, and less than kind.　　65
CLAUDIUS How is it that the clouds still hang on you?
HAMLET Not so my lord, I am too much i'th'sun. (*son*)
GERTRUDE Good Hamlet cast thy nighted colour off,
　　　　　And let thine eye look like a friend on Denmark.
　　　　　Do not forever with thy vailèd lids　　　　　　70
　　　　　Seek for thy noble father in the dust.
　　　　　Thou know'st 'tis common, all that lives must die,
　　　　　Passing through nature to eternity.
HAMLET Ay madam, it is common.
GERTRUDE　　　　　　　　　　　If it be,
　　　　　Why seems it so particular with thee?　　　　75
HAMLET Seems madam? nay it is, I know not seems.
　　　　　'Tis not alone my inky cloak, good mother,
　　　　　Nor customary suits of solemn black,
　　　　　Nor windy suspiration of forced breath,
　　　　　No, nor the fruitful river in the eye,　　　　80
　　　　　Nor the dejected haviour of the visage,
　　　　　Together with all forms, moods, shapes of grief,
　　　　　That can denote me truly. These indeed seem,
　　　　　For they are actions that a man might play,
　　　　　But I have that within which passes show –　　85
　　　　　These but the trappings and the suits of woe.
CLAUDIUS 'Tis sweet and commendable in your nature Hamlet,
　　　　　To give these mourning duties to your father;
　　　　　But you must know, your father lost a father,
　　　　　That father lost, lost his, and the survivor bound　　90
　　　　　In filial obligation for some term
　　　　　To do obsequious sorrow; but to persever
　　　　　In obstinate condolement is a course
　　　　　Of impious stubbornness, 'tis unmanly grief,

(wimpish, girly)

Claudius criticises Hamlet's continued grief, declares him next in line to the throne, but refuses him permission to return to Wittenberg University. Gertrude pleads with Hamlet to stay. He agrees to obey her request.

1 Claudius's intentions (in groups of three or four)

Claudius's lines (lines 87–117) offer many opportunities to the actor to establish the king's character and his attitude to Hamlet. Try different styles of speaking, dividing the lines into appropriate sections:

a warm and supportive to Hamlet throughout
b hard and uncompromising to his stepson, rebuking him throughout
c utterly reasonable and sincere
d addressing many lines to the court rather than to Hamlet
e expressing a variety of attitudes, feelings and intentions.

Experiment with different tones, gestures and expressions until you have a version which you think suits Claudius's intentions in each line.

2 Some puzzles (in pairs)

When actors rehearse the lines opposite, they discuss questions about the characters' motives and feelings. There are no 'right' answers to these questions, but the answers the actors agree to adopt will influence the nature of their production. Explore your own responses to the questions:

Why does Claudius rebuke Hamlet so strongly for his grief?
Why does Claudius now declare Hamlet as his heir (line 109)?
Why does Claudius refuse Hamlet permission to return to Wittenberg?
What does Claudius feel towards Hamlet (dislike, fear or . . .)?
Is Hamlet's agreement to obey his mother (line 120) sincere?
Does Claudius really think Hamlet has given 'a loving and a fair reply'?

fault offence	**bend you** accept the idea
corse corpse	**accord** agreement
unprevailing useless	**jocund health** happy toast in wine
most immediate next in line, heir	**rouse** toast (drink in honour)
retrograde opposite	**bruit** announce, declare

20

It shows a will most incorrect to heaven,   95
A heart unfortified, a mind impatient,
An understanding simple and unschooled.
For what we know must be, and is as common
As any the most vulgar thing to sense,
Why should we in our peevish opposition   100
Take it to heart? Fie, 'tis a fault to heaven,
A fault against the dead, a fault to nature,
To reason most absurd, whose common theme
Is death of fathers, and who still hath cried,
From the first corse till he that died today,   105
'This must be so.' We pray you throw to earth
This unprevailing woe, and think of us
As of a father, for let the world take note
You are the most immediate to our throne,
And with no less nobility of love   110
Than that which dearest father bears his son,
Do I impart toward you. For your intent
In going back to school in Wittenberg,
It is most retrograde to our desire,
And we beseech you bend you to remain   115
Here in the cheer and comfort of our eye,
Our chiefest courtier, cousin, and our son.
GERTRUDE Let not thy mother lose her prayers Hamlet.
I pray thee stay with us, go not to Wittenberg.
HAMLET I shall in all my best obey you madam.   120
CLAUDIUS Why, 'tis a loving and a fair reply.
Be as ourself in Denmark. Madam, come.
This gentle and unforced accord of Hamlet
Sits smiling to my heart, in grace whereof,
No jocund health that Denmark drinks today   125
But the great cannon to the clouds shall tell,
And the king's rouse the heaven shall bruit again,
Re-speaking earthly thunder. Come away.
Flourish. Exeunt all but Hamlet

Hamlet longs for death but knows suicide is forbidden by God. He is disgusted that his mother has married so soon after his father's death, but feels he must keep silent. He greets Horatio and Marcellus.

1 Hamlet's soliloquy (in small groups)

A soliloquy is spoken by a character who is alone (or thinks he or she is alone) on stage. It reveals the character's true thoughts. Experiment with one or more of the options below to help you experience Hamlet's intensity of feeling, and how he expresses despair, anger, loathing or other emotions.

a Hamlet speaks to himself, as if he were thinking aloud.

b Hamlet speaks directly to the audience.

c The soliloquy is spoken a line or two at a time by several voices.

d Prepare, on tape, a radio version of the soliloquy. Convince the listeners they have direct access to Hamlet's mind and feelings.

In your explorations, you may wish to work with these 'sections':

lines 129–32 He wishes to die, but God's law ('canon') forbids suicide.

lines 133–7 He thinks of life as tedious and foul ('rank').

lines 138–40 He recalls his dead father who was infinitely superior to Claudius ('Hyperion' = the sun-god, 'satyr' = lecherous creature, half-man, half-goat).

lines 140–2 He recalls his father's powerful love for his mother.

lines 143–5 He recalls how passionately Gertrude loved his father.

lines 146–57 He is disgusted by his mother's speedy marriage to the inferior Claudius so shortly after his father's death.

lines 158–9 He condemns the marriage, but, sorrowfully, vows silence.

---

all the uses of everything in
merely completely
beteem permit
or ere before
Niobe Queen of Thebes (who wept for her dead children even when she was turned to stone)

wants lacks
Hercules mythical Greek hero, enormously strong
gallèd sore from weeping
post hurry

22

HAMLET O that this too too solid flesh would melt,
Thaw and resolve itself into a dew, 130
Or that the Everlasting had not fixed
His canon 'gainst self-slaughter. O God, God,
How weary, stale, flat and unprofitable
Seem to me all the uses of this world!
Fie on't, ah fie, 'tis an unweeded garden 135
That grows to seed, things rank and gross in nature
Possess it merely. That it should come to this!
But two months dead – nay not so much, not two –
So excellent a king, that was to this
Hyperion to a satyr, so loving to my mother 140
That he might not beteem the winds of heaven
Visit her face too roughly – heaven and earth,
Must I remember? why, she would hang on him
As if increase of appetite had grown
By what it fed on, and yet within a month – 145
Let me not think on't; frailty, thy name is woman –
A little month, or ere those shoes were old
With which she followed my poor father's body
Like Niobe, all tears, why she, even she –
O God, a beast that wants discourse of reason 150
Would have mourned longer – married with my uncle,
My father's brother, but no more like my father
Than I to Hercules – within a month,
Ere yet the salt of most unrighteous tears
Had left the flushing in her gallèd eyes, 155
She married. Oh most wicked speed, to post
With such dexterity to incestuous sheets.
It is not, nor it cannot come to good.
But break, my heart, for I must hold my tongue.

Enter HORATIO, MARCELLUS *and* BARNARDO

HORATIO Hail to your lordship.
HAMLET   I am glad to see you well. 160
Horatio – or I do forget myself.
HORATIO The same, my lord, and your poor servant ever.
HAMLET Sir, my good friend, I'll change that name with you.
And what make you from Wittenberg, Horatio?
Marcellus. 165

23

Hamlet does not believe Horatio returned to Denmark as a truant or to attend King Hamlet's funeral, but to see Gertrude's marriage. Horatio reports that he thinks he saw Hamlet's father the previous night.

1 Changing moods

Hamlet's mood changes several times from lines 167 to 195. Identify the shifts in mood and suggest a word to describe each (for example: line 167 welcoming, lines 170–3 disbelieving but friendly).

2 An ironic contrast (in groups of five to eight)

'Thrift, thrift', says Hamlet (line 180) emphasising how quickly his mother re-married after his father's death. The leftovers from King Hamlet's funeral feast were used for the wedding breakfast of Gertrude and Claudius. Devise two tableaux (frozen pictures) to show the two images of the mourning and wedding meals, such that the first tableau ('funeral') changes slowly into the second ('marriage').

3 'My father, methinks I see my father . . .' (in pairs)

Take parts as Hamlet and Horatio. Read lines 168–95. Experiment with pauses, and with the pace of the exchange. Speak them as a quick, flowing conversation, then with long pauses.

When you have worked on the pace and rhythm of the exchange, try it in low voices. Then try it louder. Which version works best? Why?

4 'I saw him once'

When and where did Horatio see King Hamlet? On the battlefield? On a state visit? At some sport or recreation? There is of course no 'true' answer, but write an account of an imagined occasion when Horatio saw the king. Your account should reveal something about Horatio's own character and experience.

---

make you brings you
disposition nature
truster believer
Thrift penny-pinching, money-saving
coldly as cold meats (or leftovers)

Or ever before
a was he was
all in all weighing all his qualities
Season your admiration control your amazement

MARCELLUS My good lord.

HAMLET I am very glad to see you. (*To Barnardo*) Good even sir.
　　　　But what in faith make you from Wittenberg?

HORATIO A truant disposition, good my lord.

HAMLET I would not hear your enemy say so,　　　　　　　　170
　　　　Nor shall you do my ear that violence
　　　　To make it truster of your own report
　　　　Against yourself. I know you are no truant.
　　　　But what is your affair in Elsinore?
　　　　We'll teach you to drink deep ere you depart.　　　175

HORATIO My lord, I came to see your father's funeral.

HAMLET I pray thee do not mock me fellow student,
　　　　I think it was to see my mother's wedding.

HORATIO Indeed my lord, it followed hard upon.

HAMLET Thrift, thrift, Horatio. The funeral baked meats　　180
　　　　Did coldly furnish forth the marriage tables.
　　　　Would I had met my dearest foe in heaven
　　　　Or ever I had seen that day, Horatio.
　　　　My father, methinks I see my father –

HORATIO Where my lord?

HAMLET　　　　　　　　In my mind's eye, Horatio.　　　185

HORATIO I saw him once, a was a goodly king.

HAMLET A was a man, take him for all in all.
　　　　I shall not look upon his like again.

HORATIO My lord, I think I saw him yesternight.

HAMLET Saw? Who?　　　　　　　　　　　　　　　　190

HORATIO My lord, the king your father.

HAMLET　　　　　　　　　　　The king my father!

HORATIO Season your admiration for a while
　　　　With an attent ear, till I may deliver
　　　　Upon the witness of these gentlemen
　　　　This marvel to you.

HAMLET　　　　　　　For God's love let me hear.　　195

Horatio reports the sightings of the Ghost: how it was clad in armour and how it vanished at daybreak. Hamlet is troubled by what he hears. He closely questions Marcellus and Barnardo.

'A figure like your father,/ Armèd at point exactly, cap-a-pe.' The 1989 Royal National Theatre production presented a ten-foot high statue of Hamlet's father. Compare this picture with the image on page 10. Which most closely matches your imagined version of the Ghost?

at point correct in every detail
cap-a-pe from head to foot
truncheon military baton
as they had delivered exactly as they described it

address/Itself to motion began to move
Hold you the watch tonight? Are you on guard duty tonight?

HORATIO Two nights together had these gentlemen,
   Marcellus and Barnardo, on their watch
   In the dead waste and middle of the night,
   Been thus encountered. A figure like your father,
   Armèd at point exactly, cap-a-pe,   200
   Appears before them, and with solemn march
   Goes slow and stately by them. Thrice he walked
   By their oppressed and fear-surprisèd eyes
   Within his truncheon's length, whilst they, distilled
   Almost to jelly with the act of fear,   205
   Stand dumb and speak not to him. This to me
   In dreadful secrecy impart they did,
   And I with them the third night kept the watch,
   Where, as they had delivered, both in time,
   Form of the thing, each word made true and good, 210
   The apparition comes. I knew your father,
   These hands are not more like.
HAMLET   But where was this?
MARCELLUS My lord, upon the platform where we watched.
HAMLET Did you not speak to it?
HORATIO   My lord, I did,
   But answer made it none. Yet once methought 215
   It lifted up it head and did address
   Itself to motion like as it would speak;
   But even then the morning cock crew loud,
   And at the sound it shrunk in haste away
   And vanished from our sight.
HAMLET   'Tis very strange. 220
HORATIO As I do live my honoured lord 'tis true,
   And we did think it writ down in our duty
   To let you know of it.
HAMLET Indeed, indeed sirs, but this troubles me.
   Hold you the watch tonight?
MARCELLUS⎫
BARNARDO ⎬   We do, my lord.   225
HAMLET Armed say you?
MARCELLUS⎫
BARNARDO ⎬ Armed my lord.
HAMLET   From top to toe?

Hamlet continues his close questioning about the Ghost. He resolves to join the others on watch that night and to speak to the Ghost. He commands the others not to talk about what they've seen.

1 Advise the actors (in groups of four)

Take parts and speak lines 224–42 in which Hamlet questions the three men. Read in a variety of ways (for example, very fast, or slow, as Hamlet and the others think carefully about what they are to say). Then prepare detailed notes for the actors, line by line, suggesting, with reasons, suitable speaking styles.

2 'More in sorrow than in anger' (in pairs)

Show your partner 'a countenance (look) more in sorrow than in anger'. Talk together about when you yourself might use such a look (or when someone has used it towards you).

3 Marcellus and Barnardo compare notes (in pairs)

Marcellus and Barnardo have seen the Ghost three times. They have now told their news to Hamlet. Imagine they've returned to their quarters. They talk about their sightings of the Ghost, and about Hamlet's response. Improvise their conversation, using your knowledge of Scenes 1 and 2.

4 Hamlet's notebook

As you will discover in the next act, Hamlet keeps a notebook ('tables') in which he writes down some of the things he learns. Write Hamlet's notebook entry for this day. It will describe his behaviour at the court; his feelings about Claudius and Gertrude and his own moodiness; what he makes of Horatio's story; and his speculations about why his father's ghost appears to be haunting Elsinore.

---

beaver visor
tell count
grizzled grey
sable silvered black with a few
  white hairs
warrant promise, guarantee

tenable held, kept secret
hap happen
requite reward
doubt fear, suspect
Though all the earth … eyes
  however deeply buried

MARCELLUS ⎱
BARNARDO ⎰   My lord, from head to foot.

HAMLET Then saw you not his face?

HORATIO Oh yes my lord, he wore his beaver up.

HAMLET What, looked he frowningly?   230

HORATIO A countenance more in sorrow than in anger.

HAMLET Pale, or red?

HORATIO Nay very pale.

HAMLET   And fixed his eyes upon you?

HORATIO Most constantly.

HAMLET   I would I had been there.

HORATIO It would have much amazed you.   235

HAMLET Very like, very like. Stayed it long?

HORATIO While one with moderate haste might tell a hundred.

MARCELLUS ⎱
BARNARDO ⎰   Longer, longer.

HORATIO Not when I saw 't.

HAMLET   His beard was grizzled, no?

HORATIO It was as I have seen it in his life,   240
     A sable silvered.

HAMLET   I will watch tonight,
     Perchance 'twill walk again.

HORATIO   I warrant it will.

HAMLET If it assume my noble father's person,
     I'll speak to it though hell itself should gape
     And bid me hold my peace. I pray you all,   245
     If you have hitherto concealed this sight,
     Let it be tenable in your silence still,
     And whatsomever else shall hap tonight,
     Give it an understanding but no tongue.
     I will requite your loves. So fare you well: 250
     Upon the platform 'twixt eleven and twelve
     I'll visit you.

ALL   Our duty to your honour.

HAMLET Your loves, as mine to you. Farewell.

                           Exeunt all but Hamlet

My father's spirit, in arms! All is not well.
I doubt some foul play. Would the night were come.   255
Till then sit still my soul. Foul deeds will rise
Though all the earth o'erwhelm them to men's eyes.   *Exit*

Laertes warns Ophelia against Hamlet's love, saying it is merely youthful infatuation. As a prince, Hamlet is not free to choose his own wife; he must marry in the interest of the state.

1 Young love won't last! (in pairs)

In lines 5–10, Laertes stresses Hamlet's youth and the fickleness of young love. It won't last, he tells Ophelia, and makes comparisons with short-lived things: 'fashion' (passing mood), 'toy in blood' (whim of passionate youth), 'violet' (a flower of early spring) and so on. One person reads lines 5–10, pausing at each punctuation mark. In the pause, the other person repeats what has just been said, but with great emphasis. How many comparisons with short-lasting love does Laertes make? Talk together about whether you agree with Laertes's point of view.

2 Maturity comes with age (in pairs)

When Ophelia questions Laertes's assertion that Hamlet's love will be very short-lived, he replies very formally: the body ('this temple') does not only increase ('waxes') in sinews and size ('thews and bulk') but in wisdom too. Take turns reading Laertes's lines 10–14 to each other. Accompany your reading with actions to bring out the meaning.

3 Princes can't choose (in pairs)

Can a prince choose to marry whoever he wants? Laertes doesn't think so. He tells Ophelia that 'his (Hamlet's) will is not his own'. In lines 17–28, he gives reasons why a prince, unlike an ordinary person, is not free to marry anyone he chooses, because he must bear in mind the needs and interests of his country. Decide whether you think what Laertes says was true in past times – and whether it is true for princes and other royalty today.

---

necessaries belongings
convoy is assistant ships are available
the youth of primy nature the spring
suppliance pastime
crescent growing

no soil nor cautel no blemish or deceit
Carve choose
peculiar sect and force particular class and power
main voice majority opinion

Elsinore   A private room

Enter LAERTES *and his sister,* OPHELIA

LAERTES My necessaries are embarked, farewell.
And sister, as the winds give benefit
And convoy is assistant, do not sleep
But let me hear from you.

OPHELIA   Do you doubt that?

LAERTES For Hamlet, and the trifling of his favour,   5
Hold it a fashion, and a toy in blood,
A violet in the youth of primy nature,
Forward, not permanent, sweet, not lasting,
The perfume and suppliance of a minute,
No more.

OPHELIA   No more but so?

LAERTES   Think it no more.   10
For nature crescent does not grow alone
In thews and bulk, but as this temple waxes
The inward service of the mind and soul
Grows wide withal. Perhaps he loves you now,
And now no soil nor cautel doth besmirch   15
The virtue of his will; but you must fear,
His greatness weighed, his will is not his own,
For he himself is subject to his birth.
He may not, as unvalued persons do,
Carve for himself, for on his choice depends   20
The sanctity and health of this whole state,
And therefore must his choice be circumscribed
Unto the voice and yielding of that body
Whereof he is the head. Then if he says he loves you,
It fits your wisdom so far to believe it   25
As he in his peculiar sect and force
May give his saying deed, which is no further
Than the main voice of Denmark goes withal.

Laertes continues to warn Ophelia not to trust Hamlet, because young people are both vulnerable and dangerous. She reminds him to follow his own advice. Polonius urges Laertes to leave.

1 A brother gives advice (in pairs)

How does Laertes speak his advice to Ophelia: pompously? lovingly? imploringly? How does Ophelia react as her brother gives examples of the dangers that face young women? Take parts and experiment with different ways of speaking lines 29–44, and of showing Ophelia's reactions. Decide what you think is the relationship between brother and sister. For example, is Laertes genuinely affectionate or does he seem to you to have a sexist and condescending attitude? Does Laertes strike you as being much older than Ophelia?

2 Ophelia's advice to Laertes

Is Ophelia's first sentence ironic or submissive? Experiment with lines 45–51 and decide which style best fits your view of Ophelia's character.

3 'The primrose path of dalliance' (in small groups)

Prepare two mimes to show the difference between 'the steep and thorny way to heaven', and 'the primrose path of dalliance'. It will help if you think of the first as 'refusing all temptations', and the second as 'happily accepting every temptation that comes your way'.

Search out 'The Rake's Progress', a series of pictures by the eighteenth-century painter Hogarth. He may not have had Ophelia's phrase in mind, but the pictures give an accurate depiction of 'a puffed and reckless libertine' (pleasure seeker) treading the primrose path.

---

credent trustful
list his songs listen to his love talk
chaste treasure virginity
unmastered importunity uncontrolled harassment
chariest most modest
prodigal lavish

calumnious slandering
buttons buds
Contagious blastments infectious diseases
recks not his own rede disregards his own advice

Then weigh what loss your honour may sustain
If with too credent ear you list his songs,   30
Or lose your heart, or your chaste treasure open
To his unmastered importunity.
Fear it Ophelia, fear it my dear sister,
And keep you in the rear of your affection,
Out of the shot and danger of desire.   35
The chariest maid is prodigal enough
If she unmask her beauty to the moon.
Virtue itself scapes not calumnious strokes.
The canker galls the infants of the spring
Too oft before their buttons be disclosed,   40
And in the morn and liquid dew of youth
Contagious blastments are most imminent.
Be wary then, best safety lies in fear:
Youth to itself rebels, though none else near.

OPHELIA   I shall th'effect of this good lesson keep   45
As watchman to my heart. But good my brother,
Do not as some ungracious pastors do,
Show me the steep and thorny way to heaven,
Whiles like a puffed and reckless libertine
Himself the primrose path of dalliance treads,   50
And recks not his own rede.

LAERTES   Oh fear me not.

Enter POLONIUS

I stay too long – But here my father comes.
A double blessing is a double grace;
Occasion smiles upon a second leave.

POLONIUS   Yet here Laertes? Aboard, aboard for shame!   55
The wind sits in the shoulder of your sail,
And you are stayed for. There, my blessing with thee,

Polonius gives Laertes fatherly advice on speech, friendship, quarrelling, judgement, dress, money and consistency. He questions Ophelia about her relationship with Hamlet.

1 A father gives advice (in pairs)

a Just how does Polonius deliver his advice to his son? Try speaking lines 58–81 in different styles: as a pompous bureaucrat, as a loving father, as an authoritarian father, or in some other way. Talk together about what you think the lines suggest about Polonius's character.

b In lines 59–80, Polonius hands out eight sentences of advice. Imagine Laertes dares to ask his father to give a concrete practical example of each principle. One person reads Polonius's lines, pausing at each full stop. In the pause, Laertes asks 'concrete example, please'. Provide an actual example in reply (there is an example in lines 72–4).

c How do Laertes and Ophelia react? In some productions Polonius's children listen dutifully and respectfully. In others they make faces behind Polonius's back, mocking his advice. In others they silently mouth his words, showing they have heard it all many times before. Advise Laertes and Ophelia how to react to each sentence of counsel.

d Put the eight pieces of advice in order of importance, giving reasons for your decision. Then make up eight pieces of advice for a father to give to a son today.

2 Promise-keeping?

In lines 85–6, Ophelia promises to keep Laertes's words secret. Yet only three lines later she reveals to Polonius what Laertes has said. Why?

precepts moral principles
character engrave
unproportioned ill-considered
adoption tried worthiness tested
dull thy palm squander your hospitality
courage comrade

censure opinion
habit clothes
husbandry thrift, good housekeeping
Marry by Saint Mary
audience time, attention

And these few precepts in thy memory
Look thou character. Give thy thoughts no tongue,
Nor any unproportioned thought his act. 60
Be thou familiar, but by no means vulgar.
Those friends thou hast, and their adoption tried,
Grapple them unto thy soul with hoops of steel,
But do not dull thy palm with entertainment
Of each new-hatched, unfledged courage. Beware 65
Of entrance to a quarrel, but being in,
Bear't that th'opposèd may beware of thee.
Give every man thy ear, but few thy voice;
Take each man's censure, but reserve thy judgement.
Costly thy habit as thy purse can buy, 70
But not expressed in fancy: rich, not gaudy.
For the apparel oft proclaims the man,
And they in France of the best rank and station
Are of a most select and generous chief in that.
Neither a borrower nor a lender be, 75
For loan oft loses both itself and friend,
And borrowing dulls the edge of husbandry.
This above all, to thine own self be true,
And it must follow, as the night the day,
Thou canst not then be false to any man. 80
Farewell, my blessing season this in thee.
LAERTES Most humbly do I take my leave, my lord.
POLONIUS The time invites you. Go, your servants tend.
LAERTES Farewell Ophelia, and remember well
What I have said to you.
OPHELIA   'Tis in my memory locked, 85
And you yourself shall keep the key of it.
LAERTES Farewell.   *Exit Laertes*
POLONIUS What is't Ophelia he hath said to you?
OPHELIA So please you, something touching the Lord Hamlet.
POLONIUS Marry, well bethought. 90
'Tis told me he hath very oft of late
Given private time to you, and you yourself
Have of your audience been most free and bounteous.
If it be so, as so 'tis put on me,
And that in way of caution, I must tell you 95
You do not understand yourself so clearly

35

Polonius, scornful of Hamlet's love, remonstrates with Ophelia. He orders her not to believe Hamlet's love-talk. She must give up seeing him because of his royal position and his merely lustful desire.

Polonius picks up words Ophelia uses and interprets them differently: 'affection' (love/lust), 'tender' (offers/look after), 'fashion' (manner/ pretence). But does he speak harshly or affectionately?

1 Images of deceit

line 115 'springes to catch woodcocks.' 'Springes' are traps. Elizabethans thought woodcocks to be foolish birds.

lines 127–31 false appearance. Hamlet's love promises are pimps ('brokers'), like false-coloured clothes ('dye', 'investments'). They plan to do mischief ('implorators of unholy suits') when they vow true marriage ('sanctified and pious bonds').

behooves is appropriate to
Unsifted inexperienced
sterling of true value, genuine money
Roaming playing with
importuned addressed, solicited
countenance strength, support

scanter less free, more grudging
entreatments interviews, discussions
command to parley invitation to talk of love
tedder tether (rope)
In few briefly

As it behooves my daughter, and your honour.
What is between you? Give me up the truth.

OPHELIA He hath my lord of late made many tenders
Of his affection to me.   100

POLONIUS Affection? Puh! You speak like a green girl,
Unsifted in such perilous circumstance.
Do you believe his tenders as you call them?

OPHELIA I do not know my lord what I should think.

POLONIUS Marry I'll teach you. Think yourself a baby   105
That you have tane these tenders for true pay,
Which are not sterling. Tender yourself more dearly,
Or – not to crack the wind of the poor phrase,
Roaming it thus – you'll tender me a fool.

OPHELIA My lord, he hath importuned me with love   110
In honourable fashion.

POLONIUS Ay, fashion you may call it. Go to, go to.

OPHELIA And hath given countenance to his speech, my lord,
With almost all the holy vows of heaven.

POLONIUS Ay, springes to catch woodcocks. I do know,   115
When the blood burns, how prodigal the soul
Lends the tongue vows. These blazes daughter,
Giving more light than heat, extinct in both
Even in their promise as it is a-making,
You must not take for fire. From this time   120
Be something scanter of your maiden presence.
Set your entreatments at a higher rate
Than a command to parley. For Lord Hamlet,
Believe so much in him, that he is young
And with a larger tedder may he walk   125
Than may be given you. In few Ophelia,
Do not believe his vows, for they are brokers,
Not of that dye which their investments show,
But mere implorators of unholy suits,
Breathing like sanctified and pious bonds,   130
The better to beguile. This is for all:
I would not in plain terms from this time forth
Have you so slander any moment leisure
As to give words or talk with the Lord Hamlet.
Look to't I charge you. Come your ways.   135

OPHELIA I shall obey, my lord.

Exeunt

> *Just after midnight. Trumpets and gun salutes are heard. Hamlet condemns the drunkenness of the Danes and reflects that some men have a particular character fault that overwhelms reason and dignity.*

1 A custom best broken?

Hamlet explains that *A flourish of trumpets and two pieces* (cannons) *goes off* means that Claudius is celebrating with revelry ('wake'), drinking ('rouse', 'wassail'), and wild dances ('swaggering up-spring reels'). As Claudius drinks his 'draughts of Rhenish' (German wine), loud music accompanies his toast ('pledge'). Hamlet deplores this custom of the Danes, saying more honour results from not following Claudius's example ('More honoured in the breach than the observance').

Turn back to Scene 2, lines 125–8, to remind yourself of what Claudius said about tonight's revelry. Then identify, with reasons, the tone in which you think Hamlet speaks lines 8–22. Try to think of a custom that is practised today that you think would be 'more honoured in the breach than the observance'.

2 'Some vicious mole of nature . . .' (in groups of three)

In lines 23–36, Hamlet reflects on how a single character flaw ('complexion') can corrupt a person entirely. In some of his plays, Shakespeare shows the destructive effect of such a character defect. Macbeth is destroyed by ambition, Othello by jealousy, Coriolanus by pride. Laurence Olivier began his film of *Hamlet* with these lines as a voice-over, and added: 'This is the tragedy of a man who could not make up his mind'.

Talk together about whether you agree with Hamlet's view that some people are born with a character fault that will overwhelm all their virtues. Give examples. Then say what you think about Olivier beginning his film with these lines.

---

shrewdly sharply
held his wont is accustomed
two pieces goes off two cannons fire
breach breaking of it
traduced and taxed of slandered and criticised by
clepe call

Soil our addition dirty our good name
pith and marrow . . . attribute essence of our reputation
pales boundaries
o'erleavens/The form of plausive manners unbalances good behaviour

ACT 1   SCENE 4
The gun platform

Enter HAMLET, HORATIO *and* MARCELLUS

HAMLET The air bites shrewdly, it is very cold.
HORATIO It is a nipping and an eager air.
HAMLET What hour now?
HORATIO   I think it lacks of twelve.
MARCELLUS No, it is struck.
HORATIO Indeed? I heard it not. It then draws near the season   5
      Wherein the spirit held his wont to walk.
      A flourish of trumpets and two pieces goes off
      What does this mean, my lord?
HAMLET The king doth wake tonight and takes his rouse,
      Keeps wassail, and the swaggering up-spring reels,
      And as he drains his draughts of Rhenish down,   10
      The kettle-drum and trumpet thus bray out
      The triumph of his pledge.
HORATIO   Is it a custom?
HAMLET Ay marry is't,
      But to my mind, though I am native here
      And to the manner born, it is a custom   15
      More honoured in the breach than the observance.
      [This heavy-headed revel east and west
      Makes us traduced and taxed of other nations.
      They clepe us drunkards, and with swinish phrase
      Soil our addition; and indeed it takes   20
      From our achievements, though performed at height,
      The pith and marrow of our attribute.
      So, oft it chances in particular men,
      That for some vicious mole of nature in them,
      As in their birth, wherein they are not guilty,   25
      Since nature cannot choose his origin,
      By their o'ergrowth of some complexion,
      Oft breaking down the pales and forts of reason,
      Or by some habit that too much o'erleavens
      The form of plausive manners – that these men,   30

The Ghost appears, interrupting Hamlet's reflections on human nature. Hamlet addresses it as his dead father, asking why it has returned from the grave. Marcellus urges Hamlet not to follow the Ghost.

1 'The dram of eale . . .'

Lines 36–8 are obscure and probably incomplete. No one can be quite sure what Shakespeare actually wrote. Maybe the original printer made a mistake. The meaning might be that a small quantity ('dram') of 'eale' (some kind of rotting agent?) corrupts the whole of a noble enterprise.

Imagine you are editing *Hamlet*. You have reached this point at the end of Hamlet's meditation on human nature. Work out how you would edit the three lines (you can change words if you think it sensible: for example, 'eale' might become 'evil'). Suggest how you would explain their meaning.

2 Hamlet's reaction to the Ghost (in pairs)

How does Hamlet react to the Ghost? Take turns to read lines 39–57 to each other in different ways. For example, speak the lines fast, or slow, or at a varying pace. Experiment with different tones: amazed, questioning, fearful or pleading.

3 'Ministers of grace'

Hamlet is unsure about what kind of apparition he sees. Is it a good spirit from heaven or an evil goblin from hell, which has come to tempt him into eternal damnation? That problem of knowing whether the Ghost is good or bad will preoccupy Hamlet for much of the play. You will find notes on pages 258–9 to help you understand why Hamlet speaks of 'Angels', 'goblin damned', 'heaven' and 'hell' here.

stamp imprint	**cerements** shrouds, grave-clothes
livery costume (inheritance)	**enurned** buried
fortune's star bad luck	**complete steel** armour
censure opinion, judgement	**glimpses of the moon** moonlight
canonised buried in holy fashion	**impartment** message
hearsèd coffined	**removèd ground** remote place

Carrying I say the stamp of one defect,
Being nature's livery or fortune's star,
His virtues else be they as pure as grace,
As infinite as man may undergo,
Shall in the general censure take corruption   35
From that particular fault. The dram of eale
Doth all the noble substance of a doubt
To his own scandal.]

Enter GHOST

HORATIO   Look my lord, it comes!
HAMLET Angels and ministers of grace defend us!
Be thou a spirit of health, or goblin damned,   40
Bring with thee airs from heaven or blasts from hell,
Be thy intents wicked or charitable,
Thou com'st in such a questionable shape
That I will speak to thee. I'll call thee Hamlet,
King, father, royal Dane. Oh answer me.   45
Let me not burst in ignorance, but tell
Why thy canonised bones, hearsèd in death,
Have burst their cerements; why the sepulchre,
Wherein we saw thee quietly enurned,
Hath oped his ponderous and marble jaws   50
To cast thee up again. What may this mean,
That thou, dead corse, again in complete steel
Revisits thus the glimpses of the moon,
Making night hideous, and we fools of nature
So horridly to shake our disposition   55
With thoughts beyond the reaches of our souls?
Say, why is this? wherefore? What should we do?
Ghost beckons Hamlet
HORATIO It beckons you to go away with it,
As if it some impartment did desire
To you alone.
MARCELLUS   Look with what courteous action   60
It wafts you to a more removèd ground.
But do not go with it.
HORATIO   No, by no means.

41

Horatio tries to persuade Hamlet not to follow the Ghost. Hamlet is determined to follow. He threatens Horatio and Marcellus with death if they try to restrain him. He follows the Ghost.

'Go on, I'll follow thee.' A strong tradition has developed of Hamlet following the Ghost using his sword hilt as a cross to defend himself against evil. Decide whether you would wish to use that tradition if you were staging Hamlet's exit at line 86. Or would you prefer him to leave the stage with some other gesture?

a pin's fee the value of a pin
flood sea
beetles hangs
toys of desperation suicidal
 thoughts
petty arture drop of blood (little
 artery)

Nemean lion's nerve terrifying
 lion's sinews (Hercules strangled
 the lion terrorising Nemea because
 weapons could not hurt it)
waxes increases
Have after let's follow him
**Something is rotten in the state
 of Denmark** (see page 244, and
 page 262, number 5)

HAMLET It will not speak. Then I will follow it.

HORATIO Do not my lord.

HAMLET   Why, what should be the fear?
I do not set my life at a pin's fee, *my life is worth nothing*   65
And for my soul, what can it do to that,
Being a thing immortal as itself?
It waves me forth again. I'll follow it.

HORATIO What if it tempt you toward the flood my lord,
Or to the dreadful summit of the cliff   70
That beetles o'er his base into the sea,
And there assume some other horrible form
Which might deprive your sovereignty of reason,
And draw you into madness? Think of it.
[The very place puts toys of desperation,   75
Without more motive, into every brain
That looks so many fathoms to the sea
And hears it roar beneath.]

HAMLET It wafts me still. Go on, I'll follow thee.

MARCELLUS You shall not go my lord.

HAMLET   Hold off your hands.   80

HORATIO Be ruled, you shall not go.

HAMLET   My fate cries out,
And makes each petty arture in this body
As hardy as the Nemean lion's nerve.
Still am I called. Unhand me gentlemen!
By heaven I'll make a ghost of him that lets me.   85
I say away! – Go on, I'll follow thee.

                                   Exit Ghost and Hamlet

HORATIO He waxes desperate with imagination.

MARCELLUS Let's follow, 'tis not fit thus to obey him.

HORATIO Have after. To what issue will this come?

MARCELLUS Something is rotten in the state of Denmark.   90

HORATIO Heaven will direct it.

MARCELLUS   Nay let's follow him.

                                                      Exeunt

43

The Ghost says it must shortly return to its suffering but is forbidden to tell mortals of the horrors it endures. The Ghost commands Hamlet to revenge.

1 Chill the audience! (in small groups)

The Ghost hints at the terrors of its suffering. It cannot go to heaven because it died before it could confess its sins. So it must suffer dreadfully in purgatory. According to Roman Catholic belief, purgatory is the place where unconfessed sinners experience indescribable remorse as their sins are burnt and purged away before they can see God in heaven (see pages 258–9). But the Ghost says it is forbidden to tell of its terrifying ordeal ('this eternal blazon must not be').

Experiment with readings of lines 9–22 that will make the audience shrink back in their seats! Add sound effects as you think appropriate. If possible, tape-record your final version as a radio broadcast. A hint: look through some art books in the library to find pictures by Hieronymus Bosch (1450–1516), an artist who painted the tortures of the dead. They will help you to imagine the Ghost's torments.

2 'Revenge his foul and most unnatural murder' (in pairs)

Work out a tableau to show how the Ghost and Hamlet appear at line 25. Use whatever space you have available to make it as dramatically striking as possible.

My hour daybreak
bound compelled, ready
term period
harrow cruelly rip
locks hair

porpentine porcupine
eternal blazon telling of what
 happens after death
List listen

ACT 1 SCENE 5
The walls of Elsinore Castle

Enter GHOST *and* HAMLET

HAMLET Whither wilt thou lead me? Speak, I'll go no further.
GHOST Mark me.
HAMLET I will.
GHOST My hour is almost come
When I to sulph'rous and tormenting flames
Must render up myself.
HAMLET Alas poor ghost!
GHOST Pity me not, but lend thy serious hearing   5
To what I shall unfold.
HAMLET Speak, I am bound to hear.
GHOST So art thou to revenge, when thou shalt hear.
HAMLET What?
GHOST I am thy father's spirit,
Doomed for a certain term to walk the night,   10
And for the day confined to fast in fires,
Till the foul crimes done in my days of nature
Are burnt and purged away. But that I am forbid
To tell the secrets of my prison house,
I could a tale unfold whose lightest word   15
Would harrow up thy soul, freeze thy young blood,
Make thy two eyes like stars start from their spheres,
Thy knotted and combinèd locks to part
And each particular hair to stand an end
Like quills upon the fretful porpentine.   20
But this eternal blazon must not be
To ears of flesh and blood. List, list, oh list!
If thou didst ever thy dear father love –
HAMLET O God!
GHOST Revenge his foul and most unnatural murder.   25
HAMLET Murder?

45

Hamlet is eager to take immediate revenge for his father's murder. The Ghost reveals he was killed by Claudius, and expresses disgust that Gertrude now sleeps with his brother.

1 Vivid images (in small groups)

The opposite page is full of strikingly imaginative images:

lines 29–30 'wings as swift as meditation or the thoughts of love'

lines 32–3 'the fat weed that rots itself in ease on Lethe wharf'

lines 36–8 'So the whole ear of Denmark is by a forgèd process of my death rankly abused'

lines 39–40 'The serpent that did sting thy father's life now wears his crown'

lines 55–7 'So lust, though to a radiant angel linked, will sate itself in a celestial bed, and prey on garbage'.

Choose one of the images and work out a way of portraying it as a mime involving every group member. Prepare by talking together about each element in your chosen image (for example, lines 29–30: how can you relate 'wings as swift as meditation' and 'thoughts of love' to 'revenge'?)

2 Two puzzles: what do you think? (in pairs)

Talk together about your views on:

a 'O my prophetic soul! My uncle?' Had Hamlet earlier suspected that Claudius had killed his father?

b 'my most seeming virtuous queen'. Had Gertrude been unfaithful while her husband was still alive?

---

as in the best it is as even the best murder is foul
meditation thought, contemplation
apt ready to act
fat weed huge banks of weeds

Lethe a river in Hades (the world of the dead); drinking the river's water caused forgetfulness
forgèd process false account
lewdness court lust tempt
sate greedily satisfy, satiate

GHOST   Murder most foul, as in the best it is,
        But this most foul, strange, and unnatural.

HAMLET   Haste me to know't, that I with wings as swift
        As meditation or the thoughts of love   30
        May sweep to my revenge.

GHOST   I find thee apt,
        And duller shouldst thou be than the fat weed
        That rots itself in ease on Lethe wharf,
        Wouldst thou not stir in this. Now Hamlet, hear.
        'Tis given out that, sleeping in my orchard,   35
        A serpent stung me. So the whole ear of Denmark
        Is by a forgèd process of my death
        Rankly abused; but know, thou noble youth,
        The serpent that did sting thy father's life
        Now wears his crown.

HAMLET   O my prophetic soul!   40
        My uncle?

GHOST   Ay, that incestuous, that adulterate beast,
        With witchcraft of his wits, with traitorous gifts –
        O wicked wit and gifts that have the power
        So to seduce – won to his shameful lust   45
        The will of my most seeming virtuous queen.
        O Hamlet, what a falling off was there,
        From me whose love was of that dignity
        That it went hand in hand even with the vow
        I made to her in marriage, and to decline   50
        Upon a wretch whose natural gifts were poor
        To those of mine.
        But virtue as it never will be moved,
        Though lewdness court it in a shape of heaven,
        So lust, though to a radiant angel linked,   55
        Will sate itself in a celestial bed,
        And prey on garbage.
        But soft, methinks I scent the morning air;

*The Ghost tells how Claudius murdered him by pouring poison in his ear.
He died with no chance to confess his sins. He urges Hamlet to revenge,
but without harming Gertrude.*

---

1 Act out the murder (in groups of three)

Take parts as the narrator, Hamlet's father and Claudius. The narrator
slowly reads lines 59–80. The others act out what is described.

2 'No reckoning made' (in small groups)

The Ghost is horrified at having no chance before death to settle his
account with God through proper religious ceremony:

'Unhouseled': without sacrament (the bread and wine of Holy
Communion)

'disappointed': unprepared for death (by confession and
absolution)

'unaneled': unanointed (blessed by being anointed with oil).

Talk together about whether you think this horror at the lack of preparation for death is widely shared today. If an atheist (someone who
doesn't believe in God) said to you, 'I just can't experience that horror,
and so this aspect of the play doesn't grip me', what would you reply?

3 Whose line?

In some productions, line 80 is given to Hamlet. Give reasons why you
would or would not transfer it.

4 'This distracted globe'

In line 97, do you think Hamlet refers to his own 'distracted' head, to
the disturbed world, to Shakespeare's Globe Theatre, or to all, some or
none of these? Advise the actor on what to do as he says 'this distracted
globe'.

---

secure unguarded, carefree
cursèd hebenon poison
leperous distilment evil mixture
  causing leprosy
posset curdle (clotting the blood)
tetter skin disease
lazar-like like leprosy

blossoms full bloom, height
luxury lust
matin morning
gins . . . fire begins to lose its glow
couple include (with heaven and
  earth)

Brief let me be. Sleeping within my orchard,
My custom always of the afternoon,   60
Upon my secure hour thy uncle stole,
With juice of cursèd hebenon in a vial,
And in the porches of my ears did pour
The leperous distilment, whose effect
Holds such an enmity with blood of man   65
That swift as quicksilver it courses through
The natural gates and alleys of the body,
And with a sudden vigour it doth posset
And curd, like eager droppings into milk,
The thin and wholesome blood. So did it mine,   70
And a most instant tetter barked about,
Most lazar-like, with vile and loathsome crust,
All my smooth body.
Thus was I, sleeping, by a brother's hand,
Of life, of crown, of queen, at once dispatched;   75
Cut off even in the blossoms of my sin,
Unhouseled, disappointed, unaneled;
No reckoning made, but sent to my account
With all my imperfections on my head –
Oh horrible, oh horrible, most horrible!   80
If thou hast nature in thee bear it not;
Let not the royal bed of Denmark be
A couch for luxury and damnèd incest.
But howsomever thou pursues this act
Taint not thy mind, nor let thy soul contrive   85
Against thy mother aught. Leave her to heaven
And to those thorns that in her bosom lodge
To prick and sting her. Fare thee well at once.
The glow-worm shows the matin to be near,
And gins to pale his uneffectual fire.   90
Adieu, adieu, adieu. Remember me.   *Exit*
HAMLET O all you host of heaven! O earth! what else?
And shall I couple hell? Oh fie! Hold, hold, my heart,
And you my sinews grow not instant old
But bear me stiffly up. Remember thee?   95
Ay thou poor ghost, whiles memory holds a seat
In this distracted globe. Remember thee?

Hamlet determines to remember only the Ghost's commandment to revenge. He writes in his notebook. When Horatio and Marcellus find him, he avoids telling them what he knows.

1 'Smiling damnèd villain!'

Shakespeare's imagination was haunted by the image of the smiling villain. He used it to reflect the theme of deceptive appearances:

'There's daggers in men's smiles' (*Macbeth*)

'I can smile, and murder whiles I smile' (*King Henry VI, Part 3*)

'Some that smile have in their hearts, I fear, millions of mischief' (*Julius Caesar*)

'I did but smile till now' (the hypocritical Angelo in *Measure for Measure*)

'One may smile, and smile, and be a villain' (line 108 opposite).

Give reasons for whether you think playing Claudius as a 'smiler' would heighten or lessen the dramatic impact of a performance.

2 Book learning versus experience (in pairs)

Hamlet determines to forget book learning and trivial matters (lines 98–104). In some productions he writes down his thoughts about Claudius in his notebook ('tables'). In Elizabethan times, this would probably be made up of two tablets of slate or wood.

Make a drawing of Hamlet's tables, showing what he writes in them. You might include the partly obliterated proverbs ('saws'), the fresh thought of line 108 and the determination to revenge.

3 Advice, please

The actor playing Hamlet asks for your advice on how to speak lines 121–4. He says: 'Are there abrupt changes of mood and intention there?' What do you reply?

---

table/tables notebook
fond foolish
saws conventional sayings, platitudes
forms general ideas

all pressures past impressions
Illo, ho, ho the falconer's cry to his hawk
arrant absolute, complete

Yea, from the table of my memory
I'll wipe away all trivial fond records,
All saws of books, all forms, all pressures past,   100
That youth and observation copied there,
And thy commandment all alone shall live
Within the book and volume of my brain,
Unmixed with baser matter: yes, by heaven!
O most pernicious woman!   105
O villain, villain, smiling damnèd villain!
My tables – meet it is I set it down
That one may smile, and smile, and be a villain;
At least I'm sure it may be so in Denmark. [*Writing*]
So uncle, there you are. Now to my word: 110
It is 'Adieu, adieu, remember me.'
I have sworn't.

HORATIO (*Within*) My lord, my lord!
MARCELLUS *(Within)*   Lord Hamlet!

Enter HORATIO *and* MARCELLUS

HORATIO   Heavens secure him!
HAMLET So be it.
MARCELLUS Illo, ho, ho, my lord!   115
HAMLET Hillo, ho, ho, boy! Come bird, come.
MARCELLUS How is't, my noble lord?
HORATIO   What news my lord?
HAMLET Oh, wonderful!
HORATIO Good my lord, tell it.
HAMLET   No, you will reveal it.
HORATIO Not I my lord, by heaven.
MARCELLUS   Nor I my lord.   120
HAMLET How say you then, would heart of man once think it –
      But you'll be secret?
HORATIO ⎱
MARCELLUS ⎰   Ay, by heaven, my lord.
HAMLET There's ne'er a villain dwelling in all Denmark
      But he's an arrant knave.
HORATIO There needs no ghost, my lord, come from the grave, 125
      To tell us this.

Hamlet's replies puzzle Horatio. Hamlet asks the two men to keep secret all they have seen. They promise to do so. He demands they swear an oath of silence on his sword. The Ghost echoes his words.

1 'Wild and whirling words' (in groups of three)

Horatio is puzzled by Hamlet's words. To gain a sense of the rapid changes in Hamlet's language, take parts as Hamlet, Marcellus and Horatio and read lines 115–53. As you read, move around the room, with Hamlet frequently changing direction. The other two try to keep up with him.

Afterwards, talk together about how the physical movement gives additional meaning to Horatio's claim of 'wild and whirling words'. Also discuss how the activity reveals something of the state of Hamlet's mind.

2 Who hears the Ghost? (in pairs)

Do Marcellus and Horatio hear the Ghost's demand to 'swear' (line 149), or does only Hamlet hear it? Talk together about the implications of the two possibilities.

3 Swearing the oath of silence

Imagine the hilt of Hamlet's sword is shaped like a cross. Work out how he would hold it for the other two men to swear their promise of silence upon. Then decide whether you think Horatio and Marcellus are willing or unwilling to swear the oath on Hamlet's sword (see line 147). Suggest what they might be thinking at this moment.

---

circumstance formality
Saint Patrick who, in legend, released sinners from purgatory
Touching concerning

O'ermaster't overcome it
truepenny honest fellow
in the cellarage underground (beneath the stage)

HAMLET   Why right, you are i'th'right,
        And so without more circumstance at all
        I hold it fit that we shake hands and part –
        You as your business and desire shall point you,
        For every man hath business and desire,   130
        Such as it is, and for my own poor part,
        Look you, I'll go pray.
HORATIO These are but wild and whirling words, my lord.
HAMLET I'm sorry they offend you, heartily,
        Yes faith, heartily.
HORATIO   There's no offence my lord.   135
HAMLET Yes by Saint Patrick but there is Horatio,
        And much offence too. Touching this vision here,
        It is an honest ghost, that let me tell you.
        For your desire to know what is between us,
        O'ermaster't as you may. And now good friends,   140
        As you are friends, scholars, and soldiers,
        Give me one poor request.
HORATIO What is't my lord? we will.
HAMLET Never make known what you have seen tonight.
HORATIO ⎫
MARCELLUS ⎭ My lord we will not.
HAMLET   Nay but swear't.
HORATIO   In faith   145
        My lord not I.
MARCELLUS   Nor I my lord in faith.
HAMLET Upon my sword.
MARCELLUS   We have sworn my lord already.
HAMLET Indeed, upon my sword, indeed.
GHOST Swear.   *Ghost cries under the stage*
HAMLET Ha, ha, boy, sayst thou so? art thou there truepenny?   150
        Come on, you hear this fellow in the cellarage,
        Consent to swear.
HORATIO   Propose the oath my lord.
HAMLET Never to speak of this that you have seen,
        Swear by my sword.
GHOST Swear.   155

Hamlet demands that Horatio and Marcellus swear they will not reveal what has happened. They must also promise not to put on a show of knowing the true nature of any future strange behaviour by Hamlet.

1 Amusing the groundlings?

Hamlet shifts position to swear the oath as the Ghost's voice is heard from beneath the stage. He calls the Ghost 'old mole' and 'worthy pioneer' (brave miner). Do you think lines 142–64 should be played in a style to try to make the audience laugh? (In Shakespeare's time, the members of the audience standing in front of the Globe stage were called 'the groundlings'.)

2 Friends who know a secret (in pairs)

Hamlet asks his friends not to look knowing if they see him behaving oddly (lines 173–80). Show your partner what Hamlet means by 'with arms encumbered thus'. Nobody can be precisely sure if it means 'folded', so try out various possibilities.

3 'More things in heaven and earth'

In lines 166–7, Hamlet reminds Horatio that philosophy (science?) does not know everything. Learn the two lines and use them the next time someone asks you a question to which you think the answer is not known. Do you think Hamlet's words are as true today as they were in Shakespeare's time?

4 'The time is out of joint' (in small groups)

How would you expect Hamlet to say lines 189–90? Write a paragraph identifying Hamlet's motivation for speaking these words.

Hic et ubique? here and
  everywhere?
meet appropriate
antic disposition mad manner

list wished
still always
cursèd spite damned malice, evil
  fortune

HAMLET *Hic et ubique?* then we'll shift our ground.
Come hither gentlemen,
And lay your hands again upon my sword.
Never to speak of this that you have heard,
Swear by my sword.   160
GHOST Swear.
HAMLET Well said old mole, canst work i'th'earth so fast?
A worthy pioneer. Once more remove, good friends.
HORATIO O day and night, but this is wondrous strange.
HAMLET And therefore as a stranger give it welcome.   165
There are more things in heaven and earth, Horatio,
Than are dreamt of in your philosophy.
But come –
Here as before, never so help you mercy,
How strange or odd some'er I bear myself,   170
As I perchance hereafter shall think meet   *From now on I*
To put an antic disposition on –   *will have to act*
That you at such times seeing me never shall,   *crazy.*
With arms encumbered thus, or this head–shake,
Or by pronouncing of some doubtful phrase,   175
As 'Well, well, we know,' or 'We could and if we would,'
Or 'If we list to speak,' or 'There be and if they might,'
Or such ambiguous giving out, to note
That you know aught of me: this not to do,
So grace and mercy at your most need help you,   180
Swear.
GHOST Swear.
HAMLET Rest, rest, perturbèd spirit. So gentlemen,
With all my love I do commend me to you,
And what so poor a man as Hamlet is   185
May do t'express his love and friending to you,
God willing shall not lack. Let us go in together,
And still your fingers on your lips I pray. –
The time is out of joint: O cursèd spite,
That ever I was born to set it right. –   190
Nay come, let's go together.
                                        Exeunt

Looking back at Act 1
Activities for groups or individuals

1 Court circular

Imagine that a daily court circular is issued recording the activities of the royal family. Write the court circular for one day in Act 1.

2 First line

Some people argue that the first line of any Shakespeare play gives very significant indications of what the play will be about. Deduce from Barnardo's first two words some of the themes of the play.

3 Disorder

Suggestions of the disordered state of society and of individuals run through Act 1: 'The time is out of joint' (Scene 5, line 189), 'Something is rotten in the state of Denmark' (Scene 4, line 90). Identify one or two moments in each scene which show evidence of disorder. Then find a way of representing this (perhaps as a set of drawings or tableaux).

4 Claudius's notes

Politicians prepare a set of notes before making any major speech. Write the notes (a series of brief, numbered points) that Claudius prepared for himself before his first speech in Scene 2.

5 A sister and daughter gives advice

Ophelia is on the receiving end of much advice from her brother and father. But what if the roles were reversed? As Ophelia, write eight to sixteen lines of advice to Laertes and to Polonius. Would she use the same kinds of metaphor as her brother and father use?

6 What do you think?

No one knows for certain if in Scene 2, line 129 Shakespeare wrote 'solid', 'sullied' (dirty), or 'sallied' (assaulted). Explain your preference.

7 Horatio's point of view

Horatio has come to Denmark from Wittenberg University. He appears in four of the five scenes in Act 1, and seems to know a great deal about state affairs (is he a Dane?). Remind yourself quickly of all he says in this act, then write his account of all that has happened to him since he returned to Denmark.

Gertrude and Claudius, Royal Shakespeare Company, 1984. Choose a line from Scene 2 that would make an appropriate caption for this picture.

8 'To put an antic disposition on'

Hamlet tells his friends that his future behaviour may look very strange, even mad (Scene 5, lines 171–2). Brainstorm the reasons why you think Hamlet has decided to act as if he were mad.

Polonius gives Reynaldo money for Laertes in Paris. He orders Reynaldo to spy on Laertes's behaviour using devious, indirect methods. Even lies may be used to discover what Laertes is doing.

Polonius (right) tells Reynaldo that roundabout ways of questioning ('encompassment . . . question') will yield better information than direct approaches ('come you more nearer . . . touch it'). Think about how you would advise Polonius to speak in this scene to suggest his character and his role in the Danish court.

Marry by Saint Mary
Danskers Danes
means resources
keep live
Take you show, assume

Addicted given to vices
forgeries slanders, lies
wanton carefree, loose behaviour
drabbing whoring, using
 prostitutes

ACT 2 SCENE 1
A state room in the castle

Enter POLONIUS *and* REYNALDO

POLONIUS Give him this money, and these notes, Reynaldo.
REYNALDO I will my lord.
POLONIUS You shall do marvellous wisely, good Reynaldo,
    Before you visit him, to make inquire
    Of his behaviour.
REYNALDO   My lord, I did intend it.   5
POLONIUS Marry well said, very well said. Look you sir,
    Inquire me first what Danskers are in Paris,
    And how, and who, what means, and where they keep,
    What company, at what expense; and finding
    By this encompassment and drift of question   10
    That they do know my son, come you more nearer
    Than your particular demands will touch it.
    Take you as 'twere some distant knowledge of him,
    As thus, 'I know his father and his friends,
    And in part him' – do you mark this Reynaldo?   15
REYNALDO Ay, very well, my lord.
POLONIUS 'And in part him, but' – you may say – 'not well,
    But if't be he I mean, he's very wild,
    Addicted so and so' – and there put on him
    What forgeries you please; marry, none so rank   20
    As may dishonour him, take heed of that,
    But sir, such wanton, wild, and usual slips
    As are companions noted and most known
    To youth and liberty.
REYNALDO   As gaming my lord?
POLONIUS Ay, or drinking, fencing, swearing,   25
    Quarrelling, drabbing – you may go so far.
REYNALDO My lord, that would dishonour him.

Polonius continues to advise Reynaldo to use indirect methods to find out whether Laertes is guilty of improper behaviour in Paris. But Polonius loses the thread of his argument!

1 Reynaldo – the fox? (in pairs)

This is Reynaldo's only appearance in the play. The actor playing him will wish to establish his character even though he has such a small part. He might be guided by the knowledge that Reynaldo (Reynard) means 'the fox', an animal with a reputation for cunning. Take parts and read lines 1–72 in several ways to discover which works best:

a Reynaldo is an experienced secret agent, well used to spying missions

b Reynaldo thinks that Polonius is a rambling old fool

c Reynaldo is genuinely puzzled about what he's being asked to do, but wishes to be a loyal servant.

2 Losing the drift of his argument

Identify the line where Polonius begins to lose the thread of his argument. Advise the actor on how he should play this 'forgetful' episode to help establish the character of Polonius. For example, should he try to win audience sympathy for an old man's failing memory, or should he aim to get a laugh at Polonius's expense?

3 Reynaldo in Paris (in groups of three)

Improvise a scene in Paris where Reynaldo is talking with two people, trying to find out information about Laertes. Use lines 54–60 as your guide. Try it in two ways. First, Laertes has been up to no mischief at all. Second, Laertes has been behaving in ways that fulfil his father's suspicions. Which is more likely?

---

season it in the charge modify the accusation
incontinency rampant sexual misbehaviour
quaintly cleverly
unreclaimèd blood untamed passion

Of general assault that attacks everyone
fetch of warrant trick that is legitimate
prenominate already mentioned
o'ertook in's rouse drunk
Videlicet that is to say

POLONIUS Faith no, as you may season it in the charge.
  You must not put another scandal on him,
  That he is open to incontinency,   30
  That's not my meaning. But breathe his faults so quaintly
  That they may seem the taints of liberty,
  The flash and outbreak of a fiery mind,
  A savageness in unreclaimèd blood,
  Of general assault.
REYNALDO   But my good lord –   35
POLONIUS Wherefore should you do this?
REYNALDO   Ay my lord,
  I would know that.
POLONIUS   Marry sir, here's my drift,
  And I believe it is a fetch of warrant.
  You laying these slight sullies on my son,
  As 'twere a thing a little soiled i'th'working,   40
  Mark you,
  Your party in converse, him you would sound,
  Having ever seen in the prenominate crimes
  The youth you breathe of guilty, be assured
  He closes with you in this consequence,   45
  'Good sir', or so, or 'friend', or 'gentleman',
  According to the phrase and the addition
  Of man and country.
REYNALDO   Very good my lord.
POLONIUS And then sir does a this – a does – what was I about to say?
  By the mass I was about to say something. Where did I leave?   50
REYNALDO At 'closes in the consequence', at 'friend, or so', and
  'gentleman'.
POLONIUS At 'closes in the consequence' – ay marry,
  He closes with you thus: 'I know the gentleman,
  I saw him yesterday, or th'other day,   55
  Or then, or then, with such or such, and as you say,
  There was a gaming, there o'ertook in's rouse,
  There falling out at tennis', or perchance,
  'I saw him enter such a house of sale' –
  Videlicet, a brothel – or so forth. See you now,   60
  Your bait of falsehood takes this carp of truth,

Polonius dispatches Reynaldo on his spying mission to Paris. Ophelia comes to report that she has been frightened by Hamlet's strange appearance. His clothing was dishevelled and his behaviour odd.

1 A father spies on his son (in pairs)

Talk together about what you think of Polonius as a father. Is there any justification for what he orders Reynaldo to do?

2 'By indirections find directions out'

Line 64 sums up Polonius's method. What does it suggest about his character?

3 Points of view on Hamlet's madness (in groups of four)

Take parts as Claudius, Gertrude, Polonius and Ophelia. In role, offer your explanation of Hamlet's appearance from your character's point of view. Begin by saying whether you think Hamlet is really mad or just putting on an act. Then go on to say why you think he is behaving as he is. Are there any points on which all four characters agree?

4 Show the 'absent scene' (in groups of three)

Some films of the play add a scene showing Hamlet's appearance to Ophelia. Lines 75–98 are heard as a voice-over to Hamlet's behaviour. Act out your own version of this 'absent scene'. As one person slowly narrates the lines, the other two mime them.

---

of wisdom and of reach who are wise and perceptive
windlasses roundabout ways (like hunters circling their prey)
assays of bias indirect attempts (as a bowl curves towards its target)

closet private room
down-gyvèd fallen (like fetters around his ankles)
in purport in expression
perusal study

And thus do we of wisdom and of reach,
With windlasses and with assays of bias,
By indirections find directions out.
So, by my former lecture and advice,   65
Shall you my son. You have me, have you not?
REYNALDO My lord, I have.
POLONIUS   God buy ye, fare ye well.
REYNALDO Good my lord.
POLONIUS Observe his inclination in yourself.
REYNALDO I shall my lord.   70
POLONIUS And let him ply his music.
REYNALDO   Well my lord.
POLONIUS Farewell.

Exit Reynaldo

Enter OPHELIA

                 How now Ophelia, what's the matter?
OPHELIA Oh my lord, my lord, I have been so affrighted.
POLONIUS With what, i'th'name of God?
OPHELIA My lord, as I was sewing in my closet,   75
Lord Hamlet with his doublet all unbraced,
No hat upon his head, his stockings fouled,
Ungartered, and down-gyvèd to his ankle,
Pale as his shirt, his knees knocking each other,
And with a look so piteous in purport   80
As if he had been loosèd out of hell
To speak of horrors – he comes before me.
POLONIUS Mad for thy love?
OPHELIA   My lord I do not know,
But truly I do fear it.
POLONIUS   What said he?
OPHELIA He took me by the wrist, and held me hard;   85
Then goes he to the length of all his arm,
And with his other hand thus o'er his brow
He falls to such perusal of my face
As a would draw it. Long stayed he so;

63

Ophelia tells how strangely Hamlet behaved. Polonius guesses that Hamlet has been driven mad by Ophelia's rejection of his love. He decides to tell all to Claudius.

1 'I am sorry' (in pairs)

These three words from line 104 could have different meanings. Decide which of the following you prefer, because of your view of Polonius:

a Polonius is genuinely sorry for his daughter

b he feels sorry for Hamlet

c he doesn't care at all about Ophelia's or Hamlet's feelings

d he is worried about his own position as a state official who should know about such matters

e an interpretation of your own.

2 True or false? (in small groups)

In lines 112–15, Polonius says that just as older people are over-suspicious, so young people are rash and indiscreet. Talk together about whether you agree with Polonius. Give examples from your own experience.

3 Safer to tell

Polonius seems to think in lines 115–17 that it is safer to tell his suspicions to Claudius about Hamlet's love, rather than keep them secret ('close'). Although it might make trouble ('move more grief'), it is better to tell.

Look back over the scene and pick out as many examples as you can that suggest Polonius is a very cautious man, always weighing up what will bring him advantage.

---

bulk body
ecstasy madness
fordoes destroys
undertakings deeds
quoted observed

wrack dishonour, seduce
beshrew a curse on
proper to characteristic of
the younger sort young people

At last, a little shaking of mine arm,   90
And thrice his head thus waving up and down,
He raised a sigh so piteous and profound
As it did seem to shatter all his bulk,
And end his being. That done, he lets me go,
And with his head over his shoulder turned   95
He seemed to find his way without his eyes,
For out-a-doors he went without their helps
And to the last bended their light on me.

POLONIUS Come, go with me, I will go seek the king.
This is the very ecstasy of love,   100
Whose violent property fordoes itself,
And leads the will to desperate undertakings
As oft as any passion under heaven
That does afflict our natures. I am sorry.
What, have you given him any hard words of late?   105

OPHELIA No my good lord; but as you did command,
I did repel his letters, and denied
His access to me.

POLONIUS   That hath made him mad.
I am sorry that with better heed and judgement
I had not quoted him. I feared he did but trifle,   110
And meant to wrack thee, but beshrew my jealousy.
By heaven, it is as proper to our age
To cast beyond ourselves in our opinions
As it is common for the younger sort
To lack discretion. Come, go we to the king.   115
This must be known, which being kept close, might move
More grief to hide than hate to utter love.
Come.

                                                    Exeunt

Claudius has sent for Hamlet's fellow students. They are to find out the cause of Hamlet's strange behaviour. Gertrude promises Rosencrantz and Guildenstern they will be royally rewarded if they stay.

Rosencrantz and Guildenstern as portrayed in Tom Stoppard's play *Rosencrantz and Guildenstern are Dead*. Is this how you picture them? Do you think they should look and dress alike?

Moreover that not only
Sith nor since neither
neighboured to familiar with
haviour behaviour
vouchsafe your rest agree to stay
occasion favourable opportunities

glean gather, pick up
opened revealed
gentry courtesy
supply and profit help and benefit
fits befits

ACT 2 SCENE 2
The Great Hall of Elsinore Castle

Trumpet call Enter KING *and* QUEEN, ROSENCRANTZ *and*
GUILDENSTERN, *with others*

CLAUDIUS Welcome dear Rosencrantz and Guildenstern!
    Moreover that we much did long to see you,
    The need we have to use you did provoke
    Our hasty sending. Something have you heard
    Of Hamlet's transformation – so call it,   5
    Sith nor th'exterior nor the inward man
    Resembles that it was. What it should be,
    More than his father's death, that thus hath put him
    So much from th'understanding of himself,
    I cannot dream of. I entreat you both,   10
    That being of so young days brought up with him,
    And sith so neighboured to his youth and haviour,
    That you vouchsafe your rest here in our court
    Some little time, so by your companies
    To draw him on to pleasures, and to gather   15
    So much as from occasion you may glean,
    Whether aught to us unknown afflicts him thus,
    That opened lies within our remedy.
GERTRUDE Good gentlemen, he hath much talked of you,
    And sure I am, two men there is not living   20
    To whom he more adheres. If it will please you
    To show us so much gentry and good will
    As to expend your time with us a while,
    For the supply and profit of our hope,
    Your visitation shall receive such thanks   25
    As fits a king's remembrance.
ROSENCRANTZ   Both your majesties
    Might by the sovereign power you have of us
    Put your dread pleasures more into command
    Than to entreaty.

Guildenstern promises that he and Rosencrantz will do whatever Claudius commands. Polonius announces the ambassadors' return. He says he has discovered the cause of Hamlet's madness.

1 Tweedledum and Tweedledee?

Many directors seize on Gertrude's line 34 as an opportunity to make the audience laugh and to make a point about the similarity between Rosencrantz and Guildenstern. These directors advise Gertrude to speak the line in one of two ways:

Either: she is unable to distinguish which man is which, and so speaks the line as an uncertain question, unsure whether she is addressing the right person.

Or: she corrects a mistake by Claudius who has misidentified the two courtiers.

How would you advise Gertrude to speak line 34 in order to help members of the audience form their impression of Rosencrantz and Guildenstern? Would you want to get a laugh on the line by having the king or queen (or both) unable to differentiate between the two men? Try out different possibilities, including one in which Gertrude is simply reinforcing Claudius's thanks.

2 Public and private (in pairs)

Gertrude and Claudius share a brief private moment together in lines 54–8 when Gertrude expresses her unease about how quickly they married after King Hamlet's death. How would you stage the lines to emphasise the difference between their public life (as king and queen) and their domestic life (as mother and stepfather, and wife and husband)? Remember, the rest of the court on stage will be watching their every move, and hoping to overhear what they are saying.

---

in the full bent completely (like a fully drawn archery bow)
practices behaviour (or deceits)
still always
trail of policy affairs of state (or deceptions)

fruit final course of a meal
distemper illness
main major matter
sift him question Polonius (or Hamlet?) closely
brother fellow king

GUILDENSTERN   But we both obey,
          And here give up ourselves in the full bent   30
          To lay our service freely at your feet
          To be commanded.
CLAUDIUS Thanks Rosencrantz, and gentle Guildenstern.
GERTRUDE Thanks Guildenstern, and gentle Rosencrantz.
          And I beseech you instantly to visit   35
          My too much changèd son. Go some of you
          And bring these gentlemen where Hamlet is.
GUILDENSTERN Heavens make our presence and our practices
          Pleasant and helpful to him.
GERTRUDE   Ay, amen.
          Exeunt Rosencrantz and Guildenstern [and some Attendants]

          Enter POLONIUS

POLONIUS Th'ambassadors from Norway, my good lord,   40
          Are joyfully returned.
CLAUDIUS Thou still hast been the father of good news.
POLONIUS Have I my lord? Assure you, my good liege,
          I hold my duty, as I hold my soul,
          Both to my God and to my gracious king;   45
          And I do think, or else this brain of mine
          Hunts not the trail of policy so sure
          As it hath used to do, that I have found
          The very cause of Hamlet's lunacy.
CLAUDIUS Oh speak of that, that do I long to hear.   50
POLONIUS Give first admittance to th'ambassadors;
          My news shall be the fruit to that great feast.
CLAUDIUS Thyself do grace to them and bring them in.
                                        [Exit Polonius]
          He tells me, my dear Gertrude, he hath found
          The head and source of all your son's distemper.   55
GERTRUDE I doubt it is no other but the main:
          His father's death, and our o'erhasty marriage.
CLAUDIUS Well, we shall sift him.

          Enter POLONIUS, VOLTEMAND *and* CORNELIUS

                    Welcome my good friends.
          Say Voltemand, what from our brother Norway?

*Voltemand reports that the King of Norway has prevented Fortinbras
from attacking Denmark, sending him instead to invade Poland.
Polonius embarks on a long-winded explanation of Hamlet's madness.*

1 Voltemand's report (in small groups)

Much political activity has happened. To help your understanding of
Voltemand's report, try one or more of the following activities:

a Point it out! One person slowly reads aloud lines 60–85. At every
   mention of a person, everyone in the group points to a group
   member as that person (allocate parts as you read). It sounds
   complicated, but you will very quickly pick it up and find it helps
   you understand who's who. The first 'point' is in line 61, 'our'
   (Voltemand and Cornelius); the next is on 'he' (King of Norway).
   Don't worry if you do not have sufficient group members for
   everyone mentioned. Just point to objects (for example, a chair or
   table) to represent characters.

b Act it out! One person reads aloud, pausing at each punctuation
   mark. The others act out each section of Voltemand's speech.

c Write it out! The King of Norway has sent a formal letter to
   Claudius. Among other things, it asks for safe passage through
   Denmark for Fortinbras's army as it marches to invade Poland.
   Write the document in full.

2 'Brevity is the soul of wit' (in groups of three)

Take parts as Polonius, Gertrude and Claudius. Polonius speaks lines
85–92. Gertrude and Claudius work out their facial and bodily
expressions in response to Polonius's words (for example, bored,
bewildered, fascinated). Change parts and repeat. What advice would
you give to the king and queen about how they should react to each
section of Polonius's rambling introduction?

---

desires good wishes
Upon our first when we raised the
  matter
levies troops
Polack Polish nation
impotence powerlessness

borne in hand deceived
in fine in conclusion
th'assay of arms battle
allowance permission
expostulate discuss, expound
flourishes decorations

VOLTEMAND   Most fair return of greetings and desires.   60
      Upon our first, he sent out to suppress
      His nephew's levies, which to him appeared
      To be a preparation 'gainst the Polack;
      But better looked into, he truly found
      It was against your highness; whereat grieved   65
      That so his sickness, age and impotence
      Was falsely borne in hand, sends out arrests
      On Fortinbras, which he in brief obeys,
      Receives rebuke from Norway, and in fine
      Makes vow before his uncle never more   70
      To give th'assay of arms against your majesty.
      Whereon old Norway, overcome with joy,
      Gives him three thousand crowns in annual fee,
      And his commission to employ those soldiers,
      So levied as before, against the Polack;   75
      With an entreaty, herein further shown,
      That it might please you to give quiet pass
      Through your dominions for this enterprise,
      On such regards of safety and allowance
      As therein are set down.
                   [*Gives a document*]
CLAUDIUS   It likes us well,   80
      And at our more considered time we'll read,
      Answer, and think upon this business.
      Meantime, we thank you for your well-took labour.
      Go to your rest; at night we'll feast together.
      Most welcome home.
                     Exeunt Ambassadors
POLONIUS   This business is well ended.   85
      My liege, and madam, to expostulate
      What majesty should be, what duty is,
      Why day is day, night night, and time is time,
      Were nothing but to waste night, day, and time.
      Therefore, since brevity is the soul of wit   90
      And tediousness the limbs and outward flourishes,
      I will be brief. Your noble son is mad.

Polonius rambles on even though Gertrude urges him to come to the point. He reads aloud Hamlet's letter to Ophelia, and says his daughter has told him all about Hamlet's attempts to woo her.

1 'More matter with less art' (in pairs)

In spite of Gertrude's impatience, Polonius continues to play pompously with language. Find a way of speaking lines 85–108 that you think matches his character. For example, try speaking pompously, or poetically, or with embarrassment.

2 'Et cetera' (in small groups)

No one can be quite sure why Polonius says '*et cetera*' (line 112). Is it to cover up some very personal words of love that are embarrassing for a father to read? Or is it just to summarise some formal phrases in Hamlet's letter (such as 'warm greetings')? Talk together about why you think Polonius says '*et cetera*'. Then write the missing words that Polonius has declined to read.

3 Tell me everything (in pairs)

Polonius says Ophelia has told him of all her encounters with Hamlet. But how did he get the story out of her? Did she offer it willingly? Or did he bully or wheedle it out? Improvise a meeting between father and daughter where he learns all about Hamlet's 'solicitings . . . by time, by means, and place'.

4 Is it good poetry?

Hamlet clearly doesn't think much of himself as a poet ('I am ill at these numbers'). Critics are divided about the poetic quality of his four lines of verse in the letter (lines 115–18). Imagine you have been asked to comment on Hamlet's four lines of poetry. What remarks would you write to help him?

More matter with less art more information and less playing with language
figure figure of speech
Perpend consider carefully

gather and surmise draw your own conclusions
numbers verses
whilst this machine is to him as long as I live ('machine' = body)
solicitings pleadings, importunings

Mad call I it, for to define true madness,
What is't but to be nothing else but mad?
But let that go.

GERTRUDE   More matter with less art.   95

POLONIUS Madam, I swear I use no art at all.
That he is mad, 'tis true; 'tis true 'tis pity,
And pity 'tis 'tis true – a foolish figure,
But farewell it, for I will use no art.
Mad let us grant him then, and now remains   100
That we find out the cause of this effect,
Or rather say, the cause of this defect,
For this effect defective comes by cause.
Thus it remains, and the remainder thus.
Perpend.   105
I have a daughter – have while she is mine –
Who in her duty and obedience, mark,
Hath given me this. Now gather and surmise.

Reads the letter

'To the celestial, and my soul's idol, the most beautified Ophelia,' –
That's an ill phrase, a vile phrase, 'beautified' is a vile phrase – but   110
you shall hear. Thus:
'In her excellent white bosom, these, *et cetera.*'

GERTRUDE Came this from Hamlet to her?

POLONIUS Good madam stay awhile, I will be faithful.
'Doubt thou the stars are fire,   115
Doubt that the sun doth move,
Doubt truth to be a liar,
But never doubt I love.
'O dear Ophelia, I am ill at these numbers, I have not art to reckon
my groans; but that I love thee best, O most best, believe it. Adieu.   120
          'Thine evermore, most dear lady, whilst this machine is
                         to him, Hamlet.'
This in obedience hath my daughter shown me,
And, more above, hath his solicitings,
As they fell out, by time, by means, and place,   125
All given to mine ear.

CLAUDIUS   But how hath she
Received his love?

POLONIUS   What do you think of me?

CLAUDIUS As of a man faithful and honourable.

Polonius reports that he ordered Ophelia to reject Hamlet's love, so causing the prince's madness. Polonius suggests a plan: he and Claudius will spy on an arranged meeting between Ophelia and Hamlet.

1 'Played the desk, or table-book' (in groups of three)

The general sense of line 134 is that Polonius refuses to act as a mere go-between. Experiment with ways of making the imagery of the line visible. Take parts as Ophelia, Hamlet and Polonius and mime some literal meanings ('table-book' = notebook).

2 What happened? (in small groups)

In lines 141–9, Polonius describes at least eleven distinct actions. One person slowly narrates the lines, the others act out each event.

3 'Not that I know' (in pairs)

In what tone of voice does Claudius speak line 153? Talk together about what the line suggests about Claudius's attitude to Polonius.

4 'Take this from this' (in pairs)

Shakespeare often builds stage directions into his language. But just what does Polonius do at line 154? Does he touch his head and shoulder ('chop off my head')? Or does he touch his official staff of office and his hand ('dismiss me')? Work out an appropriate action to accompany the line.

5 'I'll loose my daughter to him'

'Loose' sounds like releasing a farmyard animal. Write down what line 160 suggests to you about Polonius's view of Ophelia. Consider also how he refers to her in line 138.

---

fain gladly	**prescripts** orders
given my heart a winking	**watch** sleeplessness
shut my eyes to the love-affair	**lightness** delirium, light-headedness
round directly	**declension** decline
out of thy star far above you	**arras** hanging tapestry (like a
socially	curtain covering a wall)

POLONIUS I would fain prove so. But what might you think,
      When I had seen this hot love on the wing –   130
      As I perceived it, I must tell you that,
      Before my daughter told me – what might you,
      Or my dear majesty your queen here, think,
      If I had played the desk, or table-book,
      Or given my heart a winking, mute and dumb,   135
      Or looked upon this love with idle sight –
      What might you think? No, I went round to work,
      And my young mistress thus I did bespeak:
      'Lord Hamlet is a prince out of thy star.
      This must not be.' And then I prescripts gave her,   140
      That she should lock herself from his resort,
      Admit no messengers, receive no tokens.
      Which done, she took the fruits of my advice,
      And he, repulsed – a short tale to make –
      Fell into a sadness, then into a fast,   145
      Thence to a watch, thence into a weakness,
      Thence to a lightness, and by this declension
      Into the madness wherein now he raves,
      And all we mourn for.
CLAUDIUS   Do you think 'tis this?
GERTRUDE It may be, very like.   150
POLONIUS Hath there been such a time, I'ld fain know that,
      That I have positively said, 'tis so,
      When it proved otherwise?
CLAUDIUS   Not that I know.
POLONIUS Take this from this, if this be otherwise.
      If circumstances lead me, I will find   155
      Where truth is hid, though it were hid indeed
      Within the centre.
CLAUDIUS   How may we try it further?
POLONIUS You know sometimes he walks four hours together
      Here in the lobby.
GERTRUDE   So he does indeed.
POLONIUS At such a time I'll loose my daughter to him.   160
      Be you and I behind an arras then.

Claudius agrees to Polonius's plan to spy on Hamlet. Polonius tries to make sense of Hamlet's puzzling replies and questions.

---

1 *'Enter* HAMLET *reading on a book'* (in small groups)

Each new production of the play has to take decisions on the following questions. Talk together about your own responses.

a Does Hamlet see Polonius plotting with Claudius?

b How is Hamlet dressed, and how does he behave? (This is his first appearance since he was reported mad.)

c Is Hamlet aware of anyone else on stage before Polonius greets him?

d Why, and to whom, does Polonius say 'Oh give me leave' (line 168): to Claudius? Gertrude? The Attendants? Hamlet? Try out each possibility. Decide which you think is most dramatically appropriate.

2 Cross-talk comics? (in pairs)

Some critics argue that Hamlet treats Polonius as a 'straight man' in a cross-talk comedy team. Take parts and read lines 169–212 in a variety of ways to discover if Hamlet and Polonius really do sound like a pair of comedians.

3 Fishmongers

A 'fishmonger' (line 172) could be a prostitute's pimp, a fisher for information, a person whose daughters would be both beautiful and prolific breeders of children, or a bit of nonsense by Hamlet, or something Hamlet reads out of the book he is holding. Which suggestion do you prefer?

---

thereon because of his disappointment in love
assistant for a state important civil servant
board him presently greet him immediately

God-a-mercy thank you ('God have mercy on you', a conventional reply to a social inferior)
carrion dead flesh (see page 244)
Conception becoming pregnant
harping on talking only of (like a harpist playing one string only)

Mark the encounter: if he love her not,
And be not from his reason fallen thereon,
Let me be no assistant for a state,
But keep a farm and carters.
CLAUDIUS   We will try it.   165

Enter HAMLET *reading on a book*

GERTRUDE But look where sadly the poor wretch comes reading.
POLONIUS Away, I do beseech you both, away.
        I'll board him presently.
                    Exeunt Claudius and Gertrude [and Attendants]
                    Oh give me leave.
        How does my good Lord Hamlet?
HAMLET Well, God-a-mercy.   170
POLONIUS Do you know me, my lord?
HAMLET Excellent well, y'are a fishmonger.
POLONIUS Not I my lord.
HAMLET Then I would you were so honest a man.
POLONIUS Honest my lord?   175
HAMLET Ay sir. To be honest, as this world goes, is to be one man
        picked out of ten thousand.
POLONIUS That's very true my lord.
HAMLET For if the sun breed maggots in a dead dog, being a good
        kissing carrion – Have you a daughter?   180
POLONIUS I have my lord.
HAMLET Let her not walk i'th'sun. Conception is a blessing, but as your
        daughter may conceive – Friend, look to't.
POLONIUS (*Aside*) How say you by that? Still harping on my daughter.
        Yet he knew me not at first, a said I was a fishmonger – a is far   185
        gone, far gone. And truly, in my youth I suffered much extremity
        for love, very near this. I'll speak to him again. – What do you read
        my lord?
HAMLET Words, words, words.
POLONIUS What is the matter, my lord?   190
HAMLET Between who?
POLONIUS I mean the matter that you read, my lord.

Hamlet insults Polonius who nonetheless persists in finding good sense in Hamlet's words. Polonius leaves, and Hamlet welcomes Rosencrantz and Guildenstern, exchanging sexual puns with them.

1 'The satirical rogue'

To ridicule Polonius, Hamlet quotes the author of the book he is reading. Two well-known writers mocked the handicaps of old age. Juvenal was a Roman satirist of the first century AD who ridiculed folly. Erasmus (1466–1536) was a Dutch Christian humanist who wrote *In Praise of Folly*.

Research either Juvenal or Erasmus. Report on whether you think their writings would appeal to Hamlet, and why. Alternatively, you could invent your own author and write a satirical paragraph – after all, Hamlet may be making it all up!

2 Polonius writes his report (in pairs)

As the senior officer of state in Denmark, Polonius would write or dictate a report of all his encounters with royalty. Write his report (based on lines 170–211) in which he attempts to discover 'method' (logic) in Hamlet's madness.

3 Young men joking together

Hamlet greets Rosencrantz and Guildenstern warmly. He joins in the kind of word play and sexual innuendo that was (and is?) probably typical of most male students. Fortune is turned into a female prostitute. So 'her privates we' might mean her genitals (private parts), but it could simply mean 'we are intimate with Fortune'. Similarly, 'favours' and 'secret parts' could also be *double entendres*, though their surface meanings are 'help' and 'private affairs' respectively. Which meanings do you think Hamlet and Guildenstern intend?

Slanders defamatory and false reports	**suddenly** immediately
purging discharging, exuding	**withal** with
hams thighs	**indifferent** ordinary
pregnant meaningful, apt	**button** topmost
	strumpet prostitute

HAMLET Slanders sir, for the satirical rogue says here that old men have grey beards, that their faces are wrinkled, their eyes purging thick amber and plumtree gum, and that they have a plentiful lack of wit, together with most weak hams. All which sir, though I most powerfully and potently believe, yet I hold it not honesty to have it thus set down. For yourself sir shall grow old as I am, if like a crab you could go backward. 195

POLONIUS (*Aside*) Though this be madness, yet there is method in't. – Will you walk out of the air, my lord? 200

HAMLET Into my grave?

POLONIUS Indeed that's out of the air. (*Aside*) How pregnant sometimes his replies are! a happiness that often madness hits on, which reason and sanity could not so prosperously be delivered of. I will leave him, and suddenly contrive the means of meeting between him and my daughter. – My honourable lord, I will most humbly take my leave of you. 205

HAMLET You cannot sir take from me anything that I will more willingly part withal; except my life, except my life, except my life. 210

POLONIUS Fare you well my lord.   *suicidal*

HAMLET These tedious old fools!

Enter GUILDENSTERN *and* ROSENCRANTZ

POLONIUS You go to seek the Lord Hamlet, there he is.

ROSENCRANTZ God save you sir.

[*Exit Polonius*]

GUILDENSTERN My honoured lord! 215

ROSENCRANTZ My most dear lord!

HAMLET My excellent good friends! How dost thou Guildenstern? Ah, Rosencrantz. Good lads, how do you both?

ROSENCRANTZ As the indifferent children of the earth.

GUILDENSTERN Happy in that we are not over-happy; on Fortune's cap we are not the very button. 220

HAMLET Nor the soles of her shoe?

ROSENCRANTZ Neither, my lord.

HAMLET Then you live about her waist, or in the middle of her favours?

GUILDENSTERN Faith, her privates we. 225

HAMLET In the secret parts of Fortune? Oh most true, she is a strumpet. What news?

Hamlet, Rosencrantz and Guildenstern continue their banter, but Hamlet becomes more serious. He challenges the courtiers about why they have come to Elsinore. Have they come freely or been sent for?

1 'Denmark's a prison'

Do you think Hamlet is joking or serious in claiming 'Denmark's a prison'? Identify three possible reasons why Hamlet makes his remark.

2 True or false? (in small groups)

'For there is nothing either good or bad but thinking makes it so' says Hamlet (lines 239–40). Do you believe that? Talk together about whether you agree with Hamlet's claim. Use practical examples from your own experience.

3 Verbal fencing (in groups of three)

On three or four occasions in lines 241–9, Rosencrantz and Guildenstern try to encourage Hamlet to talk about 'ambition'. Presumably they are following Claudius's instructions to discover what afflicts Hamlet. If they can get him to talk about his ambition, they will have something of real importance to report to the king. But Hamlet pushes their reasoning to an absurd conclusion. He says that if ambitions are shadows, then beggars (who have no ambitions) are more substantial ('bodies') than kings (who are filled with ambition).

The conversation between Hamlet and the courtiers might just be another example of the quick-fire word play that students at Wittenberg indulged in. Take parts and experiment with ways of speaking the lines. Bring out how Rosencrantz and Guildenstern are trying to get Hamlet to reveal his secret thoughts (for example, they might stress 'ambition'). Show how Hamlet warily fends them off. Have the image of a sword-fencing match in your mind as you speak.

---

doomsday the Day of Judgement
Fortune goddess of chance
confines, wards cells in a prison
bodies people without ambition
outstretched heroes great men, or
  ambitious actors

fay faith
sort associate
am most dreadfully attended
  have useless servants
in the beaten way of friendship
  as old friends

ROSENCRANTZ None my lord, but that the world's grown honest.

HAMLET Then is doomsday near – but your news is not true. Let me
question more in particular. What have you, my good friends, 230
deserved at the hands of Fortune, that she sends you to prison
hither?

GUILDENSTERN Prison, my lord?

HAMLET Denmark's a prison.

ROSENCRANTZ Then is the world one. 235

HAMLET A goodly one, in which there are many confines, wards, and
dungeons; Denmark being one o'th'worst.

ROSENCRANTZ We think not so my lord.

HAMLET Why then 'tis none to you,[for there is nothing either good
or bad but thinking makes it so]. To me it is a prison. 240

ROSENCRANTZ Why then your ambition makes it one; 'tis too narrow
for your mind.

HAMLET O God, I could be bounded in a nutshell, and count myself
a king of infinite space, were it not that I have bad dreams.

GUILDENSTERN Which dreams indeed are ambition, for the very 245
substance of the ambitious is merely the shadow of a dream.

HAMLET A dream itself is but a shadow.

ROSENCRANTZ Truly, and I hold ambition of so airy and light a quality
that it is but a shadow's shadow.

HAMLET Then are our beggars bodies, and our monarchs and out- 250
stretched heroes the beggars' shadows. Shall we to th'court? for by
my fay I cannot reason.

BOTH We'll wait upon you.

HAMLET No such matter. I will not sort you with the rest of my
servants; for to speak to you like an honest man, I am most 255
dreadfully attended. But in the beaten way of friendship, what make
you at Elsinore?

ROSENCRANTZ To visit you my lord, no other occasion.

HAMLET Beggar that I am, I am even poor in thanks, but I thank
you – and sure, dear friends, my thanks are too dear a halfpenny. 260
Were you not sent for? Is it your own inclining? Is it a free
visitation? Come, deal justly with me. Come, come. Nay, speak.

GUILDENSTERN What should we say my lord?

HAMLET Why, anything but to the purpose. You were sent for – and
there is a kind of confession in your looks which your modesties 265
have not craft enough to colour. I know the good king and queen
have sent for you.

*Guildenstern admits that he and Rosencrantz were sent for by Claudius.
Hamlet reflects on his melancholy and on the contrasting splendour of
man and the heavens. Rosencrantz says the players are about to arrive.*

1 From friendship to suspicion (in groups of three)

Hamlet becomes increasingly suspicious of his two friends. Why have
they come to Denmark? He 'conjures' (seriously asks) them to tell,
appealing to their 'consonancy' (youthful friendship). Take parts and
read lines 215–77. Identify where you feel Hamlet's suspicions first
begin.

2 Hamlet's melancholy (individually or in pairs)

In lines 280–90, Hamlet reflects that he has 'lost all my mirth'. He
speaks of the wonderful nature of both the world and of humankind,
but says that nothing now gives him pleasure. The earth seems 'a
sterile promontory'; the heavens 'a foul and pestilent congregation of
vapours'; and humankind, though the 'paragon' (ideal of excellence) of
animals, is merely 'dust', offering him no delight. It is possible that
Shakespeare is referring ironically to the Globe theatre: 'heavens' = the
painted canopy over the stage; 'foul and pestilent . . . vapours' = the
audience (see page 265).

Every actor who plays Hamlet spends many hours deciding how to
speak the lines. How should each section be spoken? Is Hamlet's tone
sincere, ironical, sarcastic, bitter, awe-struck – or does the mood vary
from line to line? There is no single 'right' way to speak these lines, so
work out the version you would recommend.

3 The players

Hamlet lists some members of the acting company: the king, the
knight, the lover, the humorous man (not a comic, but a man driven by
his 'humour' or moods), and the clown. Identify which of these
characters might be shown in the picture on page 84.

---

what more dear what greater
  reasons
a better proposer a more skilful
  speaker
moult no feather remain intact
express well-made
apprehension understanding

lenten frugal, thin
coted overtook
foil and target sword and shield
gratis without reward
tickle o'th'sere easily tickled to
  laughter (sere = gun trigger)

ROSENCRANTZ To what end my lord?

HAMLET That you must teach me. But let me conjure you, by the rights
of our fellowship, by the consonancy of our youth, by the obligation   270
of our ever-preserved love, and by what more dear a better proposer
can charge you withal, be even and direct with me, whether you
were sent for or no.

ROSENCRANTZ (*To Guildenstern*) What say you?

HAMLET (*Aside*) Nay then I have an eye of you. – If you love me, hold   275
not off.

GUILDENSTERN My lord, we were sent for.

HAMLET I will tell you why. So shall my anticipation prevent your
discovery, and your secrecy to the king and queen moult no feather.
I have of late, but wherefore I know not, lost all my mirth, forgone   280
all custom of exercises; and indeed it goes so heavily with my
disposition that this goodly frame, the earth, seems to me a sterile
promontory; this most excellent canopy the air, look you, this brave
o'erhanging firmament, this majestical roof fretted with golden
fire – why, it appeareth no other thing to me but a foul and pestilent   285
congregation of vapours. What a piece of work is a man! How noble
in reason, how infinite in faculties, in form and moving how express
and admirable, in action how like an angel, in apprehension how
like a god! The beauty of the world, the paragon of animals – and
yet to me, what is this quintessence of dust? Man delights not   290
me – no, nor woman neither, though by your smiling you seem to
say so.

ROSENCRANTZ My lord, there was no such stuff in my thoughts.

HAMLET Why did ye laugh then, when I said man delights not me?

ROSENCRANTZ To think, my lord, if you delight not in man, what   295
lenten entertainment the players shall receive from you. We coted
them on the way, and hither are they coming to offer you service.

HAMLET He that plays the king shall be welcome, his majesty shall have
tribute of me; the adventurous knight shall use his foil and target,
the lover shall not sigh gratis, the humorous man shall end his part   300
in peace, the clown shall make those laugh whose lungs are tickle
o'th'sere, and the lady shall say her mind freely – or the blank verse
shall halt for't. What players are they?

ROSENCRANTZ Even those you were wont to take such delight in, the
tragedians of the city.   305

HAMLET How chances it they travel? their residence, both in reputation
and profit, was better both ways.

Hamlet asks many questions about the travelling actors. Rosencrantz explains that the popularity of a company of child actors has forced the players to travel. Hamlet reflects on the fickleness of fashion.

The arrival of the players. Their 'inhibition' (ban on acting in their own theatre) has been caused by 'the late innovation' (recent change in fashion). Their reputation ('estimation') has declined because of 'an eyrie of children, little eyases, that cry out on the top of question' (a nest of child actors, as noisy as unfledged hawks). The lines refer to the 'war of the theatres' in 1600, when the success of a company of boy actors threatened the adult acting companies in London. The boys specialised in bitter satire. Some noblemen were afraid to visit the theatre for fear of mockery ('many wearing rapiers are afraid of goose-quills'). But it is possible that 'innovation' means 'political unrest' (see page 265).

wonted pace usual standard
escoted financed
quality profession (of acting)
no longer than they can sing until their voices break
tar them provoke them
went to cuffs fought
Hercules and his load Hercules with the heavens on his back (the emblem of the Globe Theatre)

make mouths sneer
ducats gold coins
picture in little miniature picture
Th'appurtenance of what is appropriate to
comply with you show you a proper welcome

ROSENCRANTZ I think their inhibition comes by the means of the late
   innovation.

HAMLET Do they hold the same estimation they did when I was in the 310
   city? Are they so followed?

ROSENCRANTZ No indeed are they not.

HAMLET How comes it? Do they grow rusty?

ROSENCRANTZ Nay, their endeavour keeps in the wonted pace, but
   there is sir an eyrie of children, little eyases, that cry out on the 315
   top of question and are most tyrannically clapped for't. These are
   now the fashion, and so be-rattle the common stages (so they call
   them) that many wearing rapiers are afraid of goose-quills, and dare
   scarce come thither.

HAMLET What, are they children? Who maintains 'em? How are they 320
   escoted? Will they pursue the quality no longer than they can sing?
   Will they not say afterwards, if they should grow themselves to
   common players – as it is most like if their means are no better, their
   writers do them wrong to make them exclaim against their own
   succession? 325

ROSENCRANTZ Faith, there has been much to do on both sides, and
   the nation holds it no sin to tar them to controversy. There was
   for a while no money bid for argument unless the poet and the player
   went to cuffs in the question.

HAMLET Is't possible? 330

GUILDENSTERN Oh there has been much throwing about of brains.

HAMLET Do the boys carry it away?

ROSENCRANTZ Ay that they do my lord, Hercules and his load too.

HAMLET It is not very strange, for my uncle is king of Denmark, and
   those that would make mouths at him while my father lived give 335
   twenty, forty, fifty, a hundred ducats apiece for his picture in little.
   'Sblood, there is something in this more than natural, if philosophy
   could find it out.

A flourish

GUILDENSTERN There are the players.

HAMLET Gentlemen, you are welcome to Elsinore. Your hands, come 340
   then. Th'appurtenance of welcome is fashion and ceremony. Let
   me comply with you in this garb, lest my extent to the players, which
   I tell you must show fairly outwards, should more appear like
   entertainment than yours. You are welcome – but my uncle-father
   and aunt-mother are deceived. 345

*Polonius enters to tell Hamlet of the players' arrival. Hamlet mocks him.
Polonius praises the actors in high-flown language. Hamlet taunts
Polonius about his daughter.*

---

1 'I know a hawk from a handsaw' (in pairs)

No one is quite sure what line 348 means. A 'hawk' might be a bird of
prey, or a plasterer's board for mortar. A 'handsaw' could be a 'hernshaw'
(heron), or a carpenter's saw. Hamlet might be saying 'I know the
difference between one thing and another – I'm not mad'. Or he may
merely be talking nonsense to bewilder Rosencrantz and Guildenstern.

Talk together about what you think Hamlet's words might mean.
For example, 'I can recognise a bird of prey (Guildenstern?) when I see
one'.

2 'Tragical – comical – historical – pastoral' (in small groups)

In lines 363–5, Shakespeare may be satirising Elizabethan scholars'
classification of plays. Polonius shows off his theatrical knowledge in a
way that invites audience laughter at the absurdity of his long-winded
list. To explore the comic potential, one person speaks the words
slowly while the others mime, in fast motion, each category he mentions
('pastoral' is a play with a country theme). You'll find 'tragical –
comical – historical – pastoral' quite a challenge!

3 'Scene individable or poem unlimited'

In lines 365–7, Polonius says twice that the actors can perform anything.
They are good at classical plays that obey the classical rules of drama
('scene individable', 'the law of writ'). They are equally skilled at plays
that ignore such rules ('poem unlimited', 'the liberty'). Why do you
think Polonius (or Shakespeare) makes these claims?

---

swaddling clouts baby clothes
Seneca/Plautus tragic/comic
  Roman dramatists
Jephtha a military leader and judge
  who sacrificed his daughter to God
'One fair daughter . . . ' Hamlet
  quotes from a song of the time

wot knows
row verse
pious chanson religious song
abridgement entertainment, or
  interruption

86

GUILDENSTERN In what my dear lord?

HAMLET I am but mad north-north-west. When the wind is southerly, I know a hawk from a handsaw.

Enter POLONIUS

POLONIUS Well be with you gentlemen.

HAMLET Hark you Guildenstern, and you too – at each ear a hearer. 350
That great baby you see there is not yet out of his swaddling clouts.

ROSENCRANTZ Happily he's the second time come to them, for they say an old man is twice a child.

HAMLET I will prophesy: he comes to tell me of the players, mark it. – You say right sir, a Monday morning, 'twas then indeed. 355

POLONIUS My lord, I have news to tell you.

HAMLET My lord, I have news to tell you. When Roscius was an actor in Rome –

POLONIUS The actors are come hither my lord.

HAMLET Buzz, buzz! 360

POLONIUS Upon my honour.

HAMLET Then came each actor on his ass –

POLONIUS The best actors in the world, either for tragedy, comedy, history, pastoral, pastoral-comical, historical-pastoral, tragical-historical, tragical-comical-historical-pastoral, scene individable or 365
poem unlimited. Seneca cannot be too heavy, nor Plautus too light. For the law of writ and the liberty, these are the only men.

HAMLET O Jephtha judge of Israel, what a treasure hadst thou!

POLONIUS What a treasure had he my lord?

HAMLET Why – 370
'One fair daughter and no more,
The which he lovèd passing well.'

POLONIUS Still on my daughter.

HAMLET Am I not i'th'right, old Jephtha?

POLONIUS If you call me Jephtha my lord, I have a daughter that I 375
love passing well.

HAMLET Nay, that follows not.

POLONIUS What follows then my lord?

HAMLET Why –
'As by lot God wot,' 380
And then you know –
'It came to pass, as most like it was,' –
the first row of the pious chanson will show you more, for look where my abridgement comes.

Hamlet welcomes the players, some of whom he recognises. He asks the principal actor to declaim a speech about Pyrrhus. Hamlet begins with the speech which tells how Pyrrhus entered Troy in the wooden horse.

1 Hamlet welcomes the players

Make a list giving as many reasons as you can for Hamlet's enthusiasm for the arrival of the players.

2 Is *Hamlet* wasted on you?

Hamlet says (line 397) that the play he is thinking of was 'caviary to the general', caviare (expensive food) to ordinary people (that is, too good for them). Some people today have the same view of Shakespeare's plays. They think that they are wasted on 'ordinary' people, and can be properly appreciated only by an élite, a small minority. What do you think? Is the play *Hamlet* 'caviary to the general' – beyond the reach of all but a select few? Organise a class debate on the question.

3 The story of Pyrrhus

Pyrrhus, like Hamlet, was a son who vowed to avenge his dead father. Lines 404–6 refer to Virgil's *Aeneid*, in which Aeneas tells Queen Dido the story of Pyrrhus, whose father Achilles was killed at the siege of Troy. Pyrrhus was one of the Greek warriors in the wooden horse ('the ominous horse') which was used to defeat the Trojans. Hamlet begins the tale of how the 'rugged' (long-haired) Pyrrhus, like a savage tiger ('th'Hyrcanian beast'), clad in black armour ('sable arms'), but covered in blood ('total gules', 'o'er-sized with coagulate gore'), sought out Priam, King of Troy, to kill him in revenge for his own father. See Activity 1 on page 90.

---

valanced bearded
beard challenge
byrlady by Our Lady (the Virgin Mary)
chopine high-heeled shoe
uncurrent gold valueless cracked coins

fly . . . see have a go at anything
sallets salads (rude bits)
indict prove guilty
tricked decorated (a heraldic term, like 'sable', 'arms', 'gules')
impasted made into paste
carbuncles fire-red precious stones

Enter the PLAYERS

Y'are welcome masters, welcome all. I am glad to see thee well. 385
Welcome good friends. Oh, my old friend! why, thy face is valanced
since I saw thee last; com'st thou to beard me in Denmark? What,
my young lady and mistress – byrlady, your ladyship is nearer to
heaven than when I saw you last by the altitude of a chopine. Pray
God your voice like a piece of uncurrent gold be not cracked within 390
the ring. Masters, you are all welcome. We'll e'en to't like French
falconers, fly at anything we see: we'll have a speech straight. Come
give us a taste of your quality: come, a passionate speech.

1 PLAYER What speech, my good lord?

HAMLET I heard thee speak me a speech once, but it was never acted, 395
or if it was, not above once, for the play I remember pleased not
the million: 'twas caviary to the general. But it was, as I received
it, and others whose judgements in such matters cried in the top
of mine, an excellent play, well digested in the scenes, set down with
as much modesty as cunning. I remember one said there were no 400
sallets in the lines to make the matter savoury, nor no matter in
the phrase that might indict the author of affectation, but called it
an honest method, as wholesome as sweet and by very much more
handsome than fine. One speech in't I chiefly loved, 'twas Aeneas'
tale to Dido, and thereabout of it especially where he speaks of 405
Priam's slaughter. If it live in your memory, begin at this line, let
me see, let me see –
    'The rugged Pyrrhus, like th'Hyrcanian beast' –
'Tis not so, it begins with Pyrrhus –
    'The rugged Pyrrhus, he whose sable arms, 410
    Black as his purpose, did the night resemble
    When he lay couchèd in the ominous horse,
    Hath now this dread and black complexion smeared
    With heraldy more dismal. Head to foot
    Now is he total gules, horridly tricked 415
    With blood of fathers, mothers, daughters, sons,
    Baked and impasted with the parching streets,
    That lend a tyrannous and a damnèd light
    To their lord's murder. Roasted in wrath and fire,
    And thus o'er-sizèd with coagulate gore, 420
    With eyes like carbuncles, the hellish Pyrrhus
    Old grandsire Priam seeks –'
So, proceed you.

The first player continues the speech from where Hamlet leaves off. He declaims how Pyrrhus finds Priam, pauses for a long moment, then slays him. The player is interrupted by Polonius, but Hamlet urges him on.

1 Go for it!

Shakespeare may be 'sending up' an older stage tradition of acting and speaking. He gives the player a speech full of high-flown language. Work out a dramatic way of reading aloud lines 426–55 (and Hamlet's lines 410–22). Try a bombastic, over-the-top, declamatory style, to match the highly coloured language. You could add exaggerated gestures and formal movements to match the style.

2 Act it out (in small groups)

As one person reads the player's speech, the others act out what he describes. The following may help you:

'Repugnant to command' = resisting orders
'fell' = cruel
'senseless Ilium' = unfeeling Troy
'Stoops to his base' = crashes to the ground
'Takes prisoner Pyrrhus' ear' = dazes him
'neutral to his will and matter' = unable to think or act
'Cyclops' = one-eyed giants who worked as blacksmiths
'Mars' = god of war.

3 Pyrrhus and Hamlet both delay

Both Hamlet and Pyrrhus are sons who seek revenge for the killing of their fathers. The player's speech contains another parallel. Pyrrhus stood still and 'Did nothing' (line 440). His inability to act forecasts Hamlet's own inaction as he delays avenging his father's murder. Some productions heavily emphasise this moment, and Hamlet echoes 'Did nothing'. Would you do the same in your own production?

---

discretion taste
milky white-haired
as a painted tyrant like a tyrant
  in a portrait
rack clouds
orb earth
proof eterne eternal protection

strumpet Fortune unpredictable
  floozy
synod gathering
fellies part of the rim of the Wheel
  of Fortune
nave hub
mobled veiled

POLONIUS 'Fore God my lord, well spoken, with good accent and good
    discretion.   425

I PLAYER   'Anon he finds him,
    Striking too short at Greeks; his antique sword,
    Rebellious to his arm, lies where it falls,
    Repugnant to command. Unequal matched,
    Pyrrhus at Priam drives, in rage strikes wide,   430
    But with the whiff and wind of his fell sword
    Th'unnervèd father falls. Then senseless Ilium,
    Seeming to feel this blow, with flaming top
    Stoops to his base, and with a hideous crash
    Takes prisoner Pyrrhus' ear; for lo, his sword,   435
    Which was declining on the milky head
    Of reverend Priam, seemed i'th'air to stick.
    So, as a painted tyrant, Pyrrhus stood,
    And like a neutral to his will and matter,
    Did nothing.   440
    But as we often see against some storm,
    A silence in the heavens, the rack stand still,
    The bold winds speechless, and the orb below
    As hush as death, anon the dreadful thunder
    Doth rend the region; so after Pyrrhus' pause,   445
    A rousèd vengeance sets him new a-work,
    And never did the Cyclops' hammers fall
    On Mars's armour, forged for proof eterne,
    With less remorse than Pyrrhus' bleeding sword
    Now falls on Priam.   450
    Out, out, thou strumpet Fortune! All you gods,
    In general synod take away her power,
    Break all the spokes and fellies from her wheel,
    And bowl the round nave down the hill of heaven
    As low as to the fiends.'   455

POLONIUS This is too long.

HAMLET It shall to th' barber's with your beard. Prithee say on.
    He's for a jig or a tale of bawdry, or he sleeps. Say on, come to
    Hecuba.

I PLAYER 'But who – ah woe! – had seen the mobled queen –'   460

HAMLET The mobled queen?

POLONIUS That's good, 'mobled queen' is good.

The player, with tears in his eyes, ends his tale of Hecuba. Hamlet orders Polonius to treat the actors hospitably. He asks the player to perform a play the next night, including a specially written speech.

1 Make him cry!

The first player ends lines 463–75 with tears in his eyes. Write a set of notes for the actor, advising him on how to finish the speech weeping, visibly moved by what he has said. Your notes should help the actor with the content and style of the lines.

Are there people in your class who can cry at will? Ask them how they do it.

2 Actors reveal society (in small groups)

Polonius stresses the low social status of the actors, saying he will 'use them according to their desert'. But for Hamlet, actors are 'the abstract and brief chronicles of the time' (lines 481–2). They show, in a dramatic form, the nature of society. Their performances are summaries and shortened stories ('abstract and brief chronicles') of certain events that occur in the time in which they live. Test out that claim in two ways:

First: by discussing how any television programme of your choice is an 'abstract and brief chronicle of the time'.

Second: by making up and acting out a short play that is somehow a mirror of today's society.

3 Is Hamlet serious?

Read line 497 in various ways: tongue-in-cheek, forcefully, as a genuine warning, or in some other tone. Decide which seems most appropriate to match what is in Hamlet's mind at this moment.

---

bisson rheum blinding tears
clout piece of cloth
diadem crown
o'er-teemèd worn out (Hecuba was said to have had a hundred children)

milch milky
passion in the gods won sympathy from the gods
desert deservings
for a need if necessary

1 PLAYER 'Run barefoot up and down, threat'ning the flames
　　　　　With bisson rheum, a clout upon that head
　　　　　Where late the diadem stood, and, for a robe,　　　　465
　　　　　About her lank and all o'er-teemèd loins
　　　　　A blanket, in th'alarm of fear caught up –
　　　　　Who this had seen, with tongue in venom steeped
　　　　　'Gainst Fortune's state would treason have pronounced.
　　　　　But if the gods themselves did see her then,　　　　470
　　　　　When she saw Pyrrhus make malicious sport
　　　　　In mincing with his sword her husband's limbs,
　　　　　The instant burst of clamour that she made,
　　　　　Unless things mortal move them not at all,
　　　　　Would have made milch the burning eyes of heaven,
　　　　　And passion in the gods.　　　　475

POLONIUS Look where he has not turned his colour, and has tears in's
　　　　eyes. Prithee no more.

HAMLET 'Tis well, I'll have thee speak out the rest of this soon. – Good
　　　　my lord, will you see the players well bestowed? Do you hear, let　480
　　　　them be well used, for they are the abstract and brief chronicles
　　　　of the time. After your death you were better have a bad epitaph
　　　　than their ill report while you live.

POLONIUS My lord, I will use them according to their desert.

HAMLET God's bodkin man, much better. Use every man after his　485
　　　　desert, and who shall scape whipping? Use them after your own
　　　　honour and dignity; the less they deserve, the more merit is in your
　　　　bounty. Take them in.

POLONIUS Come sirs.　　　　　　　　　　　　　　　*Exit Polonius*

HAMLET Follow him friends, we'll hear a play tomorrow. – Dost thou　490
　　　　hear me old friend, can you play *The Murder of Gonzago*?

1 PLAYER Ay my lord.

HAMLET We'll ha't tomorrow night. You could for a need study a
　　　　speech of some dozen or sixteen lines, which I would set down and
　　　　insert in't, could you not?　　　　495

1 PLAYER Ay my lord.

HAMLET Very well. Follow that lord, and look you mock him not.
　　　　　　　　　　　　　　　　　　　　　Exeunt Players
　　　　My good friends, I'll leave you till night. You are welcome to
　　　　Elsinore.

ROSENCRANTZ Good my lord.　　　　500
　　　　　Exeunt Rosencrantz and Guildenstern

93

Hamlet wonders at the player's ability to weep for a fictional character. He berates himself for doing nothing, even though he has real reasons for revenge. He curses Claudius, and cries for vengeance.

1 'And all for nothing?' (in small groups)

'What's Hecuba to him, or he to Hecuba?' demands Hamlet as he sees the player weeping for the sufferings of Hecuba. Faced with an actor who can cry at the imagined torments of a fictional character in a play, Hamlet reproaches himself for his own lack of action. The actor can weep 'for nothing', but Hamlet, with a murdered father, is incapable of taking revenge ('unpregnant of my cause'). Like a day-dreamer ('John-a-dreams') he does nothing.

a Talk together about whether you are sometimes more moved by a work of fiction (a play or a novel) than by what happens to you in 'real' life.

b Do you think that Hamlet is being too hard on himself? Consider in turn each of the things he calls himself and decide if they are true ('rogue', 'peasant slave', 'dull and muddy-mettled rascal', 'John-a-dreams', 'coward', 'pigeon-livered'). Why does he level these accusations at himself?

c Consider each of the seven things Hamlet calls Claudius in lines 532–3 and discuss how justified you think each description is.

2 Lists (in pairs)

Shakespeare often inserts 'lists' into his plays. The accumulation of items helps to increase the intensity of the mood being created. Pick out the following 'lists': the player's reactions (lines 506–9); what the player would do if he played Hamlet (lines 514–18); what Hamlet imagines a bully would do to him (lines 524–7); what Hamlet calls Claudius (lines 532–3). Mime one or more of the 'lists' to your partner.

---

conceit imagination
visage wanned face paled
in's aspect in his look
cleave split
Confound confuse
muddy-mettled cowardly and sluggish

peak mope
pate skull, top of the head
i'th'throat deep down
'swounds God's wounds
gall courage
kites scavenging birds

HAMLET Ay so, God bye to you. Now I am alone.
O what a rogue and peasant slave am I!
Is it not monstrous that this player here,
But in a fiction, in a dream of passion,
Could force his soul so to his own conceit   505
That from her working all his visage wanned,
Tears in his eyes, distraction in's aspect,
A broken voice, and his whole function suiting
With forms to his conceit? And all for nothing?
For Hecuba!   510
What's Hecuba to him, or he to Hecuba,
That he should weep for her? What would he do,
Had he the motive and the cue for passion
That I have? He would drown the stage with tears,
And cleave the general ear with horrid speech,   515
Make mad the guilty and appal the free,
Confound the ignorant, and amaze indeed
The very faculties of eyes and ears. Yet I,
A dull and muddy-mettled rascal, peak
Like John-a-dreams, unpregnant of my cause,   520
And can say nothing – no, not for a king,
Upon whose property and most dear life
A damned defeat was made. Am I a coward?
Who calls me villain, breaks my pate across,
Plucks off my beard and blows it in my face,   525
Tweaks me by th'nose, gives me the lie i'th'throat
As deep as to the lungs? Who does me this?
Ha, 'swounds, I should take it, for it cannot be
But I am pigeon-livered, and lack gall
To make oppression bitter, or ere this   530
I should ha' fatted all the region kites
With this slave's offal. Bloody, bawdy villain!
Remorseless, treacherous, lecherous, kindless villain!
Oh, vengeance!

Hamlet rebukes himself for his emotional outburst. He resolves to stage a play showing a murder similar to his father's. If the watching Claudius reveals his guilt, it will prove that the Ghost has spoken truly.

1 Changing moods (in groups of three or four)

Hamlet goes through several changes of mood in lines 501–58. His soliloquy contains the following sections:

line 501 dismissing Rosencrantz and Guildenstern

line 502 self-criticism

lines 503–12 wondering at the player's tears for Hecuba

lines 512–18 imagining the player's reactions to real grievances

lines 518–32 deepening self-disgust

lines 532–4 rage against Claudius

lines 535–40 self-reproach for his emotional outburst

lines 541–51 working out a plan to test the Ghost's word

lines 551–6 fear that the Ghost may be a devil, telling lies to tempt him to eternal damnation by killing Claudius

lines 557–8 elation at the thought he will prove Claudius's guilt.

Consider each section in turn. Advise Hamlet on how to communicate his changes of mood through tone, pace, rhythm, volume, movement and gesture. Try your own version of speaking the soliloquy.

2 'The play's the thing' (in pairs)

Is theatre as powerful as Hamlet claims? Talk together about whether you think a criminal, watching a play with a similar theme to his own crime, will feel guilty and remorseful.

---

the dear murderèd a murdered father
drab/scullion low-ranking servants (or prostitutes)
presently immediately
malefactions evil deeds

organ voice
tent probe
quick most tender part
a do blench he flinches
relative relevant, conclusive

Why, what an ass am I! This is most brave,   535
That I, the son of the dear murderèd,
Prompted to my revenge by heaven and hell,
Must like a whore unpack my heart with words,
And fall a-cursing like a very drab,
A scullion!   540
Fie upon't, foh! About, my brains. Hum, I have heard
That guilty creatures sitting at a play
Have by the very cunning of the scene
Been struck so to the soul, that presently
They have proclaimed their malefactions;   545
For murder, though it have no tongue, will speak
With most miraculous organ. I'll have these players
Play something like the murder of my father
Before mine uncle. I'll observe his looks,
I'll tent him to the quick. If a do blench,   550
I know my course. The spirit that I have seen
May be a devil – and the devil hath power
T'assume a pleasing shape. Yea, and perhaps,
Out of my weakness and my melancholy,
As he is very potent with such spirits,   555
Abuses me to damn me. I'll have grounds
More relative than this. The play's the thing
Wherein I'll catch the conscience of the king.   *Exit*

Turning
Point-
Decides on
his course
of action

97

Looking back at Act 2

Activities for groups or individuals

1 Hasty sending

In Tom Stoppard's *Rosencrantz and Guildenstern are Dead*, the two courtiers talk often of how they were sent for:

'An awakening, a man standing on his saddle to bang on the shutters, our names shouted in a certain dawn, a message, a summons . . .'

Make up your own version of how Claudius's hasty summons arrived. What were Rosencrantz and Guildenstern doing? What did the messenger tell them? How did they react?

2 Nine episodes

A great deal happens in Scene 2. You will find that a new action begins at the following lines: 1, 40, 85, 166, 213, 295, 338, 491 and 501. Use these lines to identify the separate events in the scene, and write a single sentence about each. Choose one line from each section that you think best expresses the dramatic action. Use your chosen lines to work out a very short enactment of the whole scene.

3 Emotional range

Hamlet appears at line 165 in Scene 2. Follow him through the scene and list ten words to show the range of emotions he experiences. Link each of your 'mood' words to a line in the script. If possible, draw a chart or graph to portray Hamlet's mood swings.

4 Catastrophe!

Imagine all Shakespeare's work was lost, except two lines from Act 2. Which two lines would you hope were saved? Why?

5 'Denmark's a prison'

Design a set for Scene 2 based on line 234.

6 Surveillance

Act 2 begins and ends with someone proposing to spy on someone else. Identify each occasion in the act which involves surveillance (observation or spying) of some kind.

Two versions of the first player declaiming the story of Pyrrhus and Priam
(Royal Shakespeare Company, 1970 and 1984).
Identify Hamlet in each picture and think about the similarities in the
portrayal of him at this moment.

Rosencrantz and Guildenstern report Hamlet's unwillingness to talk about the reasons for his madness, and his joy at news of the players. Claudius asks them to encourage Hamlet's theatrical interests.

Rosencrantz and Guildenstern report on their meeting with Hamlet. But how truthfully do they describe that conversation? Turn back to page 79 and refresh your memory by quickly reading lines 215–348. Then read aloud what they say opposite and decide if Rosencrantz and Guildenstern give Claudius a true and full account of their meeting.

1 Does Claudius suspect Hamlet? (in small groups)

In line 2, Claudius says Hamlet 'puts on' his mad act. Talk together about whether you think Claudius suspects Hamlet is not really mad at all, but just pretending – and why.

---

drift of circumstance indirect
 talk
distracted mad
forward ready, willing
sounded questioned
disposition inclination

Niggard sparse (Hamlet was
 unwilling to talk)
assay urge
o'er-raught overtook
a further edge more
 encouragement

ACT 3   SCENE 1
The Great Hall of Elsinore Castle

Enter KING, QUEEN, POLONIUS, OPHELIA, ROSENCRANTZ,
GUILDENSTERN, LORDS

CLAUDIUS And can you by no drift of circumstance
    Get from him why he puts on this confusion,
    Grating so harshly all his days of quiet
    With turbulent and dangerous lunacy?
ROSENCRANTZ He does confess he feels himself distracted,   5
    But from what cause a will by no means speak.
GUILDENSTERN Nor do we find him forward to be sounded,
    But with a crafty madness keeps aloof
    When we would bring him on to some confession
    Of his true state.
GERTRUDE   Did he receive you well?   10
ROSENCRANTZ Most like a gentleman.
GUILDENSTERN But with much forcing of his disposition.
ROSENCRANTZ Niggard of question, but of our demands
    Most free in his reply.
GERTRUDE   Did you assay him
    To any pastime?   15
ROSENCRANTZ Madam, it so fell out that certain players
    We o'er-raught on the way; of these we told him,
    And there did seem in him a kind of joy
    To hear of it. They are about the court,
    And as I think, they have already order   20
    This night to play before him.
POLONIUS   'Tis most true,
    And he beseeched me to entreat your majesties
    To hear and see the matter.
CLAUDIUS With all my heart, and it doth much content me
    To hear him so inclined.   25
    Good gentlemen, give him a further edge,
    And drive his purpose on to these delights.
ROSENCRANTZ We shall my lord.
          Exeunt Rosencrantz and Guildenstern

Claudius and Polonius prepare to spy on Hamlet to discover if his love for Ophelia has really driven him mad. Claudius's guilty conscience pricks him for the murder of King Hamlet.

1 Does Ophelia overhear? (in pairs)

Every production must decide whether Ophelia overhears Claudius's lines 28–37. Imagine that she does overhear. One person slowly reads Claudius's lines, pausing frequently. In each pause, the partner, as Ophelia, speaks her thoughts. Change roles and repeat. Then discuss whether, if you were directing the play, you would have Ophelia overhear, and the implications of each alternative.

2 Catching the conscience of the king

Line 50 reveals that the Ghost's story is true. Claudius is guilty of murder. His conscience pricks him as he hears Polonius say that a pious appearance often covers evil. Design an illustration for lines 47–9, or line 50, or lines 51–3 (just as make-up covers ugliness, so Claudius's lying words cover his evil deed), or line 54.

3 Fathers spy on children (in small groups)

Claudius and Polonius will spy on Hamlet and Ophelia: stepson and daughter. The two men have no doubts about such surveillance. They see themselves as 'lawful espials': legitimate spies. Talk together about what this action suggests about the character of each man. Do you think there are times when parents should spy on their children?

4 The women's view

Do you think Gertrude and Ophelia also fully accept spying as a legitimate practice? Decide whether you think the two women are fully consenting participants in the plot to spy on Hamlet.

---

closely secretly
Affront meet
bestow hide
wonted way usual behaviour, sanity
To both your honours to the credit of you both

Gracious your grace
colour explain
devotion's visage the show of praying
sugar o'er conceal, sweetly cover
plastering art make-up
painted deceitful

CLAUDIUS   Sweet Gertrude, leave us too,
　　　For we have closely sent for Hamlet hither,
　　　That he, as 'twere by accident, may here   30
　　　Affront Ophelia. Her father and myself,
　　　Lawful espials,
　　　Will so bestow ourselves, that seeing unseen,
　　　We may of their encounter frankly judge,
　　　And gather by him, as he is behaved,   35
　　　If't be th'affliction of his love or no
　　　That thus he suffers for.
GERTRUDE   I shall obey you.
　　　And for your part Ophelia, I do wish
　　　That your good beauties be the happy cause
　　　Of Hamlet's wildness. So shall I hope your virtues   40
　　　Will bring him to his wonted way again,
　　　To both your honours.
OPHELIA   Madam, I wish it may.
　　　　　　　　　　　[*Exit Gertrude with Lords*]
POLONIUS Ophelia walk you here. – Gracious, so please you,
　　　We will bestow ourselves. – Read on this book,
　　　That show of such an exercise may colour   45
　　　Your loneliness. – We are oft to blame in this:
　　　'Tis too much proved, that with devotion's visage,
　　　And pious action, we do sugar o'er
　　　The devil himself.
CLAUDIUS (*Aside*)   Oh, 'tis too true.
　　　How smart a lash that speech doth give my conscience!   50
　　　The harlot's cheek, beautied with plastering art,
　　　Is not more ugly to the thing that helps it
　　　Than is my deed to my most painted word.
　　　O heavy burden!
POLONIUS I hear him coming. Let's withdraw, my lord.   55
　　　　　　　　　　　Exeunt Claudius and Polonius

Hamlet reflects on death. Is it better to live or die, to endure suffering or to fight against it? The fear of what might happen after death makes us bear with life. Thought prevents us from acting.

1 'To be, or not to be, . . .' (in groups)

line 56 Hamlet wonders whether to commit suicide

lines 57–60 he wonders whether to endure or fight

lines 60–4 he looks forward to the sleep of death

lines 64–8 he is troubled with thoughts of what happens after death

lines 68–82 what stops people committing suicide, in spite of all oppressions in this life, is the fear of terrors that await the dead

lines 83–8 he decides that thinking stops us from acting.

Choose one or more of the following activities on the soliloquy:

An exercise in persuasion Share the reading, each group member speaking in turn a short sense unit. Quietly persuade your group each time you read, so that the soliloquy builds up as a developing argument.

Echo One person echoes 'To be, or not to be, that is the question' every few lines throughout a shared reading.

Speak it aloud in different ways As if Hamlet has only suicide in mind; as if Hamlet has only killing Claudius in mind; as a philosophy lecture to a group of students; as if every line, phrase or thought is a question.

A dramatic reading for radio Use sound effects, music, and short phrases from elsewhere in the play.

A set of tableaux of lines 70–4 To show the six or seven injustices of human life that Hamlet considers.

Advise Hamlet on how to speak the soliloquy in your production.

---

consummation ending
rub obstacle
shuffled off . . . coil died (shaken off the confusions of human life)
contumely humiliating insults
disprized unvalued
office people in authority

quietus release
a bare bodkin a mere dagger
fardels burdens
native hue of resolution natural determination to act
sicklied o'er unhealthily covered
orisons prayers

Enter HAMLET

HAMLET To be, or not to be, that is the question –
Whether 'tis nobler in the mind to suffer
The slings and arrows of outrageous fortune,
Or to take arms against a sea of troubles,
And by opposing end them. To die, to sleep –   60
No more; and by a sleep to say we end
The heart-ache and the thousand natural shocks
That flesh is heir to – 'tis a consummation
Devoutly to be wished. To die, to sleep –
To sleep, perchance to dream. Ay, there's the rub,   65
For in that sleep of death what dreams may come,
When we have shuffled off this mortal coil,
Must give us pause. There's the respect
That makes calamity of so long life,
For who would bear the whips and scorns of time,   70
Th'oppressor's wrong, the proud man's contumely,
The pangs of disprized love, the law's delay,
The insolence of office, and the spurns
That patient merit of th'unworthy takes,
When he himself might his quietus make   75
With a bare bodkin? Who would fardels bear,
To grunt and sweat under a weary life,
But that the dread of something after death,
The undiscovered country from whose bourn
No traveller returns, puzzles the will,   80
And makes us rather bear those ills we have
Then fly to others that we know not of?
Thus conscience does make cowards of us all,
And thus the native hue of resolution
Is sicklied o'er with the pale cast of thought,   85
And enterprises of great pitch and moment
With this regard their currents turn awry
And lose the name of action. Soft you now,
The fair Ophelia. – Nymph, in thy orisons
Be all my sins remembered.

OPHELIA   Good my lord,   90
How does your honour for this many a day?

Ophelia attempts to return Hamlet's gifts. Hamlet taunts her, saying that he once loved her, then denying it. He orders her to a nunnery and self-loathingly accuses himself of worthless vices.

1 Where to put the stress? (in pairs)

Try five different ways of speaking line 96 ('I never gave you aught'). Each time, heavily stress one different word. Talk together about how each version results in different possible interpretations.

2 Does Hamlet know? (in small groups)

Talk together about whether you think Hamlet knows he is being watched. If you think he is aware of watchers, identify the line where the realisation dawns on him and suggest who he thinks is spying on him (Claudius? Polonius? Gertrude?). Work out how you would stage this part of the scene to maximum dramatic effect.

3 Three decisions – no 'right' answers!

a But why? Draw up a list of possible reasons that might explain Hamlet's bitter treatment of Ophelia. Put them in order of 'most likely' to 'least likely'.

b 'Get thee to a nunnery.' Does Hamlet urge Ophelia to go to a convent because there she will be safe from (or renounce) the temptations and corruption of the world? Or is Hamlet being sarcastic, and by 'nunnery' mean 'brothel'? Which interpretation seems more likely to you, and why?

c Beauty will corrupt virtue more easily than virtue can make beautiful people virtuous or pure, asserts Hamlet (lines 111–14). He says that was once unbelievable ('a paradox'), but 'now the time gives it proof'. Is he thinking mainly of Ophelia or of Gertrude at this moment?

---

remembrances gifts, love-tokens
aught anything
wax grow
honest pure, a virgin
discourse to dealings with
bawd brothel-keeper

inoculate our old stock graft on to our nature
relish of it still be tainted with vice
at my beck waiting to be committed
arrant thorough, complete

HAMLET I humbly thank you, well, well, well.

OPHELIA My lord, I have remembrances of yours
　　　　That I have longèd long to re-deliver.
　　　　I pray you now receive them.

HAMLET 　　　　　　　　　　　　No, not I,　　　　95
　　　　I never gave you aught.

OPHELIA My honoured lord, you know right well you did,
　　　　And with them words of so sweet breath composed
　　　　As made the things more rich. Their perfume lost,
　　　　Take these again, for to the noble mind　　　　100
　　　　Rich gifts wax poor when givers prove unkind.
　　　　There my lord.

HAMLET Ha, ha, are you honest?

OPHELIA My lord?

HAMLET Are you fair?　　　　105

OPHELIA What means your lordship?

HAMLET That if you be honest and fair, your honesty should admit no
discourse to your beauty.

OPHELIA Could beauty, my lord, have better commerce than with
honesty?　　　　110

HAMLET Ay truly, for the power of beauty will sooner transform
honesty from what it is to a bawd, than the force of honesty can
translate beauty into his likeness. This was sometime a paradox, but
now the time gives it proof. I did love you once.

OPHELIA Indeed my lord you made me believe so.　　　　115

HAMLET You should not have believed me, for virtue cannot so
inoculate our old stock but we shall relish of it. I loved you not.

OPHELIA I was the more deceived.

HAMLET Get thee to a nunnery – why wouldst thou be a breeder of
sinners? I am myself indifferent honest, but yet I could accuse me　　　　120
of such things, that it were better my mother had not borne me.
I am very proud, revengeful, ambitious, with more offences at my
beck than I have thoughts to put them in, imagination to give them
shape, or time to act them in. What should such fellows as I do
crawling between earth and heaven? We are arrant knaves all,　　　　125
believe none of us. Go thy ways to a nunnery. Where's your father?

OPHELIA At home my lord.

HAMLET Let the doors be shut upon him, that he may play the fool
nowhere but in's own house. Farewell.

Hamlet reviles Ophelia, wishing her ill and slandering all women. She sorrows over his fall from excellence into madness. Claudius suspects Hamlet is not mad, and plans to send him to England.

1 Experiencing a tongue-lashing (in groups of eight to ten)

This activity helps bring out the devastating power of Hamlet's verbal assault on Ophelia. One person volunteers to take the part of Ophelia. The others surround her as Hamlet. The 'Hamlets' select short extracts from lines 103–43 (for example, 'are you honest?', 'Get thee to a nunnery', 'marry a fool'). The Hamlets hurl their insults at Ophelia who tries to get away from them, saying 'what means your lordship?' It can be a very cruel experience for Ophelia – so volunteers only. Afterwards, discuss how it feels to be on the receiving end of such a tongue-lashing, and the state of mind of the person who inflicts it.

2 Renaissance man (in small groups)

In lines 145–8, Ophelia paints a picture of the ideal prince. Hamlet exemplified the ideal qualities of the courtier, soldier and scholar. He was the hope and crowning glory ('expectancy and rose') of Denmark. He was the very mirror and model ('glass' and 'mould of form') of behaviour and taste, looked up to as an ideal example ('Th'observed of all observers') by everyone.

Design a series of 'before and after' contrasts. Show each of Ophelia's statements of what Hamlet was, and how those qualities are now blasted with madness ('ecstasy'). Your design could be artwork, or a number of 'before and after' tableaux based on Ophelia's lines.

---

dowry wedding gift
chaste virginal
calumny malicious lies
paintings make-up
jig dance
make . . . ignorance pretend your immorality comes from innocence

no mo no more
blown blossoming-ripe
hatch outcome
disclose result
tribute Danegeld (protection money paid by England to Denmark)

OPHELIA Oh help him you sweet heavens!   130
HAMLET If thou dost marry, I'll give thee this plague for thy dowry:
    be thou as chaste as ice, as pure as snow, thou shalt not escape
    calumny. Get thee to a nunnery, go. Farewell. Or if thou wilt needs
    marry, marry a fool, for wise men know well enough what monsters
    you make of them. To a nunnery go, and quickly too. Farewell.   135
OPHELIA O heavenly powers, restore him!
HAMLET I have heard of your paintings too, well enough. God hath
    given you one face and you make yourselves another. You jig, you
    amble, and you lisp, you nickname God's creatures, and make your
    wantonness your ignorance. Go to, I'll no more on't, it hath made   140
    me mad. I say we will have no mo marriages. Those that are married
    already, all but one shall live, the rest shall keep as they are. To
    a nunnery, go.   *Exit*
OPHELIA Oh what a noble mind is here o'erthrown!
        The courtier's, soldier's, scholar's, eye, tongue, sword,   145
        Th'expectancy and rose of the fair state,
        The glass of fashion and the mould of form,
        Th'observed of all observers, quite, quite down,
        And I of ladies most deject and wretched,
        That sucked the honey of his music vows,   150
        Now see that noble and most sovereign reason,
        Like sweet bells jangled, out of time and harsh;
        That unmatched form and feature of blown youth
        Blasted with ecstasy. Oh woe is me
        T'have seen what I have seen, see what I see.   155

                Enter KING *and* POLONIUS

CLAUDIUS Love? His affections do not that way tend;
        Nor what he spake, though it lacked form a little,
        Was not like madness. There's something in his soul
        O'er which his melancholy sits on brood,
        And I do doubt the hatch and the disclose   160
        Will be some danger; which for to prevent,
        I have in quick determination
        Thus set it down: he shall with speed to England
        For the demand of our neglected tribute.

Polonius agrees with Claudius's plan to send Hamlet to England. He proposes to spy on Gertrude's meeting with Hamlet. In Scene 2, Hamlet instructs the players on acting style.

1 A loving father? (in small groups)

'How now Ophelia?/You need not tell us what Lord Hamlet said,/We heard it all.' These are the last words in the play spoken by Polonius to his daughter. Just how does he speak them? Remember she has been on the receiving end of a brutal tongue-lashing from Hamlet. Is Polonius sympathetic, officious, uncaring or . . . ? Experiment with styles to see if you can agree on how he should speak the lines to match his character and the occasion.

In one modern-dress production of the play, Polonius produced a tape-recorder as he spoke the lines, to show he'd not only heard, but had recorded everything!

2 Managing the scene change

Work out how the action of the play can flow smoothly between Scene 1 and Scene 2.

3 'Out-Herods Herod'

Hamlet uses a noun as a verb to suggest ranting and raving more than Herod himself (Herod and Termagant were noisy, raging characters in medieval Mystery plays). Use the same technique to invent some telling comparisons of your own, for example with the name of a public figure (or someone you know). What would it be to out-Shakespeare Shakespeare? Or out-Polonius Polonius?

Haply perhaps
variable objects notable sights
something-settled partly fixed
round strict, forthright
trippingly lightly
as lief rather

robustious violent, loud-mouthed
periwig-pated wig-wearing
groundlings poorest theatre-goers
  who stood in the open yard in
  front of the stage
capable of understand

Haply the seas, and countries different,   165
With variable objects, shall expel
This something-settled matter in his heart,
Whereon his brains still beating puts him thus
From fashion of himself. What think you on't?

POLONIUS It shall do well. But yet do I believe   170
The origin and commencement of his grief
Sprung from neglected love. How now Ophelia?
You need not tell us what Lord Hamlet said,
We heard it all. My lord, do as you please,
But if you hold it fit, after the play,   175
Let his queen mother all alone entreat him
To show his grief. Let her be round with him,
And I'll be placed, so please you, in the ear
Of all their conference. If she find him not,
To England send him; or confine him where   180
Your wisdom best shall think.

CLAUDIUS   It shall be so.
Madness in great ones must not unwatched go.

Exeunt

ACT 3   SCENE 2
The Great Hall of Elsinore Castle

Enter HAMLET and two or three of the PLAYERS

HAMLET Speak the speech I pray you as I pronounced it to you,
trippingly on the tongue; but if you mouth it as many of our players
do, I had as lief the town-crier spoke my lines. Nor do not saw the
air too much with your hand thus, but use all gently; for in the
very torrent, tempest, and, as I may say, whirlwind of your passion,   5
you must acquire and beget a temperance that may give it
smoothness. Oh, it offends me to the soul to hear a robustious
periwig-pated fellow tear a passion to totters, to very rags, to split
the ears of the groundlings, who for the most part are capable of
nothing but inexplicable dumb-shows and noise. I would have such   10
a fellow whipped for o'erdoing Termagant – it out-Herods Herod.
Pray you avoid it.

*Hamlet urges moderation in acting. He defines theatre as the mirror of
nature and society. He criticises bad actors and over-ambitious clowns.
Preparations for the play begin.*

1 Shakespeare's manual for actors?

Hamlet sets himself up as an authority on acting (see also pages 265–7).
He advises that actors should aim at moderation, not excess. That
seems ironic after his unrestrained and violent words to Ophelia
shortly before. Now he lectures the players on their craft. But it may be
the voice of Shakespeare himself, commenting on the overacting of his
contemporaries. Hamlet's advice covers four topics:

Acting don't overact! (lines 1–11, 14–16, 24–9)

The purpose of theatre to mirror and critically comment on the
times (lines 17–20)

Clowns don't ad lib or laugh at your own jokes (lines 31–6)

Audiences a very mixed bunch! (lines 21–4, 33–4).

Work out a way of presenting Hamlet's advice to the players in lines
1–36. You might write a 'manual for actors', design a set of cartoons
showing 'right' and 'wrong' ways of acting, or have one person narrate
the lines as the others act out each section.

2 'Some necessary question of the play'

Every play has a set of 'necessary questions' (lines 34–5): central
themes or issues. For example, one 'necessary question' of this play is
'revenge'. But there is an irony in Hamlet's advice, because his delay in
taking his revenge can be seen as his own continued refusal to consider
that 'necessary question'.

What are the 'necessary questions' in *Hamlet*? Make a list of what
you consider to be the play's central themes. Compare your list with
those of other students and with the contents of pages 252–69.

---

warrant will do so
modesty moderation
come tardy off imperfectly done
censure judgement
profanely blasphemously
gait walk

journeymen unskilled workmen
indifferently to some extent
presently immediately
just well-balanced
As e'er . . . coped withal as I've
ever met

1 PLAYER I warrant your honour.

HAMLET Be not too tame neither, but let your own discretion be your
tutor. Suit the action to the word, the word to the action, with this   15
special observance, that you o'erstep not the modesty of nature. For
anything so o'erdone is from the purpose of playing, whose end both
at the first and now, was and is, to hold as 'twere the mirror up
to nature; to show virtue her own feature, scorn her own image,
and the very age and body of the time his form and pressure. Now   20
this overdone, or come tardy off, though it makes the unskilful
laugh, cannot but make the judicious grieve, the censure of the
which one must in your allowance o'erweigh a whole theatre of
others. Oh, there be players that I have seen play, and heard others
praise and that highly, not to speak it profanely, that neither having   25
th'accent of Christians, nor the gait of Christian, pagan, nor man,
have so strutted and bellowed that I have thought some of nature's
journeymen had made men, and not made them well, they imitated
humanity so abominably.

1 PLAYER I hope we have reformed that indifferently with us, sir.   30

HAMLET Oh reform it altogether. And let those that play your clowns
speak no more than is set down for them, for there be of them that
will themselves laugh, to set on some quantity of barren spectators
to laugh too, though in the meantime some necessary question of
the play be then to be considered. That's villainous, and shows   35
a most pitiful ambition in the fool that uses it. Go make you ready.

Exeunt Players

Enter POLONIUS, ROSENCRANTZ *and* GUILDENSTERN

How now my lord, will the king hear this piece of work?

POLONIUS And the queen too, and that presently.

HAMLET Bid the players make haste.

Exit Polonius

Will you two help to hasten them?   40

ROSENCRANTZ Ay my lord.

Exeunt Rosencrantz and Guildenstern

HAMLET What ho, Horatio!

Enter HORATIO

HORATIO Here sweet lord, at your service.

HAMLET Horatio, thou art e'en as just a man
As e'er my conversation coped withal.   45

113

Hamlet praises Horatio's well-balanced character and criticises obsequious flatterers. He urges Horatio to watch Claudius closely for any guilty reaction during the play.

1 Friendship (in small groups)

Hamlet expresses his deep friendship for Horatio (lines 46–64). It is genuine friendship not flattery, because Horatio is not wealthy ('no revenue') and so can offer no advantage ('advancement'). Hamlet admires Horatio for bearing suffering without complaint ('suffering all . . . nothing'), and for his equable temperament ('blood and judgement are so well commeddled': emotions and reason are well mixed).

Talk together about your view of how Horatio's and Hamlet's personalities are like and unlike. For example, Horatio is not 'passion's slave' (trapped by his emotions) – but is Hamlet? Then discuss how you choose your friends. Is it because they have personalities similar to or different from your own?

2 Is Hamlet embarrassed?

Does Hamlet break off in embarrassment at line 64?

3 Vivid images: flattery and fortune

Make a drawing of one or both of the images used by Hamlet:

- Lines 50–2 describe the sweet-tongued courtier ('candied tongue') who flatters vain people in high positions ('lick absurd pomp'), and bows and scrapes readily ('crook the pregnant . . . knee') for profit ('thrift').

- Lines 57–8 and 60–1 turn Fortune into a woman, buffeting and rewarding human beings, or treating them like a musical instrument ('pipe') on which she can play any tune she pleases ('sound what stops she please').

---

election choice
Sh'ath sealed she has chosen
tane taken
prithee pray you
afoot in action, presented
very comment keenest watching
occulted hidden

unkennel reveal
Vulcan's stithy god of fire's smithy (workshop)
censure of his seeming judgement of his looks
a steal aught he hides anything
idle unoccupied (or mad)

HORATIO Oh my dear lord.

HAMLET   Nay, do not think I flatter,
For what advancement may I hope from thee,
That no revenue hast but thy good spirits
To feed and clothe thee? Why should the poor be flattered?
No, let the candied tongue lick absurd pomp   50
And crook the pregnant hinges of the knee
Where thrift may follow fawning. Dost thou hear?
Since my dear soul was mistress of her choice,
And could of men distinguish her election,
Sh'ath sealed thee for herself, for thou hast been   55
As one in suffering all that suffers nothing,
A man that Fortune's buffets and rewards
Hast tane with equal thanks. And blest are those
Whose blood and judgement are so well commeddled
That they are not a pipe for Fortune's finger   60
To sound what stop she please. Give me that man
That is not passion's slave, and I will wear him
In my heart's core, ay in my heart of heart,
As I do thee. Something too much of this.
There is a play tonight before the king: 65
One scene of it comes near the circumstance
Which I have told thee of my father's death.
I prithee when thou seest that act afoot,
Even with the very comment of thy soul
Observe my uncle. If his occulted guilt   70
Do not itself unkennel in one speech,
It is a damnèd ghost that we have seen,
And my imaginations are as foul
As Vulcan's stithy. Give him heedful note,
For I mine eyes will rivet to his face,   75
And after we will both our judgements join
In censure of his seeming.

HORATIO   Well my lord.
If a steal aught the whilst this play is playing
And scape detecting, I will pay the theft.
                    Sound a flourish
HAMLET They are coming to the play. I must be idle.   80
Get you a place.

115

Hamlet revels in word-play. He puns on what Claudius and Polonius say to him, and subjects Ophelia to much sexual innuendo. He comments bitterly on Gertrude's appearance.

1 Word-play? (in groups of five)

Hamlet has just promised to be 'idle' – to appear mad. His words now are deliberately disconcerting as he seizes on meanings that neither Claudius nor Polonius nor Ophelia intend.

Claudius's line 82 means 'How are you?'. But Hamlet interprets 'fares' as meaning 'feeds', so he replies as if Claudius had asked him what he has eaten. He mocks Claudius about his earlier promise (that Hamlet should succeed him), suggesting that it is just empty air.

Hamlet also mocks Polonius, punning on 'Brutus' and 'Capitol' with 'brute' and 'capital', adding the insulting 'calf' (fool). This was also, for Shakespeare's Company, a theatrical in-joke, because Shakespeare wrote *Julius Caesar* shortly before *Hamlet*, and the same pair of actors probably played Brutus/Caesar and Hamlet/Polonius.

Hamlet's verbal treatment of Ophelia is much crueller, filled with crude sexual jokes ('country matters' = sexual intercourse, 'nothing' = female genitalia).

Take parts as Hamlet, Claudius, Polonius, Gertrude and Ophelia.

Read the opposite page several times. Stress Hamlet's puns. Then, in role, say how you think each character regards Hamlet at this moment.

2 Similarities and differences

Julius Caesar has striking parallels with *Hamlet*. In both plays, a noble, deeply thoughtful man is urged to commit a political murder to purge and purify his nation. But Brutus undertakes Caesar's assassination before the midpoint of the play; Hamlet delays throughout the play.

---

fares does, eats
cousin (used for any close relative)
chameleon lizard that changes colour (and was thought to eat only air)
capons fattened chickens

Capitol seat of government in ancient Rome
metal a pun on 'mettle' (= spirit)
your only jig-maker I'm the only comedian here

Danish march (trumpets and kettle-drums). Enter KING, QUEEN, POLONIUS, OPHELIA, ROSENCRANTZ, GUILDENSTERN *and other* LORDS *attendant, with his* GUARD *carrying torches*

CLAUDIUS How fares our cousin Hamlet?

HAMLET Excellent i'faith, of the chameleon's dish: I eat the air, promise-crammed. You cannot feed capons so.

CLAUDIUS I have nothing with this answer Hamlet, these words are not mine. 85

HAMLET No, nor mine now. – My lord, you played once i'th'university, you say.

POLONIUS That did I my lord, and was accounted a good actor.

HAMLET And what did you enact? 90

POLONIUS I did enact Julius Caesar. I was killed i'th'Capitol. Brutus killed me.

HAMLET It was a brute part of him to kill so capital a calf there. – Be the players ready? (fool)

ROSENCRANTZ Ay my lord, they stay upon your patience. 95

GERTRUDE Come hither my dear Hamlet, sit by me.

HAMLET No good mother, here's metal more attractive. (He'd rather sit by Ophelia)

POLONIUS Oh ho, do you mark that?

HAMLET Lady, shall I lie in your lap?

OPHELIA No my lord. 100

HAMLET I mean, my head upon your lap?

OPHELIA Ay my lord.

HAMLET Do you think I meant country matters?

OPHELIA I think nothing my lord.

HAMLET That's a fair thought to lie between maids' legs. 105

OPHELIA What is, my lord?

HAMLET Nothing.

OPHELIA You are merry my lord.

HAMLET Who, I?

OPHELIA Ay my lord. 110

HAMLET O God, your only jig-maker. What should a man do but be merry? for look you how cheerfully my mother looks, and my father died within's two hours.

OPHELIA Nay, 'tis twice two months my lord.

Hamlet comments bitterly on his mother's hasty second marriage. The dumb-show presents a mirror-image of the murder of Hamlet's father. Hamlet again vents his cynicism on Ophelia.

Hamlet and the court watch the dumb-show (Royal Shakespeare Company 1992). In Elizabethan drama, a dumb-show (mime) often preceded the play, summarising the action ('imports the argument'). This dumb-show presents a sleeping king being murdered by a man who steals both his crown and queen. It is a mirror-image of what Claudius did to his brother. How will Claudius behave as he sees his own villainy being acted out in front of him? He might ignore it altogether (as he talks lovingly to Gertrude). Or he might gradually realise what it means, but can react in very different ways (with fear, suspicion, anger or in some other way). Or he might watch it imperturbably, utterly calm.
Work out how you think Claudius should behave, and why. Suggest what Claudius does at each point in the dumb-show. Then act it out!

sables expensive mourning clothes
byrlady by the Virgin Mary
a must build . . . on he must build churches or be forgotten
hobby-horse prostitute, or character in a morris dance
Hoboys oboes

makes show of protestation shows her love
mutes silent actors
miching mallecho sneaky villainy
naught improper, rude
posy of a ring a motto engraved on a ring

HAMLET So long? Nay then let the devil wear black, for I'll have a suit   115
of sables. O heavens! die two months ago, and not forgotten yet?
Then there's hope a great man's memory may outlive his life half
a year, but byrlady a must build churches then, or else shall a suffer
not thinking on, with the hobby-horse, whose epitaph is, 'For O,
for O, the hobby-horse is forgot.'   120

Hoboys play. The dumb-show enters

Enter a KING *and a* QUEEN, *very lovingly, the Queen embracing him. She
kneels and makes show of protestation unto him. He takes her up, and declines
his head upon her neck. He lies him down upon a bank of flowers. She, seeing
him asleep, leaves him. Anon comes in another man, takes off his crown, kisses
it, pours poison in the sleeper's ears, and leaves him. The Queen returns,
finds the King dead, and makes passionate action. The poisoner, with some
two or three mutes, comes in again, seeming to condole with her. The dead
body is carried away. The poisoner woos the Queen with gifts. She seems
harsh awhile, but in the end accepts his love.*   Exeunt

OPHELIA What means this my lord?
HAMLET Marry this is miching mallecho, it means mischief.
OPHELIA Belike this show imports the argument of the play?

Enter PROLOGUE

HAMLET We shall know by this fellow; the players cannot keep counsel,
they'll tell all.   125
OPHELIA Will a tell us what this show meant?
HAMLET Ay, or any show that you'll show him. Be not you ashamed
to show, he'll not shame to tell you what it means.
OPHELIA You are naught, you are naught. I'll mark the play.

PROLOGUE For us and for our tragedy,   130
Here stooping to your clemency,
We beg your hearing patiently.

HAMLET Is this a prologue, or the posy of a ring?
OPHELIA 'Tis brief my lord.
HAMLET As woman's love.   135

The player king speaks of thirty years of loving and holy marriage. The player queen expresses worries about his health, but vows not to marry again. He replies that vows are often broken.

1 Stereotyping (in small groups)

The player queen says that women's fear and love are equal ('hold quantity'), either extreme or barely felt (lines 148–9). One student's reaction to that was 'Rubbish!'. But another student argued that it is inappropriate to judge this 'play scene' as if it represents ordinary life. She said 'It's so obviously artificial – a theatrical convention'. Join in the argument, saying why you agree or disagree with either student.

2 Gertrude's reactions (in pairs)

One person reads the player queen's speeches, pausing after each unit of meaning (usually about two or three lines). In each pause, the other person, as Gertrude, speaks what Gertrude thinks as she hears and sees herself portrayed on stage with her first husband.

3 Language and movement (in groups of four)

The players' speeches sound very formal. This is because both players speak in rhymed couplets, use stylised language, and make classical references: for example, Phoebus (Apollo, the sun god), Tellus (goddess of the earth).

Work out an equally stylised and ritualistic style of moving and acting to fit the formality of the language. As two persons speak the lines, the other two play out the words with ceremonious, stylised gestures and movement.

Phoebus' cart the sun
Neptune's salt wash the sea
Tellus' orbèd ground the earth
borrowed sheen reflected light
Hymen god of marriage
Unite commutual . . . bands join
  in marriage

distrust you worry about you
operant powers . . . do faculties
  (eyesight, and so on) are failing
wormwood bitter
instances motives
base . . . thrift thoughts of money

Enter the PLAYER KING *and* QUEEN

PLAYER KING Full thirty times hath Phoebus' cart gone round
    Neptune's salt wash and Tellus' orbèd ground,
    And thirty dozen moons with borrowed sheen
    About the world have times twelve thirties been,
    Since love our hearts, and Hymen did our hands,   140
    Unite commutual in most sacred bands.
PLAYER QUEEN So many journeys may the sun and moon
    Make us again count o'er ere love be done.
    But woe is me, you are so sick of late,
    So far from cheer and from your former state,   145
    That I distrust you. Yet though I distrust,
    Discomfort you my lord it nothing must.
    For women's fear and love hold quantity,
    In neither aught, or in extremity.
    Now what my love is, proof hath made you know;   150
    And as my love is sized, my fear is so.
    [Where love is great, the littlest doubts are fear;
    Where little fears grow great, great love grows there.]
PLAYER KING Faith, I must leave thee love, and shortly too:
    My operant powers their functions leave to do;   155
    And thou shalt live in this fair world behind,
    Honoured, beloved; and haply one as kind
    For husband shalt thou –
PLAYER QUEEN   Oh confound the rest!
    Such love must needs be treason in my breast.
    In second husband let me be accurst: 160
    None wed the second but who killed the first.
HAMLET That's wormwood, wormwood.
PLAYER QUEEN The instances that second marriage move
    Are base respects of thrift, but none of love.
    A second time I kill my husband dead   165
    When second husband kisses me in bed.
PLAYER KING I do believe you think what now you speak,
    But what we do determine oft we break.

The player king argues that strong intentions don't last, because time makes us forget. Changing social conditions change the emotions. But the player queen swears she will never remarry.

1 It won't last! (in small groups)

The player king's speech is a sustained reflection on the theme that strong intentions don't last. In rhyming couplets, he argues repeatedly that time wears away resolutions ('Purpose'), however passionately ('of violent birth') they were originally declared. This reflects Hamlet's situation. He has sworn passionately to revenge his father's murder, but he procrastinates: time may wear away his resolution.

One person reads lines 167–96, two lines at a time. After each pair of lines, the others say 'Hamlet, your desire for revenge will fade' (or a similar sentence of your own). Afterwards, talk together about whether you agree with the player king's view that strong intentions won't last (the desire for revenge will fade, the widow will forget her previous vow and remarry, and so on).

2 Money brings you friends? (in pairs)

Lines 181–90 echo the Roman philosopher Cicero. He wrote that friendship ('love', 'favourite') changes with circumstances ('fortune'). When someone has wealth, they also have friends. But when a rich person loses their money, they are deserted by their friends.

Read lines 181–90, two lines at a time. Discuss each pair of lines to test whether they reflect what Cicero claimed. Then talk together about whether you believe that having money brings you friends.

---

validity strength, sticking power
enactures actions
is not for aye does not last
 eternally
flies deserts him
poor advanced poor man
 promoted
not needs is rich
in want is poor

seasons him turns him into
devices still plans always
anchor's cheer hermit's food and
 condition (poverty and loneliness)
scope future
blanks the face of joy changes a
 happy face to a sad one
here and hence in this world and
 the next

Purpose is but the slave to memory,
Of violent birth but poor validity,   170
Which now like fruit unripe sticks on the tree,
But fall unshaken when they mellow be.
Most necessary 'tis that we forget
To pay ourselves what to ourselves is debt.
What to ourselves in passion we propose,   175
The passion ending, doth the purpose lose.
The violence of either grief or joy
Their own enactures with themselves destroy.
Where joy most revels, grief doth most lament;
Grief joys, joy grieves, on slender accident.   180
This world is not for aye, nor 'tis not strange
That even our loves should with our fortunes change,
For 'tis a question left us yet to prove,
Whether love lead fortune, or else fortune love.
The great man down, you mark his favourite flies;   185
The poor advanced makes friends of enemies,
And hitherto doth love on fortune tend;
For who not needs shall never lack a friend,
And who in want a hollow friend doth try
Directly seasons him his enemy.   190
But orderly to end where I begun,
Our wills and fates do so contrary run
That our devices still are overthrown;
Our thoughts are ours, their ends none of our own.
So think thou wilt no second husband wed,   195
But die thy thoughts when thy first lord is dead.
PLAYER QUEEN Nor earth to me give food, nor heaven light,
Sport and repose lock from me day and night,
[To desperation turn my trust and hope,
An anchor's cheer in prison be my scope,]   200
Each opposite that blanks the face of joy
Meet what I would have well, and it destroy;
Both here and hence pursue me lasting strife,
If once a widow, ever I be wife.

HAMLET If she should break it now!   205

The player king sleeps. Hamlet hints that he knows Claudius is a murderer. He again subjects Ophelia to bitter sexual innuendo, and curses Lucianus, urging him to speak. Lucianus poisons the player king.

1 Promises, promises (in pairs)

Gertrude's judgement on the player queen has become a famous saying ('The lady doth protest too much methinks': she is over the top (too rash) with her promises of everlasting love). Talk together about what lies behind Gertrude's comment. Does she recognise herself in the play?

2 Hamlet shows his hand?

Hamlet almost reveals his knowledge of Claudius's guilt when he seizes on the king's 'offence' and turns it into poison, traps and murder. But just how does Hamlet speak lines 214–20? Savagely? Off-handedly? Laughingly? Advise the actor.

3 Taunting Ophelia (in small groups)

Ophelia again has to endure Hamlet's bitter sexual language. His first reply is doubly obscene (he could add a commentary, like a puppet-master, to Ophelia and her lover's flirting; or 'puppets' = sexual organs). Then he seizes on her word 'keen' making it explicitly sexual. (To reduce his desire he would make her pregnant and so groan in childbirth.) Finally, he twists 'better and worse', implying that wives mistake (betray) their husbands. Talk together about why you think Hamlet directs so much sexual venom towards Ophelia and what she may think and feel about his words.

4 Lucianus

Lucianus speaks the language of melodrama. Judging by Hamlet's admonition ('Pox, leave thy damnable faces and begin') he overacts too. Invent movement, expressions and gestures for lines 231–6.

---

fain . . . beguile I would gladly while away
Tropically metaphorically
free souls clear consciences
galled jade saddle-sore horse
withers neck joints
unwrung not hurt

dallying making love
croaking . . . revenge (Hamlet misquotes an old play)
Confederate season good opportunity, perfect time
Hecat queen of witches
usurp overthrow, destroy

PLAYER KING 'Tis deeply sworn. Sweet, leave me here awhile;
    My spirits grow dull, and fain I would beguile
    The tedious day with sleep.
               Sleeps
PLAYER QUEEN   Sleep rock thy brain,
    And never come mischance between us twain.   *Exit*

HAMLET Madam, how like you this play?   210
GERTRUDE The lady doth protest too much methinks.
HAMLET Oh but she'll keep her word.
CLAUDIUS Have you heard the argument? Is there no offence in't?
HAMLET No, no, they do but jest, poison in jest, no offence i'th'world.
CLAUDIUS What do you call the play?   215
HAMLET The Mousetrap. Marry how? Tropically. This play is the
    image of a murder done in Vienna. Gonzago is the duke's name,
    his wife Baptista. You shall see anon. 'Tis a knavish piece of work,
    but what o' that? Your majesty, and we that have free souls, it
    touches us not. Let the galled jade winch, our withers are unwrung.   220

              Enter LUCIANUS

This is one Lucianus, nephew to the king.
OPHELIA You are as good as a chorus my lord.
HAMLET I could interpret between you and your love if I could see the
    puppets dallying.
OPHELIA You are keen my lord, you are keen.   225
HAMLET It would cost you a groaning to take off mine edge.
OPHELIA Still better and worse.
HAMLET So you mistake your husbands. Begin, murderer. Pox, leave
    thy damnable faces and begin. Come, the croaking raven doth
    bellow for revenge.   230

LUCIANUS Thoughts black, hands apt, drugs fit, and time agreeing,
    Confederate season, else no creature seeing.
    Thou mixture rank, of midnight weeds collected,
    With Hecat's ban thrice blasted, thrice infected,
    Thy natural magic and dire property   235
    On wholesome life usurp immediately.
         Pours the poison in his ears

Claudius abruptly leaves the play, calling for light. Hamlet is delighted that his plot succeeded. He believes the Ghost has told the truth and that Claudius has revealed his guilt.

1 Claudius reacts

Just how does Claudius react to Hamlet's words? Some productions show him terrified and agitated, and his confusion is reflected in his courtiers' behaviour. In other productions his exit is calm and dignified. Suggest, with reasons, how you would stage lines 237–45.

2 Hamlet exults

Hamlet's joy at the success of his plan knows no bounds. First he sings an old song: wounded ('strucken') deer were believed to go off on their own to weep, while the unwounded male ('hart ungalled') played on unconcerned.

Then Hamlet says that even if everything else fails, the success of the play would gain him the exotic dress and footwear ('feathers' and 'razed shoes') of an actor. It would purchase him a whole share in an acting company, like Shakespeare's own, where leading actors were entitled to a percentage ('fellowship/share') of the admission money.

Hamlet sings another old song that parallels the situation in Denmark where the good king ('Jove') is dead ('dismantled') and a villain ('pajock') rules in his place. So the Ghost has told the truth!

Work out Hamlet's movements to match his language in lines 246–68.

---

for's estate for his lands and title
is extant still exists
anon soon
false fire blank ammunition (make-believe)
turn Turk get worse

razed decorated with cuts
Damon close friend (from the legendary friendship of Damon and Pythias)
perdy by God (*par dieu*)
vouchsafe grant

HAMLET A poisons him i'th'garden for's estate. His name's Gonzago.
The story is extant, and written in very choice Italian. You shall
see anon how the murderer gets the love of Gonzago's wife.
OPHELIA The king rises.   240
HAMLET What, frighted with false fire?
GERTRUDE How fares my lord?
POLONIUS Give o'er the play. (stop the play)
CLAUDIUS Give me some light. Away!
LORDS Lights, lights, lights!   245

Exeunt all but Hamlet and Horatio

HAMLET Why, let the strucken deer go weep,
    The hart ungallèd play,
  For some must watch while some must sleep,
    Thus runs the world away.
Would not this, sir, and a forest of feathers, if the rest of my fortunes   250
turn Turk with me, with two provincial roses on my razed shoes,
get me a fellowship in a cry of players, sir?
HORATIO Half a share.
HAMLET A whole one I.
  For thou dost know, O Damon dear,   255
    This realm dismantled was
  Of Jove himself, and now reigns here
    A very, very – pajock.
HORATIO You might have rhymed.
HAMLET O good Horatio, I'll take the ghost's word for a thousand   260
pound. Didst perceive?
HORATIO Very well my lord.
HAMLET Upon the talk of the poisoning?
HORATIO I did very well note him.

Enter ROSENCRANTZ *and* GUILDENSTERN

HAMLET Ah ha! – Come, some music! Come, the recorders!   265
  For if the king like not the comedy,
    Why then – belike he likes it not, perdy.
Come, some music!
GUILDENSTERN Good my lord, vouchsafe me a word with you.
HAMLET Sir, a whole history.   270
GUILDENSTERN The king, sir –
HAMLET Ay sir, what of him?

Hamlet disconcerts Guildenstern by deliberately misunderstanding him.
He mocks Rosencrantz too, but agrees to visit Gertrude. Hamlet denies
any hope of becoming king.

1 Shaking off old friends (in groups of three)

Take parts as Hamlet, Rosencrantz and Guildenstern, and read lines
269–336. Change roles so that everyone has a chance to read Hamlet.
Emphasise the words with which Hamlet mocks the two courtiers.
Notice particularly that lines 301–2 are the only time in the play that
Hamlet uses the royal 'we'. Afterwards, talk together about the ways in
which Hamlet clearly shows that their friendship is at an end.

2 'Pickers and stealers'

Work out some gestures Hamlet might make as he says line 304.

3 Is it a threat? (in pairs)

Does Rosencrantz threaten Hamlet with imprisonment in lines 305–7?
Or does he have some other meaning in mind?

Suggest what seems most likely to be Rosencrantz's meaning at this
moment, and advise the actor on how to speak the lines.

4 A stale proverb

Hamlet says at line 308 that he lacks 'advancement' (has no ambition –
or hope – to rule Denmark). But Rosencrantz assures Hamlet that he
will succeed Claudius as king. Hamlet responds (line 311) with a
proverb: 'While the grass grows, the starving horse dies.' Think of one
or two reasons why Hamlet makes this reply.

---

distempered disturbed
choler anger
purgation cure, cleansing
discourse talk
frame order
breed kind
admiration astonishment

no sequel no consequence
closet bedroom or private room
trade business
pickers and stealers hands (from
the *Book of Common Prayer* 'keep
my hands from picking and
stealing')

GUILDENSTERN Is in his retirement marvellous distempered.

HAMLET With drink sir?

GUILDENSTERN No my lord, rather with choler.   275

HAMLET Your wisdom should show itself more richer to signify this
to his doctor, for, for me to put him to his purgation would perhaps
plunge him into far more choler.

GUILDENSTERN Good my lord, put your discourse into some frame,
and start not so wildly from my affair.   280

HAMLET I am tame sir, pronounce.

GUILDENSTERN The queen your mother, in most great affliction of
spirit, hath sent me to you.

HAMLET You are welcome.

GUILDENSTERN Nay good my lord, this courtesy is not of the right   285
breed. If it shall please you to make me a wholesome answer, I will
do your mother's commandment. If not, your pardon and my return
shall be the end of my business.

HAMLET Sir, I cannot.

ROSENCRANTZ What, my lord?   290

HAMLET Make you a wholesome answer; my wit's diseased. But, sir,
such answer as I can make, you shall command, or rather, as you
say, my mother. Therefore no more, but to the matter. My mother,
you say.

ROSENCRANTZ Then thus she says. Your behaviour hath struck her   295
into amazement and admiration.

HAMLET O wonderful son that can so stonish a mother! But is there
no sequel at the heels of this mother's admiration? Impart.

ROSENCRANTZ She desires to speak with you in her closet ere you go
to bed.   300

HAMLET We shall obey, were she ten times our mother. Have you any
further trade with us?

ROSENCRANTZ My lord, you once did love me.

HAMLET And do still, by these pickers and stealers.

ROSENCRANTZ Good my lord, what is your cause of distemper? You   305
do surely bar the door upon your own liberty if you deny your griefs
to your friend.

HAMLET Sir, I lack advancement.

ROSENCRANTZ How can that be, when you have the voice of the king
himself for your succession in Denmark?   310

HAMLET Ay sir, but while the grass grows – the proverb is something
musty.

Hamlet bitterly accuses Guildenstern of treating him as a mere musical instrument, to be made to say anything at someone else's wish. He demonstrates that process on Polonius.

1 'You would pluck out the heart of my mystery'

Even after four hundred years of performances and criticism, no one can be sure what is Hamlet's inmost essence – his 'mystery'. You will find an activity on page 246 that will help you gain some further understanding of Hamlet – though it certainly doesn't claim to pluck out the heart of his mystery.

2 Playing on Polonius

To show Rosencrantz and Guildenstern how they are treating him, Hamlet does the same to Polonius. He plays upon him like a recorder making him say anything that he, Hamlet, chooses. So Polonius is made to say he sees the imaginary shapes Hamlet suggests are in the clouds.

Some directors and critics challenge this view of Polonius as a silly old man humouring someone he thinks is a lunatic. They argue that Polonius replies in a dignified and tolerant manner, showing that he knows that Hamlet is trying to make fun of him. And certain critics have tried to show that 'camel', 'weasel' and 'whale' are symbols for certain themes of the play.

a Direct Polonius as to how he should behave in lines 337–47.

b Work out an explanation of how 'camel', 'weasel' and 'whale' could have significance in the play. You don't have to be too serious about it. You could invent some spoof criticism – which is likely to be just as good as quite a lot of the criticism written about the play!

---

withdraw be private
recover the wind of me direct me (like hunters keeping upwind of their prey)
toil net
ventages/stops finger holes
mystery innermost secrets

compass range
'Sblood God's blood
fret irritate, or add a fret on a lute
th'mass the Roman Catholic Mass
bent utmost limit (like a stretched bow)

Enter the PLAYERS *with recorders*

Oh, the recorders. Let me see one. To withdraw with you – Why do you go about to recover the wind of me, as if you would drive me into a toil?   315

GUILDENSTERN O my lord, if my duty be too bold, my love is too unmannerly.

HAMLET I do not well understand that. Will you play upon this pipe?

GUILDENSTERN My lord, I cannot.

HAMLET I pray you.   320

GUILDENSTERN Believe me I cannot.

HAMLET I do beseech you.

GUILDENSTERN I know no touch of it my lord.

HAMLET 'Tis as easy as lying. Govern these ventages with your fingers and thumb, give it breath with your mouth, and it will discourse   325 most eloquent music. Look you, these are the stops.

GUILDENSTERN But these cannot I command to any utterance of harmony. I have not the skill.

HAMLET Why look you now how unworthy a thing you make of me. You would play upon me, you would seem to know my stops, you   330 would pluck out the heart of my mystery, you would sound me from my lowest note to the top of my compass – and there is much music, excellent voice, in this little organ, yet cannot you make it speak. 'Sblood, do you think I am easier to be played on than a pipe? Call me what instrument you will, though you can fret me, you cannot   335 play upon me.

Enter POLONIUS

God bless you sir.

POLONIUS My lord, the queen would speak with you, and presently.

HAMLET Do you see yonder cloud that's almost in shape of a camel?

POLONIUS By th'mass, and 'tis like a camel indeed.   340

HAMLET Methinks it is like a weasel.

POLONIUS It is backed like a weasel.

HAMLET Or like a whale?

POLONIUS Very like a whale.

HAMLET Then I will come to my mother by and by. – They fool me   345 to the top of my bent. – I will come by and by.

Hamlet threatens bloody revenge. He decides to visit Gertrude to upbraid but not harm her. Claudius, fearing Hamlet's growing dangerousness, briefs Rosencrantz and Guildenstern to take Hamlet to England.

1 The language of revenge (in pairs)

In lines 349–53, Hamlet uses the language of the traditional revenger in Elizabethan drama (see pages 252–5). Talk together about whether you think the lines are out of character with Hamlet's personality, reducing him to a stereotype of traditional Revenge Tragedy.

2 'I will speak daggers to her'

Hamlet intends to 'speak daggers' to his mother but not to hurt her physically. He is horrified because she has married Claudius, but does he suspect her of anything else? Make a list of all the things he is likely to accuse her of. Check how accurate your predictions are when you read Scene 4.

3 A scene change

In Shakespeare's Globe Theatre the scenes flowed quickly and smoothly without long intervals for scene-changing. Most modern productions also aim at one scene flowing directly into the next. Work out how you would stage the change from Scene 2 to Scene 3. Might Claudius actually glimpse Hamlet at line 1?

Contagion evil
Soft careful!
Nero Roman emperor who murdered his mother
How in my words somever however much in my speech

shent punished, shamed
seals action
commission letters of instruction
The terms of our estate my status as king
provide make preparations

POLONIUS I will say so. *Exit*

HAMLET By and by is easily said. – Leave me, friends.

Exeunt all but Hamlet

'Tis now the very witching time of night,
When churchyards yawn, and hell itself breathes out   350
Contagion to this world. Now could I drink hot blood,
And do such bitter business as the day
Would quake to look on. Soft, now to my mother.
O heart, lose not thy nature; let not ever
The soul of Nero enter this firm bosom.   355
Let me be cruel, not unnatural:
I will speak daggers to her but use none.
My tongue and soul in this be hypocrites,
How in my words somever she be shent,
To give them seals never my soul consent.   *Exit* 360

ACT 3   SCENE 3
The king's private chapel

Enter CLAUDIUS, ROSENCRANTZ *and* GUILDENSTERN

CLAUDIUS I like him not, nor stands it safe with us
To let his madness range. Therefore prepare you:
I your commission will forthwith dispatch,
And he to England shall along with you.
The terms of our estate may not endure   5
Hazard so near us as doth hourly grow
Out of his brows.

GUILDENSTERN   We will ourselves provide.
Most holy and religious fear it is
To keep those many many bodies safe
That live and feed upon your majesty.   10

133

Rosencrantz contrasts the private individual with a king. Everyone depends upon the ruler: when he dies, everyone suffers. Polonius reports that he will spy on Hamlet and Gertrude.

1 Flattery

Rosencrantz mouths the flattering belief that all tyrants love to hear: everything and everybody depend on the monarch ('That spirit'). In Tudor England the ruling class made it the official ideology. But many Elizabethans did not believe it.

Rosencrantz uses two striking images. First, the king's death ('cess'), like a whirlpool ('gulf'), draws everything in to disaster. The second image is that of a huge ('massy') wheel, the king at the centre, everybody else firmly attached ('mortised and adjoined'). When the wheel breaks, every tiny part ('annexment') suffers.

a Choose either the whirlpool or wheel image and illustrate it (or you could illustrate the 'sigh/groan' image of lines 22–3).

b Research 'the Elizabethan World Picture' (the belief in a harmonious hierarchical society, depending on the king at the top). Shakespeare presents the belief clearly in *Troilus and Cressida* Act 1 Scene 3, lines 77–123. But there, as here, a scheming character (Ulysses) speaks, so you need to be wary of taking it as the truth.

c Advise Claudius about how to react to Rosencrantz's flattery, especially when he hears the words 'the cess of majesty'. Does he recall his murder of King Hamlet?

2 More flattery

Polonius suggests that the idea of spying on Hamlet and Gertrude was the king's suggestion (line 30). In fact, Polonius himself proposed it. Do you think he is flattering the king, protecting himself, or has some other motive?

---

single and peculiar life private individual
noyance harm
weal health
boisterous tumultuous
a general groan the sorrow of everyone

fetters chains
arras hanging tapestry
tax him home criticise him strongly
'Tis meet it's fitting
partial biased
of vantage also

ROSENCRANTZ The single and peculiar life is bound
            With all the strength and armour of the mind
            To keep itself from noyance; but much more
            That spirit upon whose weal depends and rests
            The lives of many. The cess of majesty   15
            Dies not alone, but like a gulf doth draw
            What's near it with it. It is a massy wheel
            Fixed on the summit of the highest mount,
            To whose huge spokes ten thousand lesser things
            Are mortised and adjoined, which when it falls,   20
            Each small annexment, petty consequence,
            Attends the boisterous ruin. Never alone
            Did the king sigh, but with a general groan.
CLAUDIUS Arm you I pray you to this speedy voyage,
            For we will fetters put about this fear   *Realises that*   25
            Which now goes too free-footed.   *Hamlet knows*
ROSENCRANTZ   We will haste us. *everything*
                        Exeunt Rosencrantz and Guildenstern

                    Enter POLONIUS

POLONIUS My lord, he's going to his mother's closet.
            Behind the arras I'll convey myself
            To hear the process. I'll warrant she'll tax him home,
            And as you said, and wisely was it said,   30
            'Tis meet that some more audience than a mother,
            Since nature makes them partial, should o'erhear
            The speech of vantage. Fare you well my liege,
            I'll call upon you ere you go to bed
            And tell you what I know.
CLAUDIUS   Thanks, dear my lord.   35
                                    Exit Polonius

Claudius hopes for divine mercy for his brother's murder. But he knows that pardon is impossible while he retains the fruits of his crime, even though villainy can triumph on earth. He tries to pray.

1 The conscience of the king (in small groups)

Claudius agonises over his dilemma. He has committed murder, yet hopes for heavenly pardon. He knows that although he might escape judgement on earth, there is no escape for him in heaven, except God's forgiveness through prayer and true repentance. Though he finds he is in no state to pray or repent, he calls on angels to help, and kneels to pray.

Each person speaks a section of the soliloquy then hands on to the next person. Read around the group in different ways:

- a line at a time
- a sentence at a time
- up to any punctuation mark
- saying only one powerful word from each line
- a 'sense unit' of your own choice.

Try to make your reading sound like a developing argument that Claudius is having with himself. Experiment with whispers, fear, puzzlement and anger. Can you find moments of hope in the soliloquy?

After your explorations, decide on the style you most prefer and make a presentation of Claudius's lines to the class.

2 A mirror of Hamlet?

Lines 41–3 echo Hamlet's indecision. Claudius wants to pray, but cannot. What stops him?

---

rank stinking, rotten
primal eldest first and oldest (in the Bible the killing of Abel by Cain)
inclination desire
will determination
forestallèd prevented
corrupted currents wicked ways
Offence's gilded hand rich criminals

wicked prize profits from crimes
above/There heaven
shuffling deceit
Even . . . evidence to tell our wickedest sins
limèd trapped (like a bird snared by lime)
assay attempt

Oh my offence is rank, it smells to heaven; Feels guilty
It hath the primal eldest curse upon't,
A brother's murder. Pray can I not,
Though inclination be as sharp as will.
My stronger guilt defeats my strong intent,   40
And like a man to double business bound,
I stand in pause where I shall first begin,
And both neglect. What if this cursèd hand
Were thicker than itself with brother's blood,
Is there not rain enough in the sweet heavens   45
To wash it white as snow? Whereto serves mercy
But to confront the visage of offence?
And what's in prayer but this two-fold force,
To be forestallèd ere we come to fall,
Or pardoned being down? Then I'll look up,   50
My fault is past. But oh, what form of prayer
Can serve my turn? 'Forgive me my foul murder'?
That cannot be, since I am still possessed
Of those effects for which I did the murder,
My crown, mine own ambition, and my queen.   55
May one be pardoned and retain th'offence?
In the corrupted currents of this world
Offence's gilded hand may shove by justice,
And oft 'tis seen the wicked prize itself
Buys out the law. But 'tis not so above;   60
There is no shuffling, there the action lies
In his true nature, and we ourselves compelled
Even to the teeth and forehead of our faults
To give in evidence. What then? What rests?
Try what repentance can. What can it not?   65
Yet what can it when one cannot repent?
Oh wretched state! Oh bosom black as death!
Oh limèd soul that struggling to be free
Art more engaged! Help, angels! – Make assay:
Bow stubborn knees, and heart with strings of steel   70
Be soft as sinews of the new-born babe.
All may be well.
                    [*He kneels*]

137

Hamlet refrains from killing Claudius because the king is praying, and so would go to heaven. Hamlet resolves to kill him at a sinful moment, and thus send him to hell. But Claudius has prayed in vain.

1 Hamlet delays

Hamlet does not kill Claudius because the king is praying. Hamlet's own father suffers after death because Claudius killed him at a moment when he was unprepared for heaven ('grossly, full of bread' = full of sin, no opportunity to fast), not having confessed his sins. Hamlet therefore decides to wait for a moment ('hent' = opportunity) when Claudius is committing a sin. Killing Claudius then, when he has no thought of heaven in his mind, will surely send Claudius to hell.

Experiment with dramatic ways of presenting Hamlet's lines. You will find that inter-cutting Hamlet's lines with Claudius's soliloquy on page 137 can lead to fascinating discoveries.

pat instantly, neatly
a is a-praying he's praying
would be scanned needs study
hire and salary legal payment (not punishment)
broad blown in full blossom
as flush full of life

audit account with God
in our circumstance . . . thought it is generally believed
purging cleansing
fit and seasoned fully prepared
relish of salvation hope of heaven
physic medicine

Enter HAMLET

HAMLET Now might I do it pat, now a is a-praying,
And now I'll do't – and so a goes to heaven,
And so am I revenged. That would be scanned.   75
A villain kills my father, and for that,
I his sole son do this same villain send
To heaven.
Why, this is hire and salary, not revenge.
A took my father grossly, full of bread,   80
With all his crimes broad blown, as flush as May,
And how his audit stands who knows save heaven?
But in our circumstance and course of thought
'Tis heavy with him. And am I then revenged
To take him in the purging of his soul,   85
When he is fit and seasoned for his passage?
No.
Up sword, and know thou a more horrid hent,
When he is drunk asleep, or in his rage,
Or in th'incestuous pleasure of his bed,   90
At game a-swearing, or about some act
That has no relish of salvation in't –
Then trip him that his heels may kick at heaven,
And that his soul may be as damned and black
As hell whereto it goes. My mother stays.   95
This physic but prolongs thy sickly days.   *Exit*
CLAUDIUS My words fly up, my thoughts remain below.
Words without thoughts never to heaven go.   *Exit*

Polonius advises Gertrude to speak sharply to her son, and then hides.
Hamlet is vehemently critical of Gertrude, making her fear for her life.
Her alarm makes Polonius call for help – with fatal results.

1 Read through the scene (in groups of three)

To gain a first impression, take parts and read through the whole scene. The same person can read Polonius and the Ghost.

2 Where is the scene set?

Scene 4 is known as 'the closet scene'. A closet was a private room. But for the last hundred years the stage convention has been to set it in Gertrude's bedroom. This usually has the effect of heightening the impression of Hamlet having an Oedipus complex (a desire to sleep with his mother – see page 248). Laurence Olivier's film heavily emphasised this Oedipal interpretation.

Imagine you are directing the play and you have a leading Shakespeare scholar as your consultant. She says to you: 'In Shakespeare's day "closet" meant private room, and the Oedipus complex hadn't been thought of, so I advise you not to bring a bed on stage.' Do you take her advice? Why or why not?

3 The killing of Polonius

Hamlet thrusts his sword through the arras, killing Polonius. How would you stage the killing to bring out aspects of both men's characters?

---

straight immediately
lay home deal firmly with, talk severely
your grace . . . and him like a firescreen you have shielded Hamlet from criticism
round outspoken, firm

warrant assure, promise
rood holy cross of Christ
I'll set . . . speak I'll fetch others to correct you
glass mirror
ducat gold coin ('I'll bet I've killed him')

ACT 3   SCENE 4
Gertrude's private room

Enter GERTRUDE *and* POLONIUS

POLONIUS A will come straight. Look you lay home to him.
　　　　Tell him his pranks have been too broad to bear with,
　　　　And that your grace hath screened and stood between
　　　　Much heat and him. I'll silence me e'en here.
　　　　Pray you be round with him.　　　　　　　　　　　　5
HAMLET (*Within*) Mother, mother, mother!
GERTRUDE I'll warrant you, fear me not. Withdraw, I hear him coming.
　　　　[*Polonius hides himself behind the arras*]

Enter HAMLET

HAMLET Now mother, what's the matter?
GERTRUDE Hamlet, thou hast thy father much offended.
HAMLET Mother, you have my father much offended.　　　　10
GERTRUDE Come, come, you answer with an idle tongue.
HAMLET Go, go, you question with a wicked tongue.
GERTRUDE Why, how now Hamlet?
HAMLET　　　　　　　　　　What's the matter now?
GERTRUDE Have you forgot me?
HAMLET　　　　　　　　　No by the rood, not so.
　　　　You are the queen, your husband's brother's wife,　　　15
　　　　And, would it were not so, you are my mother.
GERTRUDE Nay, then I'll set those to you that can speak.
HAMLET Come, come and sit you down, you shall not budge.
　　　　You go not till I set you up a glass
　　　　Where you may see the inmost part of you.　　　　　20
GERTRUDE What wilt thou do? thou wilt not murder me?
　　　　Help, help, ho!
POLONIUS (*Behind*) What ho! Help, help, help!
HAMLET (*Draws*) How now, a rat? Dead for a ducat, dead.
　　　　　　　　　　Kills Polonius
POLONIUS (*Behind*) Oh, I am slain!

*Hamlet dismisses the dead Polonius as a meddling fool. He accuses
Gertrude of shamefully defiling true love and marriage, making heaven
blush with shame.*

---

1 Did she know? (in small groups)

'As kill a king?' echoes Gertrude (line 30). But did she know that
Claudius had murdered her first husband? On stage, a clue is often
given in the way Gertrude behaves as she speaks these four words. Talk
together about whether you think Gertrude knew anything about the
murder. Advise her on how to deliver the line.

2 A just epitaph?

'Wretched, rash, intruding fool.' Would Ophelia or the queen accept
this as an appropriate epitaph for Polonius? Invent the four words each
of them would substitute for Hamlet's callous dismissal. Choose four
words of your own to describe Polonius.

3 'What have I done . . . ?'

Hamlet does not answer Gertrude's question directly, but embarks on
a densely-packed diatribe against her. He includes the image of
prostitutes being branded ('blister') on the forehead, and says she has
torn the heart ('plucks the very soul') out of the marriage contract ('the
body of contraction'), making religion a meaningless jumble ('rhapsody')
of words. Her act makes heaven blush ('glow') with shame, and the
earth sad and sickened as if Doomsday had come.

Identify in lines 40–51 the eight consequences of Gertrude's 'act'
(some are given in the paragraph above). Call up a picture in your mind
for each. Compare your 'mental pictures' with those of other students.
(The eight consequences end with these words: modesty, hypocrite,
there, oaths, soul, words, glow, act).

---

thy better the king
damnèd custom wicked habits
brazed hardened (like brass)
proof and bulwark armoured
  strongly
sense feeling
grace and blush innocence

dicers' oaths gamblers' promises
solidity and compound mass
  the world
tristful visage sad face
the doom the Day of Judgement
index list of sins

GERTRUDE   Oh me, what hast thou done?   25
HAMLET Nay I know not, is it the king?
GERTRUDE Oh what a rash and bloody deed is this!
HAMLET A bloody deed? Almost as bad, good mother,
      As kill a king and marry with his brother.
GERTRUDE As kill a king?
HAMLET   Ay lady, 'twas my word.   30
      [*Lifts up the arras and reveals the body of Polonius*]
      Thou wretched, rash, intruding fool, farewell.
      I took thee for thy better. Take thy fortune.
      Thou find'st to be too busy is some danger. −
      Leave wringing of your hands. Peace! Sit you down
      And let me wring your heart, for so I shall   35
      If it be made of penetrable stuff,
      If damnèd custom have not brazed it so,
      That it be proof and bulwark against sense.
GERTRUDE What have I done, that thou dar'st wag thy tongue
      In noise so rude against me?
HAMLET   Such an act   40
      That blurs the grace and blush of modesty,
      Calls virtue hypocrite, takes off the rose
      From the fair forehead of an innocent love
      And sets a blister there, makes marriage vows
      As false as dicers' oaths. Oh such a deed   45
      As from the body of contraction plucks
      The very soul, and sweet religion makes
      A rhapsody of words. Heaven's face doth glow;
      Yea, this solidity and compound mass,
      With tristful visage as against the doom,   50
      Is thought-sick at the act.
GERTRUDE   Ay me, what act,
      That roars so loud and thunders in the index?

> *Hamlet compares his father with Claudius: the good man against the bad. He berates Gertrude for not seeing the difference, and deplores her inability to control her sexual desires.*

1 Two pictures

Hamlet shows Gertrude two miniature portraits ('counterfeit presentment') to compare his father and Claudius. He presents his father as god-like: 'Hyperion' = the sun god; 'Jove' = king of the gods; 'Mars' = Roman god of war; 'Mercury' = winged messenger of the gods.

Work out how Hamlet shows the portraits. In many productions Hamlet has his father's picture on a chain around his neck. Gertrude wears her husband's picture similarly. But might there be portraits on the wall?

2 Can't you tell the difference? (in pairs)

Hamlet lectures his mother in lines 65–88 on not being able to tell the difference between her two husbands, and on her sexuality. Take turns at reading the lines. Put as much feeling of disgust as you can into your reading. Put yourself in Gertrude's place. What does she feel at being subjected to such a tongue-lashing?

3 Blaming parents (in small groups)

In lines 82–8, Hamlet demands to know how young people can be expected to control their passions, if mothers can't control theirs ('mutine in a matron's bones' = run riot in a mother's body). When middle-age ('frost') is highly sexually active ('doth burn') and intellect helps to satisfy desire ('reason panders will'), then there is no shame in anyone's passion. Talk together about whether Hamlet's anger at his mother's sexuality is typical of young people today.

---

station posture
New-lighted recently landed
mildewed ear rotten ear of corn
batten greedily feed
Sense sexual desire
motion emotions
apoplexed paralysed
ecstasy madness

thralled enslaved
But it . . . difference but it could choose good from bad
cozened cheated
hoodman-blind blind man's buff
sans all without anything else
so mope be so stupid

HAMLET Look here upon this picture, and on this,
The counterfeit presentment of two brothers.
See what a grace was seated on this brow; 55
Hyperion's curls, the front of Jove himself,
An eye like Mars, to threaten and command;
A station like the herald Mercury,
New-lighted on a heaven-kissing hill;
A combination and a form indeed, 60
Where every god did seem to set his seal
To give the world assurance of a man.
This was your husband. Look you now what follows.
Here is your husband, like a mildewed ear
Blasting his wholesome brother. Have you eyes? 65
Could you on this fair mountain leave to feed
And batten on this moor? Ha! have you eyes?
You cannot call it love, for at your age
The heyday in the blood is tame, it's humble,
And waits upon the judgement; and what judgement 70
Would step from this to this? [Sense sure you have,
Else could you not have motion, but sure that sense
Is apoplexed, for madness would not err,
Nor sense to ecstasy was ne'er so thralled,
But it reserved some quantity of choice 75
To serve in such a difference.] What devil was't
That thus hath cozened you at hoodman-blind?
[Eyes without feeling, feeling without sight,
Ears without hands or eyes, smelling sans all,
Or but a sickly part of one true sense 80
Could not so mope.]
O shame, where is thy blush? Rebellious hell,
If thou canst mutine in a matron's bones,
To flaming youth let virtue be as wax
And melt in her own fire. Proclaim no shame 85
When the compulsive ardour gives the charge,
Since frost itself as actively doth burn,
And reason panders will.

Hamlet expresses his disgust at Gertrude's sexuality. She pleads with him to stop. He reviles Claudius. The Ghost reminds Hamlet of his mission and urges him to comfort Gertrude. She is amazed by his words.

'*Enter* GHOST': an eighteenth-century staging. The first published version of the play had the stage direction 'Enter the Ghost in his nightgown'. In one production the Ghost sat alongside Hamlet and put its arm around Hamlet's shoulders, whispering the lines. Work out how you would stage the Ghost's entry, appearance (nightgown? armour?), movement and manner of speech.

1 Speaking daggers

'The product of a very sick mind.' What comments would you make on this judgement by a student on Hamlet's lines 91–4 ('enseamèd' = greasy, semen-stained; 'stewed' = like prostitutes, 'stews' were brothels)?

grainèd indelibly stained
leave their tinct lose their stain
tithe tenth part
vice clown in medieval morality
  plays, dressed in multi-coloured
  costume ('A king of shreds and
  patches')

cutpurse thief
tardy slow
whet sharpen
amazement bewilderment
Conceit imagination
bend your eye look
th'incorporal bodyless

GERTRUDE   O Hamlet, speak no more.
    Thou turn'st my eyes into my very soul,
    And there I see such black and grainèd spots   90
    As will not leave their tinct.
HAMLET   Nay, but to live
    In the rank sweat of an enseamèd bed,
    Stewed in corruption, honeying and making love
    Over the nasty sty.
GERTRUDE   Oh speak to me no more.
    These words like daggers enter in my ears.   95
    No more sweet Hamlet.
HAMLET   A murderer and a villain,
    A slave that is not twentieth part the tithe
    Of your precedent lord, a vice of kings,
    A cutpurse of the empire and the rule,
    That from a shelf the precious diadem stole   100
    And put it in his pocket.
GERTRUDE   No more!

Enter GHOST

HAMLET A king of shreds and patches –
    Save me and hover o'er me with your wings,
    You heavenly guards! – What would your gracious figure?
GERTRUDE Alas he's mad!   105
HAMLET Do you not come your tardy son to chide,
    That lapsed in time and passion lets go by
    Th'important acting of your dread command? Oh say!
GHOST Do not forget. This visitation
    Is but to whet thy almost blunted purpose.   110
    But look, amazement on thy mother sits.
    Oh step between her and her fighting soul:
    Conceit in weakest bodies strongest works.
    Speak to her, Hamlet.
HAMLET   How is it with you lady?
GERTRUDE Alas, how is't with you,   115
    That you do bend your eye on vacancy,
    And with th'incorporal air do hold discourse?
    Forth at your eyes your spirits wildly peep,

Gertrude, unable to see the Ghost, is bewildered by Hamlet's behaviour. Hamlet fears that his impulse to revenge might soften to pity. He says he is not mad, and urges Gertrude to repent.

1 The mind's construction in the face?

Hamlet says the combination of the Ghost's appearance and plea for justice would make even stones feel pity ('form and cause conjoined … capable'). Hamlet implores the Ghost to turn his gaze away because it weakens his impulse to revenge (lines 126–9). Write three sentences that describe respectively the facial expressions of Hamlet, Gertrude and the Ghost. Use clues in the script.

2 Why can't Gertrude see the Ghost? (in pairs)

Talk together about whether you think Gertrude's inability to see the Ghost signifies her moral blindness, or whether there are other possible explanations.

3 Images of corruption (in small groups)

Hamlet rejects Gertrude's accusation that he is mad. It's your crime ('trespass') not my madness that has called up the Ghost, he says. To believe otherwise is just an ointment ('unction') to cover ('skin and film') the corruption deep and growing within her (lines 145–50). He attributes virtue to himself and vice to Gertrude: she is the one who should repent. In these sick ('pursy') times, virtue must ask forgiveness of vice.

How does Hamlet speak lines 140–56? Does he plead with her, trying to appeal to her reason with rational argument? Or does he speak vehemently and accusingly, stressing intensely all the words to do with madness and corruption? Experiment with ways of speaking the lines to express Hamlet's emotional state at this point in the play.

in th'alarm woken by call to battle	**portal** door
bedded smoothed down	**coinage** creation
excrements outgrowths (hair)	**ecstasy/Is very cunning**
stern effects intention to revenge	in madness invents
want true colour lose its real	**gambol** leap, shy away
character	**curb and woo** flatter
habit as he lived everyday clothes	**leave** permission

And, as the sleeping soldiers in th'alarm,
Your bedded hair, like life in excrements,   120
Start up and stand an end. O gentle son,
Upon the heat and flame of thy distemper
Sprinkle cool patience. Whereon do you look?
HAMLET On him, on him! Look you how pale he glares.
His form and cause conjoined, preaching to stones,   125
Would make them capable. – Do not look upon me,
Lest with this piteous action you convert
My stern effects. Then what I have to do
Will want true colour: tears perchance for blood.
GERTRUDE To whom do you speak this?   130
HAMLET Do you see nothing there?
GERTRUDE Nothing at all, yet all that is I see.
HAMLET Nor did you nothing hear?
GERTRUDE No, nothing but ourselves.
HAMLET Why, look you there – look how it steals away –   135
My father in his habit as he lived –
Look where he goes, even now out at the portal.

Exit Ghost

GERTRUDE This is the very coinage of your brain.
This bodiless creation ecstasy
Is very cunning in.
HAMLET   Ecstasy?   140
My pulse as yours doth temperately keep time,
And makes as healthful music. It is not madness
That I have uttered. Bring me to the test,
And I the matter will reword, which madness
Would gambol from. Mother, for love of grace,   145
Lay not that flattering unction to your soul,
That not your trespass but my madness speaks;
It will but skin and film the ulcerous place,
Whiles rank corruption, mining all within,
Infects unseen. Confess yourself to heaven,   150
Repent what's past, avoid what is to come,
And do not spread the compost on the weeds
To make them ranker. Forgive me this my virtue,
For in the fatness of these pursy times
Virtue itself of vice must pardon beg,   155
Yea, curb and woo for leave to do him good.

149

Hamlet pleads with Gertrude not to sleep with Claudius tonight: that abstinence will begin what can become a virtuous habit. He claims to be heaven's agent in killing Polonius.

1 Custom – or naive psychology? (in small groups)

'Custom' destroys sensibility, but it also can result in virtue, argues Hamlet (lines 162–71). Good things, as well as bad, can come about through habitual practice. If Gertrude doesn't sleep with Claudius tonight, that will make it easier for her to refrain the next night, and on further nights. Discuss whether you agree with Hamlet's argument, or whether you think abstinence just stores up emotion that leads to a later explosion. Will Gertrude follow Hamlet's advice?

2 What's the missing word?

No one knows what Shakespeare intended to write in line 170. The word is missing in all the earliest printed editions. Which word do you think would fit? Suggestions have been: curb, master, aid, shame, speed, quell, house, lodge and oust.

3 Laying off the blame (in pairs)

Hamlet has blamed his mother for his vehement language. Now he places the responsibility for Polonius's death on heaven, not on himself (lines 174–6). Talk together about whether this suggests a shiftiness in Hamlet's character. Make a list of the possible causes of the death of Polonius and rank them in order of likelihood.

4 'I must be cruel only to be kind' (in small groups)

Hamlet's line 179 has become part of everyday language. Give examples from your own experience of when you have used it (or when it has been said to or about you).

---

cleft my heart in twain broken my heart in two
sense finer feelings, sensibility
Of habits devil the evil spirit of all habits
frock or livery clothing or uniform

Refrain don't go to bed with him
wondrous potency amazing power
scourge and minister whip and officer who wields it
bestow dispose of
remains behind lies ahead

GERTRUDE Oh Hamlet, thou hast cleft my heart in twain.
HAMLET Oh throw away the worser part of it
      And live the purer with the other half.
      Good night – but go not to my uncle's bed;   160
      Assume a virtue if you have it not.
      [That monster custom, who all sense doth eat,
      Of habits devil, is angel yet in this,
      That to the use of actions fair and good
      He likewise gives a frock or livery   165
      That aptly is put on.] Refrain tonight,
      And that shall lend a kind of easiness
      To the next abstinence, [the next more easy,
      For use almost can change the stamp of nature,
      And either…the devil, or throw him out,   170
      With wondrous potency.] Once more good night,
      And when you are desirous to be blessed,
      I'll blessing beg of you. For this same lord,
      I do repent; but heaven hath pleased it so,
      To punish me with this, and this with me,   175
      That I must be their scourge and minister.
      I will bestow him, and will answer well
      The death I gave him. So again, good night.
      I must be cruel only to be kind;
      Thus bad begins, and worse remains behind.   180
      One word more good lady.
GERTRUDE   What shall I do?

Hamlet urges Gertrude not to reveal his pretended madness to Claudius. He threatens her. She promises to keep silent. Hamlet plans to kill Rosencrantz and Guildenstern who are involved in a plot against him.

1 Irony or sarcasm?

Lines 183–92 are heavily ironic, even sarcastic. Hamlet seems to order Gertrude to reveal his secrets to Claudius. But line 182 makes his intention clear: she is not to do as he commands. Advise the actor playing Hamlet on how to speak lines 182–92.

2 'The famous ape'

No one knows the story for sure. Perhaps lines 194–7 mean: an ape took a bird cage onto a roof, released the birds, and seeing them fly, decided to imitate them ('try conclusions') – with disastrous results! Hamlet may be using the fable to threaten his mother: if she reveals his secrets to the king, she too will come to grief ('and break your own neck down'). Invent another interpretation that seems plausible.

3 Mining and countermining

Attackers besieging a city often dug tunnels (mines) under the walls and packed them with explosives to demolish the defences. The defenders dug countermines underneath ('in one line') to blow up the besiegers' tunnels. Thus the 'engineer' (miner) was 'hoist with his own petar' (blown up with his own bomb). See page 262, 'Imagery'.

4 To cut or not to cut?

The lines in square brackets (lines 203–11) suggest that Hamlet already has plans to kill Rosencrantz and Guildenstern. As Act 5 Scene 2 shows, that may not be true. Imagine you are directing the play and are urged to cut the lines for that reason. What do you reply?

---

bloat flabby, bloated
wanton lustfully
reechy filthy
ravel unravel, explain
craft pretence, cunning
paddock/gib toad/cat

dear concernings important matters
adders fanged poisonous snakes
mandate orders
delve dig
crafts plots

HAMLET Not this by no means that I bid you do:
Let the bloat king tempt you again to bed,
Pinch wanton on your cheek, call you his mouse,
And let him for a pair of reechy kisses,   185
Or paddling in your neck with his damned fingers,
Make you to ravel all this matter out,
That I essentially am not in madness,
But mad in craft. 'Twere good you let him know,
For who that's but a queen, fair, sober, wise,   190
Would from a paddock, from a bat, a gib,
Such dear concernings hide? Who would do so?
No, in despite of sense and secrecy,
Unpeg the basket on the house's top,
Let the birds fly, and like the famous ape,   195
To try conclusions, in the basket creep
And break your own neck down.
GERTRUDE Be thou assured, if words be made of breath,
And breath of life, I have no life to breathe
What thou hast said to me.   200
HAMLET I must to England, you know that?
GERTRUDE   Alack,
I had forgot. 'Tis so concluded on.
HAMLET [There's letters sealed, and my two schoolfellows,
Whom I will trust as I will adders fanged,
They bear the mandate. They must sweep my way   205
And marshal me to knavery. Let it work,
For 'tis the sport to have the engineer
Hoist with his own petar, an't shall go hard
But I will delve one yard below their mines
And blow them at the moon. Oh 'tis most sweet   210
When in one line two crafts directly meet.]
This man shall set me packing.
I'll lug the guts into the neighbour room.
Mother, good night. Indeed, this counsellor
Is now most still, most secret, and most grave,   215
Who was in life a foolish prating knave.
Come sir, to draw toward an end with you.
Good night mother.
                    Exit Hamlet tugging in Polonius; [Gertrude remains]

Looking back at Act 3
Activities for groups or individuals

1 Hamlet: speech, action and response

Hamlet appears in each of the four scenes in Act 3. To further your understanding of his relationships with other characters, copy the table below onto a large sheet of paper and complete the blank spaces.

Scene	Hamlet speaks to or about	A typical line or lines	Hamlet's mood and intention
1	Ophelia		
2	The players		
	Horatio		
	Claudius		
	Polonius		
	Gertrude		
	Ophelia		
	Rosencrantz and Guildenstern		
3	Claudius		
4	Gertrude		

2 Attitudes to Hamlet

Consider each character listed in the table above. Write a sentence for each of them, expressing their attitude to Hamlet as they encounter him in Act 3, and whether they think he is mad. Then rank the characters in order of what you judge to be Hamlet's feelings towards them in Act 3. The person he loves most goes at the top of your list; the person he hates most goes at the bottom.

3 Hamlet as playwright

Hamlet asked the first player to learn 'a speech of some dozen or sixteen lines' he would write specially for *The Murder of Gonzago* play. No one knows for certain if those lines actually were spoken in Scene 2. Try to identify (giving reasons) which lines were Hamlet's. If you think none of the lines were his, write a dozen lines that you think he would have inserted.

Hamlet and Gertrude. Find lines from Scene 4 that could make suitable captions for each picture. Talk together about what you think the director of each production might have in mind about the mother–son relationship.

Gertrude tells Claudius that Hamlet has killed Polonius. Claudius fears that he himself might have been the victim and that he will be blamed for Polonius's death. He lies about his love for Hamlet.

1 Continuity of action?

At the end of Act 3 the stage direction, '*Gertrude remains*', is in square brackets because it does not appear in one of the early editions of the play. As director of a production, give advice to Gertrude about whether she should remain on stage until the arrival of Claudius, Rosencrantz and Guildenstern in this scene, or whether she should exit and re-enter with Claudius. Which is the more dramatically convincing?

Similarly, decide whether you will include line 4, 'Bestow this place on us a little while'. Justify your decision by talking about why Rosencrantz and Guildenstern are dismissed without speaking (and why Shakespeare brought them on in the first place. See also their brief appearance on page 159.)

2 Claudius and Gertrude alone (in pairs)

Take parts and read lines 5–32. Suggest how the king and queen behave towards each other as they speak. Remember that this is the only time they are alone together in the play.

3 Gertrude's promise (in small groups)

Gertrude has just promised Hamlet she will keep his secret (Act 3 Scene 4, lines 198–200). She seems to keep her word because she tells Claudius at least four times that Hamlet is mad (lines 7, 8, 11 and 25).

Talk together about whether you think this is the point in the play where Gertrude begins to assert her loyalty to her son over loyalty to her husband.

---

profound heaves deep sighs and shudders
translate explain
contend dispute
lawless unruly
brainish apprehension frenzied state of mind
providence foresight

short confined
out of haunt out of the public eye
divulging becoming generally known
pith core, essence
ore . . . pure pure metal shining among crude ones

ACT 4   SCENE 1
Gertrude's private room

Enter CLAUDIUS with ROSENCRANTZ and GUILDENSTERN

CLAUDIUS There's matter in these sighs, these profound heaves.
        You must translate, 'tis fit we understand them.
        Where is your son?
GERTRUDE [Bestow this place on us a little while.]
                  [*Exeunt Rosencrantz and Guildenstern*]
        Ah mine own lord, what have I seen tonight!   5
CLAUDIUS What, Gertrude? How does Hamlet?
GERTRUDE Mad as the sea and wind, when both contend
        Which is the mightier. In his lawless fit,
        Behind the arras hearing something stir,
        Whips out his rapier, cries 'A rat, a rat!',   10
        And in this brainish apprehension kills
        The unseen good old man.
CLAUDIUS   Oh heavy deed!
        It had been so with us had we been there.
        His liberty is full of threats to all,
        To you yourself, to us, to everyone.   15
        Alas, how shall this bloody deed be answered?
        It will be laid to us, whose providence
        Should have kept short, restrained, and out of haunt,
        This mad young man. But so much was our love,
        We would not understand what was most fit,   20
        But like the owner of a foul disease,
        To keep it from divulging, let it feed
        Even on the pith of life. Where is he gone?
GERTRUDE To draw apart the body he hath killed,
        O'er whom his very madness, like some ore   25
        Among a mineral of metals base,
        Shows itself pure; a weeps for what is done.

Claudius decides to send Hamlet away from Denmark. He orders Rosencrantz and Guildenstern to join with others to find Polonius's body and take it to the chapel. He hopes he can avoid slanderous accusations.

1 'We will ship him hence'
List the advantages to Claudius of sending Hamlet into exile away from Denmark.

2 Puzzle it out!
There is a puzzling end to Scene 1. The dots at line 40 suggest that two words are missing. Lines 41 to 44 are in square brackets because they do not appear in the folio version of the play, printed later than other versions (see page 262).

Decide which of the following two courses of action you would recommend to a director of the play:

a Insert 'For slander' in place of the dots in line 40. In such a version, Claudius would be expressing his hope that though slanderous rumours about him may circulate, they may miss their mark if he briefs his 'wisest friends' well.

b Cut the dots and the lines in brackets. If you choose this option, justify your cutting of the reference to slander.

3 What's going on? (in pairs)
Imagine that, between their exit at line 37 and their entry in Scene 2 at line 4, Rosencrantz and Guildenstern discuss the situation. Improvise a dialogue in which they consider Hamlet's actions and 'madness', and their own position.

4 'Oh here they come'
Experiment with ways of speaking 'Oh here they come' (lines 3–4). Then give reasons for how you think Hamlet should speak it.

---

countenance condone, accept
join you with give
untimely wrongly, inappropriately
o'er the world's diameter to the ends of the world
level accurately

blank target
name reputation
woundless invulnerable
Compounded mixed, blended
kin related

CLAUDIUS Oh Gertrude, come away!
　　　The sun no sooner shall the mountains touch
　　　But we will ship him hence, and this vile deed　　　　30
　　　We must with all our majesty and skill
　　　Both countenance and excuse. Ho, Guildenstern!

Enter Rosencrantz and Guildenstern

　　　Friends both, go join you with some further aid.
　　　Hamlet in madness hath Polonius slain,
　　　And from his mother's closet hath he dragged him.　　35
　　　Go seek him out, speak fair, and bring the body
　　　Into the chapel. I pray you haste in this.
　　　　　　　　Exeunt Rosencrantz and Guildenstern
　　　Come Gertrude, we'll call up our wisest friends
　　　And let them know both what we mean to do
　　　And what's untimely done.   ...   ...　　　　　　40
　　　[Whose whisper o'er the world's diameter,
　　　As level as the cannon to his blank,
　　　Transports his poisoned shot, may miss our name
　　　And hit the woundless air.] Oh come away,
　　　My soul is full of discord and dismay.　　　　　　45
　　　　　　　　　　　　　　　　　Exeunt

ACT 4　SCENE 2
A corridor in the castle

Enter HAMLET

HAMLET Safely stowed.
GENTLEMEN (*Within*) Hamlet! Lord Hamlet!
HAMLET But soft, what noise? Who calls on Hamlet? Oh here they
　　come.

Enter ROSENCRANTZ *and* GUILDENSTERN

ROSENCRANTZ What have you done my lord with the dead body?　　5
HAMLET Compounded it with dust whereto 'tis kin.

Hamlet's replies bewilder Rosencrantz and Guildenstern. He does not reveal where Polonius's body is hidden. Claudius feels he cannot punish Hamlet severely because Hamlet is popular in Denmark.

1 Hamlet's smokescreen

Identify the different strategies used by Hamlet in lines 9–27 to avoid telling Rosencrantz and Guildenstern where Polonius's body is hidden. Suggest how this episode could be played to maximum dramatic effect.

2 Play with metaphor! (in pairs)

Hamlet uses metaphor to sum up Rosencrantz's nature: he is a sponge, or he is like food to be sucked and swallowed by a king in the same way that an ape eats. Hamlet also plays with metaphor to divert Rosencrantz from his attempt to find out the whereabouts of Polonius.

Make up your own metaphors to describe each of the following characters:

- Hamlet (a chameleon? changeable weather?)
- Guildenstern (a toad?)
- Horatio (a solid rock? a buttress?)
- Claudius
- Gertrude.

3 'The body is with the king . . .'

Offer some advice to the actor about the 'business' (stage actions) Hamlet might use as he speaks his enigmatic lines 24–5.

4 'Hide fox, and all after!' (in groups of three)

In some productions, Hamlet runs away as he speaks line 27, chased by the two courtiers. But consider other possibilities and work out a departure from the stage for the three characters. Reflect on how the hunting image might be applicable to the play as a whole.

---

replication reply
countenance favour, goodwill
gleaned gathered, harvested
knavish sarcastic

the strong law strict restraints
distracted muddled, irrational
like . . . eyes love him for his looks rather than for sound reasons

ROSENCRANTZ Tell us where 'tis, that we may take it thence and bear
it to the chapel.

HAMLET Do not believe it.

ROSENCRANTZ Believe what?   10

HAMLET That I can keep your counsel and not mine own. Besides, to
be demanded of a sponge, what replication should be made by the
son of a king?

ROSENCRANTZ Take you me for a sponge my lord?

HAMLET Ay sir, that soaks up the king's countenance, his rewards, his   15
authorities. But such officers do the king best service in the end:
he keeps them like an ape in the corner of his jaw, first mouthed
to be last swallowed. When he needs what you have gleaned, it is
but squeezing you, and, sponge, you shall be dry again.

ROSENCRANTZ I understand you not my lord.   20

HAMLET I am glad of it, a knavish speech sleeps in a foolish ear.

ROSENCRANTZ My lord, you must tell us where the body is, and go
with us to the king.

HAMLET The body is with the king, but the king is not with the body.
The king is a thing –   25

GUILDENSTERN A thing my lord?

HAMLET Of nothing. Bring me to him. Hide fox, and all after!

Exeunt

ACT 4   SCENE 3
A state room

Enter CLAUDIUS and two or three ATTENDANTS

CLAUDIUS I have sent to seek him, and to find the body.
How dangerous is it that this man goes loose,
Yet must not we put the strong law on him;
He's loved of the distracted multitude,
Who like not in their judgement, but their eyes;   5

Claudius reflects that he must use desperate methods. Hamlet is brought in. He taunts Claudius with images of the corruption of dead bodies, then reveals where Polonius's body is hidden.

The 1970 Royal Shakespeare Company production showed Hamlet stripped and beaten by Rosencrantz and Guildenstern. How would you present the stage direction at line 15?

1 Through the guts of a beggar

In taunting Claudius, Hamlet stresses corruption ('worms') and the levelling nature of death: a king may go 'a progress' (a royal journey) through the guts of a beggar. Hamlet also puns on the Diet ('convocation') of Worms (a town in Germany) where in 1521 the Protestant Martin Luther defended his anti-papal views. The worms are 'politic' because they infiltrate the body in the same way as Polonius has insinuated his way into Hamlet's privacy. Make a series of drawings to illustrate the sequence (lines 19–29) that Hamlet sees as inevitable for everyone, including kings.

---

scourge punishment
weighed noted
Deliberate pause planned
appliance remedies
variable service different dishes
  in a menu

i'th'other place hell
A will stay till you come he
  won't move (in the theatre,
  Hamlet's ironic remark often makes
  the audience laugh)

And where 'tis so, th'offender's scourge is weighed,
But never the offence. To bear all smooth and even,
This sudden sending him away must seem
Deliberate pause. Diseases desperate grown
By desperate appliance are relieved,   10
Or not at all.

Enter ROSENCRANTZ

How now, what hath befallen?
ROSENCRANTZ Where the dead body is bestowed, my lord,
We cannot get from him.
CLAUDIUS   But where is he?
ROSENCRANTZ Without, my lord, guarded, to know your pleasure.
CLAUDIUS Bring him before us.
ROSENCRANTZ   Ho! bring in my lord.   15

Enter HAMLET *and* GUILDENSTERN

CLAUDIUS Now Hamlet, where's Polonius?
HAMLET At supper.
CLAUDIUS At supper? Where?
HAMLET Not where he eats, but where a is eaten. A certain convocation
of politic worms are e'en at him. Your worm is your only emperor   20
for diet: we fat all creatures else to fat us, and we fat ourselves for
maggots. Your fat king and your lean beggar is but variable service,
two dishes, but to one table; that's the end.
CLAUDIUS Alas, alas.
HAMLET A man may fish with the worm that hath eat of a king, and   25
eat of the fish that hath fed of that worm.
CLAUDIUS What dost thou mean by this?
HAMLET Nothing but to show you how a king may go a progress
through the guts of a beggar.
CLAUDIUS Where is Polonius?   30
HAMLET In heaven, send thither to see. If your messenger find him not
there, seek him i'th'other place yourself. But if indeed you find him
not within this month, you shall nose him as you go up the stairs
into the lobby.
CLAUDIUS Go seek him there.   35
HAMLET A will stay till you come.

[*Exeunt Attendants*]

Claudius tells Hamlet that a ship and attendants wait to take him to England. Hamlet bids Claudius an ironic farewell. Claudius reveals he has written letters ordering Hamlet's immediate execution in England.

1 Hamlet's suspicions

At line 44, Claudius replies to Hamlet's positive acceptance of the impending trip to England with: 'So is it if thou knew'st our purposes'. The words have sinister implications: Claudius is planning to have Hamlet killed. Hamlet responds: 'I see a cherub that sees them' (line 45). At whom (or what) does Hamlet look when he says 'cherub', and why does he use that word? Give reasons for your choice, and consider whether you think Hamlet suspects that Claudius intends to have him killed.

2 'One flesh'

Work out how Hamlet speaks lines 48–9 (for example, with loathing, humour, calm logic, or with some other feeling or combination of feelings). Imagine you are a director. Advise the actor on how to speak these lines by suggesting what is in Hamlet's mind at this moment.

3 'Do it England' (in pairs)

Claudius's soliloquy (lines 54–64) suggests that Denmark has recently won a great victory over England, whose 'cicatrice' (battle-scar) 'looks raw and red'. Claudius now has great power over England. It voluntarily ('free awe') pays him tribute money, and is very unlikely to ignore his royal wishes ('sovereign process').

One person reads aloud lines 54–64. The other says 'England' each time Claudius refers to England (there are eight references). Change roles and repeat, then talk together about how you think Claudius might deliver the soliloquy. For example, would it have more or less dramatic effect if he addressed it to a map, clearly visible to the audience?

do tender have concern for	**imports** means, implies
bark ship	**congruing** leading, agreeing
at foot closely	**present** immediate
else leans on is connected with	**hectic** fever
at aught as having any value	**haps** fortunes
coldly set look at with indifference	

CLAUDIUS Hamlet, this deed, for thine especial safety,
Which we do tender, as we dearly grieve
For that which thou hast done, must send thee hence
With fiery quickness. Therefore prepare thyself.   40
The bark is ready and the wind at help,
Th'associates tend, and everything is bent
For England.
HAMLET   For England?
CLAUDIUS   Ay Hamlet.
HAMLET   Good.
CLAUDIUS So is it if thou knew'st our purposes.
HAMLET I see a cherub that sees them. But come, for England! Farewell   45
dear mother.
CLAUDIUS Thy loving father, Hamlet.
HAMLET My mother. Father and mother is man and wife, man and wife
is one flesh, and so, my mother. Come, for England.   *Exit*
CLAUDIUS Follow him at foot, tempt him with speed aboard.   50
Delay it not, I'll have him hence tonight.
Away, for everything is sealed and done
That else leans on th'affair. Pray you make haste.
                [Exeunt Rosencrantz and Guildenstern]
And England, if my love thou hold'st at aught,
As my great power thereof may give thee sense,   55
Since yet thy cicatrice looks raw and red
After the Danish sword, and thy free awe
Pays homage to us – thou mayst not coldly set
Our sovereign process, which imports at full,
By letters congruing to that effect,   60
The present death of Hamlet. Do it England,
For like the hectic in my blood he rages,
And thou must cure me. Till I know 'tis done,
Howe'er my haps, my joys were ne'er begun.   *Exit*

Fortinbras sends a captain to ask Claudius for permission to pass through Danish territory. The captain tells Hamlet the army will fight for a tiny, unprofitable part of Poland. Hamlet reflects on a sick society.

Fortinbras and his army. The Russian film director Kozintsev's imaginative re-creation of Scene 4.

would aught wishes to negotiate
in his eye face to face
softly quietly, carefully
How purposed with what purpose
main entire country
addition exaggeration
ducats gold coins
ranker rate greater price

in fee outright
Will not debate . . . straw will not be enough to resolve this trivial matter
impostume abscess, inner sore
without outside
God buy you God be with you

ACT 4 SCENE 4
The sea coast near Elsinore

Enter FORTINBRAS *with his army*

FORTINBRAS Go captain, from me greet the Danish king.
        Tell him that by his licence, Fortinbras
        Craves the conveyance of a promised march
        Over his kingdom. You know the rendezvous.
        If that his majesty would aught with us,   5
        We shall express our duty in his eye,
        And let him know so.
CAPTAIN   I will do't, my lord.
FORTINBRAS Go softly on.

                  [Exit Fortinbras, with the army]

      [Enter HAMLET, ROSENCRANTZ, *etc.*

HAMLET Good sir, whose powers are these?
CAPTAIN They are of Norway sir.   10
HAMLET How purposed sir I pray you?
CAPTAIN Against some part of Poland.
HAMLET Who commands them sir?
CAPTAIN The nephew to old Norway, Fortinbras.
HAMLET Goes it against the main of Poland sir,   15
        Or for some frontier?
CAPTAIN Truly to speak, and with no addition,
        We go to gain a little patch of ground
        That hath in it no profit but the name.
        To pay five ducats, five, I would not farm it,   20
        Nor will it yield to Norway or the Pole
        A ranker rate, should it be sold in fee.
HAMLET Why then the Polack never will defend it.
CAPTAIN Yes, it is already garrisoned.
HAMLET Two thousand souls and twenty thousand ducats   25
        Will not debate the question of this straw.
        This is th'impostume of much wealth and peace,
        That inward breaks, and shows no cause without
        Why the man dies. I humbly thank you sir.
CAPTAIN God buy you sir.   *[Exit]*

Hamlet criticises his delay in revenging his father's death. Is it forgetfulness or too much thought that stops him? Prompted by his encounter with Fortinbras's army, he resolves to speed to his revenge.

1 Spurs to revenge (in small groups)

Hamlet's soliloquy contains five sections:

lines 32–3 'How all occasions . . . revenge!': everything I encounter prompts me to revenge

lines 33–46 'What is a man . . . exhort me': answers to my own question, 'What is a man . . . ?' and reflections on my delay

lines 47–56 'Witness . . . stake': the principal example 'exhorting' me to revenge. Fortinbras teaches me that honour must always be defended

lines 56–65 'How stand I . . . slain': I have great cause, yet do nothing, but I see thousands of men about to die for a trivial cause

lines 65–6 'Oh from this time forth . . . nothing worth': From now on, I will pursue only revenge.

Read the soliloquy around the group. In turn, each person reads up to a punctuation mark, then hands on. Try to read as if you are persuading someone of the argument you are developing. Alternatively, you could prepare a choral reading of the soliloquy. Experiment with everyone reading together (for example, the first line) or a variety of voices within the group. Emphasise, echo and repeat words and phrases that seem central to Hamlet's argument. After your reading talk together about:

- how Hamlet convinces himself that he should not delay in revenging his father's death
- how many times he deludes himself in line 45
- whether you believe that his thoughts will really be 'bloody' from now.
- how you would advise the actor to speak the soliloquy on stage.

---

inform against rebuke
good and market profit
large discourse powerful
  intelligence
fust go stale
Bestial oblivion animal
  forgetfulness

craven scruple cowardly restraint
mass and charge numbers and
  cost
Makes . . . event mocks death
Whereon . . . the cause where
  there is not enough room to fight
continent large enough container

ROSENCRANTZ   Will't please you go my lord?   30
HAMLET I'll be with you straight; go a little before.

                          [Exeunt all but Hamlet]

How all occasions do inform against me,
And spur my dull revenge! What is a man
If his chief good and market of his time
Be but to sleep and feed? A beast, no more.   35
Sure he that made us with such large discourse,
Looking before and after, gave us not
That capability and god-like reason
To fust in us unused. Now whether it be
Bestial oblivion, or some craven scruple   40
Of thinking too precisely on th'event –
A thought which quartered hath but one part wisdom
And ever three parts coward – I do not know
Why yet I live to say this thing's to do,
Sith I have cause, and will, and strength, and means   45
To do't. Examples gross as earth exhort me.
Witness this army of such mass and charge,
Led by a delicate and tender prince,
Whose spirit with divine ambition puffed
Makes mouths at the invisible event,   50
Exposing what is mortal and unsure
To all that fortune, death and danger dare,
Even for an egg-shell. Rightly to be great
Is not to stir without great argument,
But greatly to find quarrel in a straw   55
When honour's at the stake. How stand I then,
That have a father killed, a mother stained,
Excitements of my reason and my blood,
And let all sleep, while to my shame I see
The imminent death of twenty thousand men,   60
That for a fantasy and trick of fame
Go to their graves like beds, fight for a plot
Whereon the numbers cannot try the cause,
Which is not tomb enough and continent
To hide the slain. Oh from this time forth,   65
My thoughts be bloody or be nothing worth.   *Exit*]

Gertrude refuses to see Ophelia, but is told that Ophelia is mad and needs pity. Gertrude agrees to admit Ophelia, but expresses guilt and misgivings about the future.

1 Why is Gertrude reluctant to see Ophelia?
(in groups of three)

Talk together about possible reasons why Gertrude is reluctant to see or speak to Ophelia. For example, it may be because she doesn't care for her (is that likely?), or because she cannot bear to see what her son has done to Ophelia. Explore other possibilities.

2 Does Gertrude share Claudius's secret? (in pairs)

Gertrude expresses guilt in lines 17–20. Is it because she shares, or suspects, Claudius's secret, and feels guilty because of that knowledge? Look again at the scenes in which Gertrude has appeared (Act 1 Scene 2; Act 2 Scene 2; Act 3 Scenes 1, 2 and 4; Act 4 Scene 1). One person looks for evidence to support the view that Gertrude does not know that Claudius killed King Hamlet. The other person's task is to find evidence that Gertrude does know that Claudius killed King Hamlet. Present each argument in as powerful a way as possible.

3 'Enter OPHELIA *distracted*'

Before you turn the page make three predictions about what Ophelia will talk about as she enters the court. Remember that 'mad' people often reveal their obsessions in what they say, even if their speech seems 'distracted'.

---

importunate persistent
distract mad
What would she have? what does she want?
hems clears her throat
Spurns . . . straws gets angry at little things

to collection to work out a meaning
yawn guess
conjectures suppositions, ideas
ill-breeding suspicious, trouble-makers'
toy trifle
amiss misfortune

ACT 4   SCENE 5
The Great Hall of Elsinore Castle

Enter HORATIO, GERTRUDE *and a* GENTLEMAN

GERTRUDE I will not speak with her.
GENTLEMAN She is importunate, indeed distract;
    Her mood will needs be pitied.
GERTRUDE   What would she have?
GENTLEMAN She speaks much of her father, says she hears
    There's tricks i'th'world, and hems, and beats her heart,   5
    Spurns enviously at straws, speaks things in doubt
    That carry but half sense. Her speech is nothing,
    Yet the unshapèd use of it doth move
    The hearers to collection. They yawn at it,
    And botch the words up fit to their own thoughts,   10
    Which, as her winks and nods and gestures yield them,
    Indeed would make one think there might be thought,
    Though nothing sure, yet much unhappily.
HORATIO 'Twere good she were spoken with, for she may strew
    Dangerous conjectures in ill-breeding minds.   15
GERTRUDE Let her come in.
                         [Exit Gentleman]
    (*Aside*) To my sick soul, as sin's true nature is,
    Each toy seems prologue to some great amiss.
    So full of artless jealousy is guilt,
    It spills itself in fearing to be spilt.   20

Enter OPHELIA *distracted*

OPHELIA Where is the beauteous majesty of Denmark?

Ophelia's first song recalls the death of her father. She replies enigmatically to Claudius then sings a song about the loss of virginity.

Helena Bonham Carter as Ophelia in Zeffirelli's 1991 film. How closely does she match your image of Ophelia driven into madness?

cockle hat a hat with a shell emblem, worn by pilgrims
shoon shoes
imports means
shrowd death sheet, shroud
Larded decorated

good dild you God yield (reward) you
Conceit thoughts
betime early
dupped undid

GERTRUDE How now Ophelia?

OPHELIA   *She sings*

    How should I your true love know
      From another one?
    By his cockle hat and staff   25
      And his sandal shoon.

GERTRUDE Alas sweet lady, what imports this song?

OPHELIA Say you? Nay, pray you mark.

    He is dead and gone lady,   *Song*
      He is dead and gone;   30
    At his head a grass-green turf,
      At his heels a stone.

  Oho!

GERTRUDE Nay but Ophelia –

OPHELIA Pray you mark.   35

    White his shrowd as the mountain snow –   *Song*

Enter CLAUDIUS

GERTRUDE Alas, look here my lord.

OPHELIA   Larded all with sweet flowers,
      Which bewept to the grave did not go
    With true-love showers.   40

CLAUDIUS How do you, pretty lady?

OPHELIA Well good dild you. They say the owl was a baker's daughter.
Lord, we know what we are, but know not what we may be. God
be at your table.

CLAUDIUS Conceit upon her father.   45

OPHELIA Pray let's have no words of this, but when they ask you what
it means, say you this –

    Tomorrow is Saint Valentine's day,   *Song*
      All in the morning betime,
    And I a maid at your window,   50
      To be your Valentine.

    Then up he rose and donned his clothes
      And dupped the chamber door;
    Let in the maid that out a maid
      Never departed more.   55

CLAUDIUS Pretty Ophelia!

*Ophelia sings of betrayed love. She talks distractedly. Claudius reflects
that sorrows never come alone: Polonius killed, the citizens restless,
Ophelia mad and Laertes a prey to rumour among the people.*

1 Reason in her madness? (in pairs)

When Ophelia entered at line 21, you were invited to make predictions
about what she would talk about (see page 170). Were your predictions
accurate? Use what Ophelia has said between lines 21 and 72 to identify
how her madness reflects what has happened – or what she thinks has
happened. Note:

'Indeed la!' may be an ironic response to Claudius
'Gis' = Jesus
'tumbled' = had sex with.

2 Ophelia's appearance

In the 1993 Royal Shakespeare Company production, Ophelia appeared
dressed in her dead father's clothes. Either sketch what you think
Ophelia looks like in this scene, or collect pictures to convey your
impressions of her appearance.

3 Battalions of sorrows (in groups of four or five)

In lines 74–95, Claudius reflects that sorrows never come alone, but all
together ('not single spies,/But in battalions'). He lists the troubles
that beset him: Polonius's death, Hamlet's exile, suspicious citizens,
the secret burial of Polonius, Ophelia's madness, and the returned
Laertes surrounded by rumour mongers ('wants not buzzers') who
stop at nothing ('nothing stick') to invent lies.

One person reads lines 74–95 while the others mime each action
described.

Afterwards, talk together about which of these 'sorrows' Claudius
feels most deeply about, and why.

---

remove banishment
greenly naively, foolishly
In hugger-mugger in secret
as much containing as serious as
Feeds . . . clouds imagines all
 kinds of things

necessity, of matter beggared
 they are obliged, lacking facts
Will nothing stick will stop at
 nothing
arraign accuse
murdering piece a small cannon
superfluous death multiple deaths

OPHELIA Indeed la! Without an oath I'll make an end on't.

By Gis and by Saint Charity,
    Alack and fie for shame,
Young men will do't if they come to't –   60
    By Cock, they are to blame.

Quoth she, 'Before you tumbled me,
    You promised me to wed.'

He answers –

So would I ha' done, by yonder sun,   65
    And thou hadst not come to my bed.

CLAUDIUS How long hath she been thus?

OPHELIA I hope all will be well. We must be patient, but I cannot
choose but weep to think they would lay him i'th' cold ground. My
brother shall know of it, and so I thank you for your good counsel.   70
Come, my coach. Good night ladies, good night sweet ladies, good
night, good night.   *Exit*

CLAUDIUS Follow her close, give her good watch I pray you.

                                                        [*Exit Horatio*]

Oh this is the poison of deep grief, it springs
All from her father's death, [and now behold –]   75
Oh Gertrude, Gertrude,
When sorrows come, they come not single spies,
But in battalions. First, her father slain;
Next, your son gone, and he most violent author
Of his own just remove; the people muddied,   80
Thick and unwholesome in their thoughts and whispers
For good Polonius' death – and we have done but greenly
In hugger-mugger to inter him; poor Ophelia
Divided from herself and her fair judgement,
Without the which we are pictures, or mere beasts;   85
Last, and as much containing as all these,
Her brother is in secret come from France,
Feeds on his wonder, keeps himself in clouds,
And wants not buzzers to infect his ear
With pestilent speeches of his father's death,   90
Wherein necessity, of matter beggared,
Will nothing stick our person to arraign
In ear and ear. O my dear Gertrude, this,
Like to a murdering piece, in many places
Gives me superfluous death.   95

A messenger tells Claudius that Laertes and an angry mob are coming, and that some of the rioters proclaim that Laertes should be king. Laertes bursts in and demands to know what happened to his father.

1 'The rabble' enter (in pairs)

The ordinary people of Denmark rarely appear in the play. Here, they are briefly glimpsed, supporting Laertes. Work out how page 177 could be acted out to present the Danish people to greatest dramatic effect.

2 'You false Danish dogs!'

The actor playing Gertrude says: 'I just don't believe Gertrude would say lines 109–10. There's nothing in the play up to this point that suggests she could speak like that.' What do you reply? It may help you to know that Gertrude uses an image from hunting: dogs follow a trail of scent, but if they run 'counter', they follow the trail in the wrong direction.

3 Laertes's complaint

List reasons for Laertes's anger with Claudius. Some of his reasons will be personal, others political. Notice the imagery of branding a prostitute that Laertes uses to express his feelings in lines 118–21.

Attend! attention!	**head** advance party
Swissers Swiss guards	**ratifiers and props** supporters
overpeering of his list breaking its boundary	**counter** wrong-headed, improper
flats shore	**That drop. . . . calm** cool feelings
impitious impetuous, without pity	**cuckold** deceived husband

A noise within

GERTRUDE Alack, what noise is this?

CLAUDIUS Attend! Where are my Swissers? Let them guard the door.

Enter a MESSENGER

What is the matter?

MESSENGER   Save yourself my lord.
The ocean, overpeering of his list,
Eats not the flats with more impitious haste   100
Than young Laertes in a riotous head
O'erbears your officers. The rabble call him lord,
And, as the world were now but to begin,
Antiquity forgot, custom not known,
The ratifiers and props of every word,   105
They cry 'Choose we! Laertes shall be king.'
Caps, hands and tongues applaud it to the clouds,
'Laertes shall be king, Laertes king!'

GERTRUDE How cheerfully on the false trail they cry!
Oh this is counter, you false Danish dogs!   110

A noise within

CLAUDIUS The doors are broke.

Enter LAERTES *with others*

LAERTES Where is this king? – Sirs, stand you all without.

ALL No, let's come in.

LAERTES I pray you give me leave.

ALL We will, we will.   115

LAERTES I thank you. Keep the door.

                              [*Exeunt followers*]
                     O thou vile king,
Give me my father.

GERTRUDE   Calmly, good Laertes.

LAERTES That drop of blood that's calm proclaims me bastard,
Cries cuckold to my father, brands the harlot
Even here, between the chaste unsmirchèd brow   120
Of my true mother.

Claudius is unafraid to face the wrath of Laertes. Claudius claims to be protected by the divine aura of kingship. He urges Laertes to distinguish between friends and foes, and says he is innocent of Polonius's death.

---

1 How do they speak? (in pairs)

Take parts as Claudius and Laertes. Speak the lines opposite several times, experimenting with different tones, volumes and pauses. For example, try Claudius as impatient or calm. Laertes's tone could be enraged, emphatic or despairing.

2 A fourth revenger

Like Hamlet, Laertes swears to avenge his father's death. This is the fourth revenge plot in the play (see page 252). The others are Hamlet's revenge of his father's death; Fortinbras's campaign to win back lands lost by his father; and Pyrrhus's slaughter of Priam in revenge for his own father's death. Concentrate on Hamlet and Laertes, and list the differences between their motives for revenge, and how the two characters react to their revenge mission.

Identify some lines earlier in the play where Hamlet's language is similar in tone to Laertes's lines 130–6.

3 'You will draw both friend and foe . . .' (in pairs)

In lines 139–43, Claudius asks Laertes if in his revenge he will kill the innocent and guilty alike, like reckless gamblers sweeping up all the stakes ('soopstake') whether they have won or lost. Laertes replies he will kill only Polonius's murderers and treat his friends kindly, like the pelican that was believed to pierce its breast to feed its young with its own blood.

Talk together about how appropriate or inappropriate you think the images are to each speaker's character (Claudius as a gambler, Laertes as a kind parent).

---

hedge surround
Acts little of his will cannot do
  what it would like to
vows promises of loyalty
both the worlds I give to
  negligence I care not for heaven
  or hell

husband manage
Repast feed
sensibly with feeling
level well-aimed

CLAUDIUS   What is the cause, Laertes,
That thy rebellion looks so giant-like? –
Let him go, Gertrude, do not fear our person.
There's such divinity doth hedge a king
That treason can but peep to what it would,   125
Acts little of his will. – Tell me Laertes,
Why thou art thus incensed. – Let him go Gertrude. –
Speak man.
LAERTES   Where is my father?
CLAUDIUS   Dead.
GERTRUDE   But not by him.
CLAUDIUS Let him demand his fill.
LAERTES How came he dead? I'll not be juggled with.   130
To hell allegiance, vows to the blackest devil,
Conscience and grace to the profoundest pit!
I dare damnation. To this point I stand,
That both the worlds I give to negligence,
Let come what comes, only I'll be revenged   135
Most throughly for my father.
CLAUDIUS   Who shall stay you?
LAERTES My will, not all the world.
And for my means, I'll husband them so well,
They shall go far with little.
CLAUDIUS   Good Laertes,
If you desire to know the certainty   140
Of your dear father, is't writ in your revenge
That, soopstake, you will draw both friend and foe,
Winner and loser?
LAERTES   None but his enemies.
CLAUDIUS Will you know them then?
LAERTES To his good friends thus wide I'll ope my arms,   145
And like the kind life-rendering pelican,
Repast them with my blood.
CLAUDIUS   Why now you speak
Like a good child and a true gentleman.
That I am guiltless of your father's death,
And am most sensibly in grief for it,   150
It shall as level to your judgement pierce
As day does to your eye.

*Laertes is appalled by Ophelia's madness. It moves him even more
strongly to revenge. Ophelia sings again of death.
She distributes herbs and flowers.*

After her song, to which characters does Ophelia give the flowers and herbs
in lines 174–81? Think of the symbolic significance of each of the herbs
and flowers, and write notes suggesting which she gives to whom. The
herbs and flowers include fennel (flattery), columbines (ingratitude and
infidelity), rue (sorrow), daisy (springtime, love), and violets (sweetness).

1 Two puzzles

In line 171, 'wheel' might mean 'refrain', 'spinning-wheel' or the
Wheel of Fortune, which brought either good fortune (when you were
on the top of the wheel) or bad fortune (when you were at the bottom);
'false steward' may be from a traditional ballad – no one knows. Justify
your own preferred meanings for each.

---

sense and virtue power and
  effectiveness
our scale turn the beam revenge
  tilts the scales our way
fine refined
instance part
bier funeral carriage

a-down with lower tone (also a
  refrain)
nothing's nonsense is
matter sense
document lesson
thoughts melancholy
favour good end

A noise within: 'Let her come in'

LAERTES   How now, what noise is that?

Enter OPHELIA

O heat dry up my brains, tears seven times salt
Burn out the sense and virtue of mine eye!   155
By heaven, thy madness shall be paid with weight
Till our scale turn the beam. O rose of May,
Dear maid, kind sister, sweet Ophelia –
O heavens, is't possible a young maid's wits
Should be as mortal as an old man's life?   160
Nature is fine in love, and where 'tis fine,
It sends some precious instance of itself
After the thing it loves.

OPHELIA   They bore him bare-faced on the bier   *Song*
    Hey non nonny, nonny, hey nonny,   165
    And in his grave rained many a tear –
Fare you well my dove.

LAERTES   Hadst thou thy wits, and didst persuade revenge,
    It could not move thus.

OPHELIA   You must sing a-down a-down, and you call him a-down-a.   170
Oh how the wheel becomes it. It is the false steward that stole his
master's daughter.

LAERTES   This nothing's more than matter.

OPHELIA   There's rosemary, that's for remembrance – pray you, love,
remember – and there is pansies, that's for thoughts.   175

LAERTES   A document in madness, thoughts and remembrance fitted.

OPHELIA   There's fennel for you, and columbines. There's rue for you,
and here's some for me; we may call it herb of grace a Sundays.
Oh you must wear your rue with a difference. There's a daisy. I
would give you some violets, but they withered all when my father   180
died. They say a made a good end.

[*Sings*]
For bonny sweet Robin is all my joy.

LAERTES   Thought and affliction, passion, hell itself,
She turns to favour and to prettiness.

Ophelia again sings about her father's death. Claudius sympathises with Laertes's grief, and makes an offer: if Claudius proves to blame, Laertes can be king. If not, Claudius will help Laertes find justice and revenge.

1 Interpreting Ophelia's behaviour

Imagine that the doctor at the court of Elsinore has been on-stage throughout Scene 5. Write the doctor's case notes on Ophelia.

2 Claudius's strategy (in pairs)

Claudius has been trying to control and direct Laertes's anger, but the entrance of Ophelia and her effect on Laertes have made his attempt more difficult. Laertes's anger is refuelled.

Take parts and read lines 196–214 several times. Think especially about whether you should leave a long pause before Laertes says 'Let this be so' in line 207. Then talk together about how Claudius manages to salvage the situation and turn Laertes's passion for revenge to his own ends.

3 What happens next? (in pairs)

The scene ends with Claudius requesting Laertes to leave with him. Discuss what you think they will talk about. Think about the two men's feelings and attitudes as they talk. Will Claudius be sympathetic to Laertes? Will Laertes be hot-blooded and angry, or will he listen coolly? Improvise their off-stage conversation.

4 The silent Gertrude

Gertrude does not speak in the scene after line 128. Write a paragraph suggesting what she might be feeling and how she would react during lines 129–214.

All flaxen was his poll his hair was white
God buy you God be with you
commune with share
of whom of whichever
collateral indirect

touched guilty
lend grant
labour work
hatchment coat of arms
ostentation display of mourning

| OPHELIA | And will a not come again? | *Song* | 185 |

And will a not come again?
    No, no, he is dead,
    Go to thy death-bed,
He never will come again.
His beard was as white as snow,   190
All flaxen was his poll,
    He is gone, he is gone,
    And we cast away moan,
God-a-mercy on his soul.

And of all Christian souls, I pray God. God buy you.   *Exit*   195
LAERTES Do you see this, O God?
CLAUDIUS Laertes, I must commune with your grief,
    Or you deny me right. Go but apart,
    Make choice of whom your wisest friends you will,
    And they shall hear and judge 'twixt you and me.   200
    If by direct or by collateral hand
    They find us touched, we will our kingdom give,
    Our crown, our life, and all that we call ours,
    To you in satisfaction. But if not,
    Be you content to lend your patience to us,   205
    And we shall jointly labour with your soul
    To give it due content.
LAERTES   Let this be so.
    His means of death, his obscure funeral,
    No trophy, sword, nor hatchment o'er his bones,
    No noble rite, nor formal ostentation,   210
    Cry to be heard, as 'twere from heaven to earth,
    That I must call't in question.
CLAUDIUS   So you shall.
    And where th'offence is, let the great axe fall.
    I pray you go with me.
                                                           Exeunt

Hamlet's letter reveals that he has been captured in a sea battle. By doing a deal with the pirates he has returned to Denmark. He has sent letters to the king, and urgently wishes to meet Horatio.

1 Hamlet and the pirates (in groups of four or more)

Imagine the scene where Hamlet has boarded the pirate ship. They would be puzzled to find out who he was, where he was going and why he needed to return to Denmark. Some of them may wish to kill him. Others see him as a valuable prisoner whom they can exchange for a large ransom.

Improvise the scene where Hamlet persuades the pirates to spare him and to help him return to Denmark. Start with him being threatened by them. What is the deal that he strikes with the pirates?

2 Horatio reads the letter

You are the director of a film of *Hamlet*. Films have greater opportunities than stage productions: settings can be changed instantly; a character's thoughts can be presented visually; 'realistic' settings can be used.

Work out how you will film Scene 6. For example, Horatio's reading might be done as a voice-over, while the film shows the action described. Re-write the scene as a film script.

3 What kind of scene?

Why do you think Shakespeare makes this a 'letter-scene', rather than showing the action on the ships? Try to find three or four reasons.

and please if it please
Ere before
of very warlike appointment heavily armed
put on a compelled valour were obliged to be brave

thieves of mercy thieves with compassion
repair thou return, come
for the bore of the matter for the weight of their meaning

ACT 4 SCENE 6
A room in the castle

Enter HORATIO *with an* ATTENDANT

HORATIO What are they that would speak with me?
ATTENDANT Seafaring men sir, they say they have letters for you.
HORATIO Let them come in.

> [*Exit Attendant*]

I do not know from what part of the world
I should be greeted, if not from Lord Hamlet.   5

Enter SAILORS

1 SAILOR God bless you sir.
HORATIO Let him bless thee too.
1 SAILOR A shall sir, and please him. There's a letter for you sir, it came
from th'ambassador that was bound for England, if your name be
Horatio, as I am let to know it is.   10
HORATIO (*Reads the letter*) 'Horatio, when thou shalt have overlooked
this, give these fellows some means to the king; they have letters
for him. Ere we were two days old at sea, a pirate of very warlike
appointment gave us chase. Finding ourselves too slow of sail, we
put on a compelled valour, and in the grapple I boarded them. On   15
the instant they got clear of our ship, so I alone became their
prisoner. They have dealt with me like thieves of mercy, but they
knew what they did: I am to do a good turn for them. Let the king
have the letters I have sent, and repair thou to me with as much
speed as thou wouldest fly death. I have words to speak in thine   20
ear will make thee dumb, yet are they much too light for the bore
of the matter. These good fellows will bring thee where I am.
Rosencrantz and Guildenstern hold their course for England. Of
them I have much to tell thee. Farewell.

> He that thou knowest thine,   25
> Hamlet.'

Come, I will give you way for these your letters,
And do't the speedier that you may direct me
To him from whom you brought them.

> *Exeunt*

185

Claudius claims that Hamlet not only killed Polonius but was intent on killing him, too. He explains that he did not punish Hamlet for two reasons: love of Gertrude, and Hamlet's popularity with the people.

1 Are Claudius's reasons plausible?

Claudius gives two reasons why he did not take action against Hamlet (see above). What evidence can you find in the play for these reasons? Suggest other possible reasons that might explain Claudius's delay in acting against Hamlet.

Claudius begins to plot with Laertes against Hamlet. From the Royal Shakespeare Company's modern dress production, 1988.

my acquittance seal confirm my
  innocence
Sith since
knowing understanding
feats deeds
capital deserving of death
mainly mightily, greatly
unsinewed weak
conjunctive closely joined with
sphere orbit

but by her move without her
count account
gender populace
spring lime-rich water
gyves chains (vices)
Too slightly timbered not thick
  enough
Stood challenger . . .
  perfections was more perfect
  than all other women

ACT 4   SCENE 7
A state room in the castle

Enter CLAUDIUS and LAERTES

CLAUDIUS Now must your conscience my acquittance seal,
   And you must put me in your heart for friend,
   Sith you have heard, and with a knowing ear,
   That he which hath your noble father slain
   Pursued my life.
LAERTES   It well appears. But tell me   5
   Why you proceeded not against these feats,
   So crimeful and so capital in nature,
   As by your safety, wisdom, all things else.
   You mainly were stirred up.
CLAUDIUS   Oh for two special reasons,
   Which may to you perhaps seem much unsinewed,   10
   But yet to me they're strong. The queen his mother
   Lives almost by his looks, and for myself,
   My virtue or my plague, be it either which,
   She's so conjunctive to my life and soul,
   That as the star moves not but in his sphere,   15
   I could not but by her. The other motive,
   Why to a public count I might not go,
   Is the great love the general gender bear him,
   Who, dipping all his faults in their affection,
   Work like the spring that turneth wood to stone,   20
   Convert his gyves to graces, so that my arrows,
   Too slightly timbered for so loud a wind,
   Would have reverted to my bow again,
   And not where I had aimed them.
LAERTES And so have I a noble father lost,   25
   A sister driven into desperate terms,
   Whose worth, if praises may go back again,
   Stood challenger on mount of all the age
   For her perfections. But my revenge will come.

Claudius assures Laertes that he will not let Hamlet's actions go unpunished. A messenger brings letters from Hamlet, telling of his return to Denmark. Laertes welcomes the chance to be revenged on Hamlet.

1 Reading between the lines (in pairs)

Imagine you are Hamlet writing his letter to Claudius. One person reads up to a punctuation mark, then pauses. In each pause, the partner speaks Hamlet's thoughts on what he has just written.

2 'Naked?'

Claudius is puzzled by Hamlet describing himself as 'set naked on your kingdom'. This probably doesn't mean that he is literally without clothes – but what can it mean? How many explanations can you find for the word? Which seem most appropriate to the play?

3 Point it out! (in groups of six or more)

One person slowly reads the whole page, emphasising each pronoun or name ('your', 'you', 'Hamlet', and so on). The others point emphatically to the character (or characters) mentioned each time (cast the parts as you read). Pointing out of the words in the script in this way can help increase your understanding. (This function of the words is technically known as deixis (pronounced 'dyke-sis'): here, the use of pronouns to identify who is taking part in the discussion, and who is being referred to.)

---

flat unfeeling
pastime trivial
abuse trick
no such thing no such thing has
 happened
hand handwriting

character style (or handwriting)
devise help
warms inflames, does good
o'errule me to a peace force me
 to be friendly

CLAUDIUS Break not your sleeps for that. You must not think   30
        That we are made of stuff so flat and dull
        That we can let our beard be shook with danger
        And think it pastime. You shortly shall hear more.
        I loved your father, and we love ourself,
        And that I hope will teach you to imagine –   35

Enter a MESSENGER *with letters*

        How now? What news?
MESSENGER   Letters my lord from Hamlet.
        This to your majesty, this to the queen.
CLAUDIUS From Hamlet? Who brought them?
MESSENGER Sailors my lord they say, I saw them not;
        They were given me by Claudio – he received them   40
        Of him that brought them.
CLAUDIUS   Laertes, you shall hear them. –
        Leave us.

                                        Exit Messenger

[*Reads*] 'High and mighty, you shall know I am set naked on your
kingdom. Tomorrow shall I beg leave to see your kingly eyes, when
I shall, first asking your pardon thereunto, recount th'occasion of   45
my sudden and more strange return.

                                        Hamlet.'

        What should this mean? Are all the rest come back?
        Or is it some abuse, and no such thing?
LAERTES Know you the hand?
CLAUDIUS   'Tis Hamlet's character. Naked?   50
        And in a postscript here he says alone.
        Can you devise me?
LAERTES I'm lost in it my lord. But let him come –
        It warms the very sickness in my heart
        That I shall live and tell him to his teeth   55
        'Thus didest thou!'
CLAUDIUS   If it be so, Laertes –
        As how should it be so? – how otherwise? –
        Will you be ruled by me?
LAERTES   Ay my lord,
        So you will not o'errule me to a peace.

Claudius begins to hatch a new plot to kill Hamlet. He says that Hamlet envies Laertes, but delays naming the reason for that envy. Instead, Claudius talks of Lamord, an accomplished French soldier.

1 Why does Claudius delay? (in small groups)

Claudius's plot against Hamlet is going to 'work him to an exploit . . . under the which he shall not choose but fall'. He does not immediately tell Laertes of his plan. Instead he talks of 'a quality' of Laertes. When Laertes asks him what that quality is (line 75), Claudius again does not reply directly but calls the unnamed quality 'a very riband in the cap of youth', (mere ribbon, little more than a decoration on a cap). Yet this quality is 'needful' (or necessary), because it suits youth in the same way that 'health and graveness' suit older people. Claudius then goes on to talk about the Frenchman, Lamord.

As an actor playing Claudius, put the following questions to your director (the rest of the group) as you work out how to read these lines:

a Why do I delay in revealing my scheme?

b Why am I emphasising youth at this point?

Add any further questions you want to ask about the lines.

2 Lamord (in pairs)

Claudius makes Lamord sound a splendid character. He is described as a 'gallant' (fine young man) seeming to be 'incorpsed and demi-natured' (part of the same body) with his horse. He 'topped' (surpassed) Claudius's imagination ('thought', 'forgery') of any feat of horsemanship ('shapes and tricks'). Discuss why Shakespeare included this description of Lamord in the play. It may be because Lamord sounds like the French 'la mort' – death. Or it may be to make comparisons and contrasts with Hamlet and Laertes. Or it may be to add another insight into Claudius's character. What do you think?

---

checking at abandoning
exploit plot
ripe in my device ready in my scheming
uncharge the practice not suspect trickery
The rather the better

organ agent
falls right falls into place
unworthiest siege least account
sables dark clothes
weeds sober garments
can well are skilful
brooch jewel in the crown

190

CLAUDIUS To thine own peace. If he be now returned, 60
    As checking at his voyage, and that he means
    No more to undertake it, I will work him
    To an exploit, now ripe in my device,
    Under the which he shall not choose but fall,
    And for his death no wind of blame shall breathe, 65
    But even his mother shall uncharge the practice
    And call it accident.
[LAERTES   My lord, I will be ruled,
    The rather if you could devise it so
    That I might be the organ.
CLAUDIUS   It falls right.
    You have been talked of since your travel much, 70
    And that in Hamlet's hearing, for a quality
    Wherein they say you shine. Your sum of parts
    Did not together pluck such envy from him
    As did that one, and that in my regard
    Of the unworthiest siege.
LAERTES   What part is that my lord? 75
CLAUDIUS A very riband in the cap of youth,
    Yet needful too, for youth no less becomes
    The light and careless livery that it wears
    Than settled age his sables and his weeds
    Importing health and graveness.] Two months since 80
    Here was a gentleman of Normandy.
    I've seen myself, and served against, the French,
    And they can well on horseback, but this gallant
    Had witchcraft in't. He grew unto his seat,
    And to such wondrous doing brought his horse 85
    As had he been incorpsed and demi-natured
    With the brave beast. So far he topped my thought,
    That I in forgery of shapes and tricks
    Come short of what he did.
LAERTES   A Norman was't?
CLAUDIUS A Norman.
LAERTES Upon my life Lamord. 90
CLAUDIUS   The very same.
LAERTES I know him well, he is the brooch indeed
    And gem of all the nation.

Claudius relates Lamord's praise of Laertes's swordsmanship. Laertes asks what is the point of Claudius's words. Claudius talks of how love fades with time. Laertes is resolute for revenge.

1 To cut or not to cut (in large groups)

Lines 99–101 and 113–22 are in square brackets. They did not appear in the Folio version of Shakespeare's plays (see page 262). The first passage reports that Laertes was a superior swordsman, one of the best fencers in France. In the second passage Claudius reflects on how time kills love, goodness dies of its own excess, and intentions simply fade away if not quickly carried out.

Imagine you are about to put on the play. Will you include these lines in square brackets, or cut them? Divide the group in half to argue for and against cutting the lines. Those arguing to include the lines might stress how the second passage echoes the theme of delay.

2 An insight into Claudius? (in pairs)

Read lines 109–24 in two ways. First, with Claudius always looking at Laertes and consciously persuading him to carry out the revenge. Second, with Claudius drifting off into an internal meditation about how love fades with time. Which style do you prefer and why?

3 Persuasion: direct and indirect (in groups of three)

Claudius's talk about Lamord, then about how time kills love, seems indirect and circuitous. He is delaying outlining his plot to Laertes, and also reflecting on delay itself. His strategy is indirect persuasion. Talk together about why you think Claudius is avoiding getting directly to the point. At line 63 he said he had a plan. Why doesn't he simply reveal it?

---

made confession told the truth
art and exercise . . . defence skill and mastery in swordplay
Th'escrimers the master swordsmen
play swordfence
passages of proof events that bear me out

qualifies moderates, dulls
abate extinguish
is at a like goodness still remains good always
plurisy (disease resulting from) excess
quick heart

CLAUDIUS He made confession of you,
　　　　　And gave you such a masterly report　　　　　　　95
　　　　　For art and exercise in your defence,
　　　　　And for your rapier most especial,
　　　　　That he cried out 'twould be a sight indeed
　　　　　If one could match you. [Th'escrimers of their nation
　　　　　He swore had neither motion, guard, nor eye,　　　100
　　　　　If you opposed them.] Sir, this report of his
　　　　　Did Hamlet so envenom with his envy
　　　　　That he could nothing do but wish and beg
　　　　　Your sudden coming o'er to play with you.
　　　　　Now out of this –
LAERTES 　　　　　　　　　What out of this, my lord?　　　105
CLAUDIUS Laertes, was your father dear to you?
　　　　　Or are you like the painting of a sorrow,
　　　　　A face without a heart?
LAERTES 　　　　　　　　　Why ask you this?
CLAUDIUS Not that I think you did not love your father,
　　　　　But that I know love is begun by time,　　　　　110
　　　　　And that I see, in passages of proof,
　　　　　Time qualifies the spark and fire of it.
　　　　　[There lives within the very flame of love
　　　　　A kind of wick or snuff that will abate it,
　　　　　And nothing is at a like goodness still,　　　　　115
　　　　　For goodness, growing to a plurisy,
　　　　　Dies in his own too much. That we would do,
　　　　　We should do when we would, for this 'would' changes,
　　　　　And hath abatements and delays as many
　　　　　As there are tongues, are hands, are accidents;　　120
　　　　　And then this 'should' is like a spendthrift sigh,
　　　　　That hurts by easing. But to the quick of th'ulcer –]
　　　　　Hamlet comes back; what would you undertake
　　　　　To show yourself in deed your father's son
　　　　　More than in words?
LAERTES 　　　　　　　　　To cut his throat i'th'church.　　　125

*Claudius plans a duel in which one of the swords will not be blunted.
Laertes offers to poison the sharpened foil. To make Hamlet's death
certain, Claudius proposes to poison Hamlet's drink.*

1 'No place indeed should murder sanctuarize'

Line 126 might mean 'no church should give protection (sanctuary) to
a murderer like Hamlet' or 'no better place to do the murder of
Hamlet'. Which do you think Claudius intends?

2 The plot thickens (in pairs)

After careful preparation, Claudius has increased Laertes's hatred of
Hamlet ('To cut his throat i'th'church', line 125). Laertes now plots
with Claudius a devious and seemingly foolproof murder of Hamlet.
The two men build upon each other's wickedness in devising ways of
ensuring Hamlet's death in a duel. The plot to kill Hamlet involves a
duelling sword, sharp ('unbated') and poisoned. With it, Laertes will
strike Hamlet in a deceitful thrust ('pass of practice'). A poisoned drink
will kill Hamlet if Laertes fails to kill him with his sword.

Take parts and read the script opposite. Then talk together to
discover how far you agree with the following statements:

a It is surprising that Laertes has brought a poison ('unction') with
  him.

b Hamlet is accurately described by Claudius as 'remiss, most
  generous, and free from all contriving' ('remiss' = unsuspecting,
  'contriving' = deviousness).

c Claudius has all the details of his plot already in his mind, and
  only pretends to think up the 'back or second' (the poisoned cup).

3 Does Claudius hope for Laertes's death?

What motivation might Claudius have for Laertes's death in the duel?

---

sanctuarize protect
keep close stay
in fine finally
peruse the foils inspect the
  swords
mountebank quack doctor
cataplasm dressing, antidote

simples medicinal herbs
shape plot, design
drift aim
assayed tried
blast in proof fail
preferred offered
nonce occasion

CLAUDIUS No place indeed should murder sanctuarize;
 Revenge should have no bounds. But, good Laertes,
 Will you do this, keep close within your chamber;
 Hamlet, returned, shall know you are come home;
 We'll put on those shall praise your excellence,   130
 And set a double varnish on the fame
 The Frenchman gave you; bring you in fine together,
 And wager on your heads. He being remiss,
 Most generous, and free from all contriving,
 Will not peruse the foils, so that with ease,   135
 Or with a little shuffling, you may choose
 A sword unbated, and in a pass of practice
 Requite him for your father.
LAERTES   I will do't,
 And for that purpose I'll anoint my sword.
 I bought an unction of a mountebank,   140
 So mortal that but dip a knife in it,
 Where it draws blood no cataplasm so rare,
 Collected from all simples that have virtue
 Under the moon, can save the thing from death
 That is but scratched withal. I'll touch my point   145
 With this contagion, that if I gall him slightly,
 It may be death.
CLAUDIUS   Let's further think of this,
 Weigh what convenience both of time and means
 May fit us to our shape. If this should fail,
 And that our drift look through our bad performance,   150
 'Twere better not assayed. Therefore this project
 Should have a back or second, that might hold
 If this did blast in proof. Soft, let me see.
 We'll make a solemn wager on your cunnings –
 I ha't!   155
 When in your motion you are hot and dry,
 As make your bouts more violent to that end,
 And that he calls for drink, I'll have preferred him
 A chalice for the nonce, whereon but sipping,
 If he by chance escape your venomed stuck,   160
 Our purpose may hold there. But stay, what noise?

                    Enter GERTRUDE

How, sweet queen!

                    195

Gertrude tells how Ophelia drowned: she fell from a willow as she attempted to hang flowers and was pulled under by her clothes. Laertes unsuccessfully fights back tears. Claudius lies about calming Laertes.

'Ophelia' by the Victorian painter, Millais.

1 'There is a willow . . .'

Explore lines 166–83 in one of the following ways:

a Work in pairs. One person reads the lines aloud. The other listens and studies the picture. Exchange roles and repeat. Identify particular lines or words that Millais used as a basis for his painting. Talk together about what elements of the script are missing from the painting.

b Work in groups of four to eight. Prepare a choral reading of the lines. Decide which lines you will read together and which will be read by a single voice. Try echoing and repeating some lines or words to discover if it increases emotional intensity. Add music or other sound effects if you wish.

---

askant leaning over
hoar grey
liberal free-speaking
pendant hanging
cronet coronet, garland
sliver branch
lauds hymns

incapable of uncomprehending
indued adapted
lay song
trick way
The woman will be out I'll have finished crying
douts douses, extinguishes

GERTRUDE One woe doth tread upon another's heel,
　　　　So fast they follow. Your sister's drowned, Laertes.
LAERTES Drowned! Oh where?　　　　　　　　　　　　165
GERTRUDE There is a willow grows askant a brook,
　　　　That shows his hoar leaves in the glassy stream.
　　　　Therewith fantastic garlands did she make,
　　　　Of crow-flowers, nettles, daisies, and long purples,
　　　　That liberal shepherds give a grosser name,　　170
　　　　But our cold maids do dead men's fingers call them.
　　　　There on the pendant boughs her cronet weeds
　　　　Clamb'ring to hang, an envious sliver broke,
　　　　When down her weedy trophies and herself
　　　　Fell in the weeping brook. Her clothes spread wide,　175
　　　　And mermaid-like awhile they bore her up,
　　　　Which time she chanted snatches of old lauds
　　　　As one incapable of her own distress,
　　　　Or like a creature native and indued
　　　　Unto that element. But long it could not be　　180
　　　　Till that her garments, heavy with their drink,
　　　　Pulled the poor wretch from her melodious lay
　　　　To muddy death.
LAERTES　　　　　　　　Alas, then she is drowned?
GERTRUDE Drowned, drowned.
LAERTES Too much of water hast thou, poor Ophelia,　185
　　　　And therefore I forbid my tears. But yet
　　　　It is our trick; nature her custom holds,
　　　　Let shame say what it will. When these are gone,
　　　　The woman will be out. Adieu my lord,
　　　　I have a speech of fire that fain would blaze,　190
　　　　But that this folly douts it.　　　　　　*Exit*
CLAUDIUS　　　　　　　　Let's follow, Gertrude.
　　　　How much I had to do to calm his rage!
　　　　Now fear I this will give it start again.
　　　　Therefore let's follow.
　　　　　　　　　　　　　　　　　　Exeunt

Looking back at Act 4
Activities for groups or individuals

1 Claudius: a complex character

Act 4 begins and ends with Claudius lying to Gertrude. In Scene 1 he claims to love Hamlet; in Scene 7 he says he tried to calm Laertes's rage. Claudius also lies to Hamlet in Scene 3, telling him he is being sent to England 'for thine especial safety'. But Claudius is not simply a liar. He displays other aspects of his character in Act 4. Check through each scene in which he appears and compile a list of the different qualities he shows. Present your findings as a collage of quotations.

2 Seven scenes, seven settings

Each of the seven scenes in Act 4 takes place in a different location. Design a stage set to enable the action to flow swiftly and continuously. Your set should be simple, but should convey a definite sense of place for each scene.

3 Ophelia's songs

'Ophelia's songs show that her true nature is quite different from that she has shown up to Act 4. She is by no means as innocent or naive as she appears.' Consider each song in turn and talk together about whether you agree with this student's view of Ophelia.

4 Honour?

In Act 4, Hamlet, Fortinbras and Laertes are each much concerned with 'honour'. Design a coat of arms for each man to show the similarities and differences in their conceptions of 'honour'.

5 The citizens' views of the court

The 'ordinary people' of Denmark appear in the play only very briefly in Scene 5, supporting Laertes. Improvise a conversation between some of Denmark's citizens as they try to work out what is happening at the castle. Some may have relatives working at the court who have overheard snatches of what has been said. Truth may be mixed with rumour, and with opinions on who should be king. Remember that the people are the 'distracted multitude' that love Hamlet and now welcome Laertes.

Father, lover, brother. Throughout the play, Ophelia is dominated by her father, lover and brother. Her father makes her reveal her secrets (Act 1) and uses her so that he can spy on Hamlet (Act 2). Her brother counsels her against Hamlet (Act 1) but is driven to tears by her madness (Act 4). Hamlet denies he loves her, and subjects her to a cruel tongue-lashing (Act 3). Use the pictures as a basis for telling Ophelia's story in a style you think appropriate.

Two gravediggers discuss Ophelia's death. They think she committed suicide, but is being allowed a Christian burial because of her high rank.

1 Two gravediggers – and a graveyard (in pairs)

The mood of the play switches abruptly to comedy – in a graveyard. Take parts and read lines 1–50. Then talk together about why you think Shakespeare makes this shift of place and atmosphere. Work out how you would set this scene, and decide how the gravediggers are dressed. In the 1993 Royal Shakespeare Company production, the first gravedigger (Clown) wore the top hat and black clothes of a funeral director.

2 Suicide

Lines 8–17 echo a famous Elizabethan law case: the suicide of Sir James Hales in 1554. Suicides were traditionally denied a Christian burial and forfeited their lands, but Sir James's widow took the case to court. In the court case there was much talk of the three parts of an act (lines 9–10) and whether Sir James went to the water or the water came to him.

Invent stage 'business' (actions) to accompany lines 13–17 as the Clown makes clear his meaning.

3 Mistakes show meaning (in small groups)

There are comic characters in other Shakespeare plays who similarly mangle the language and yet give insights into the central concerns of the play. Here, the first gravedigger (Clown) mistakes 'salvation' for damnation; '*se offendendo*' for *se defendendo* (self-defence); 'Argal' for *Ergo* (therefore). Discuss how all three expressions reflect something significant about *Hamlet*.

---

straight immediately, properly (as appropriate to a Christian burial)
crowner . . . her coroner has held an inquest
goodman delver gravedigger
will he, nill he willy-nilly (whether he wants to or not)

quest law law of inquests
countenance permission
even-Christen ordinary fellow Christians
Adam the first man
confess thyself – and be hanged (a proverb)

ACT 5   SCENE 1
A graveyard near the castle

Enter two CLOWNS (gravediggers)

CLOWN Is she to be buried in Christian burial, when she wilfully seeks
her own salvation?

OTHER I tell thee she is, therefore make her grave straight. The crowner
hath sat on her, and finds it Christian burial.

CLOWN How can that be, unless she drowned herself in her own   5
defence?

OTHER Why, 'tis found so.

CLOWN It must be *se offendendo*, it cannot be else. For here lies the
point: if I drown myself wittingly, it argues an act, and an act hath
three branches – it is to act, to do, to perform. Argal, she drowned   10
herself wittingly.

OTHER Nay, but hear you goodman delver –

CLOWN Give me leave. Here lies the water – good. Here stands the
man – good. If the man go to this water and drown himself, it is
will he, nill he, he goes – mark you that. But if the water come to   15
him, and drown him, he drowns not himself. Argal, he that is not
guilty of his own death shortens not his own life.

OTHER But is this law?

CLOWN Ay marry is't, crowner's quest law.

OTHER Will you ha' the truth on't? If this had not been a gentlewoman, 20
she should have been buried out o' Christian burial.

CLOWN Why, there thou sayst – and the more pity that great folk
should have countenance in this world to drown or hang themselves
more than their even-Christen. Come, my spade; there is no ancient
gentlemen but gardeners, ditchers, and gravemakers; they hold up   25
Adam's profession.

OTHER Was he a gentleman?

CLOWN A was the first that ever bore arms.

OTHER Why, he had none.

CLOWN What, art a heathen? How dost thou understand the scripture?   30
The scripture says Adam digged. Could he dig without arms? I'll
put another question to thee. If thou answerest me not to the
purpose, confess thyself –

201

*The gravedigger's question puzzles his mate; the answer praises
gravediggers. The gravedigger sings about becoming old. Hamlet
speculates on whose skull has been thrown out of the grave.*

The gravediggers, Royal National Theatre, 1987.

1 Two puzzles

a Who (or what or where) is Yaughan (line 50)? No one knows.
Invent a plausible suggestion ('stoup' = tankard).

b 'the hand of little employment hath the daintier sense'. Do you
think lines 58–9 mean that people who don't work have finer
feelings than those who do? Or that the less often you do
something, the more emotional impact it's likely to have on you?
Or is Hamlet echoing the player king's sentiments that custom
deadens the senses (as the previous line suggests: 'property of
easiness' = unworrying job)?

Go to! get on with it!
frame structure
unyoke stop work
Mass by the Mass
mend his pace go faster
behove enjoyment, advantage
meet better

jowls hurls
Cain killed his brother Abel (with
  a donkey's jawbone)
pate head
o'erreaches outwits
circumvent outwit

OTHER Go to!

CLOWN What is he that builds stronger than either the mason, the   35
shipwright, or the carpenter?

OTHER The gallows-maker, for that frame outlives a thousand tenants.

CLOWN I like thy wit well in good faith. The gallows does well, but
how does it well? It does well to those that do ill. Now, thou dost
ill to say the gallows is built stronger than the church; argal, the   40
gallows may do well to thee. To't again, come.

OTHER Who builds stronger than a mason, a shipwright, or a carpenter?

CLOWN Ay, tell me that, and unyoke.

OTHER Marry, now I can tell.

CLOWN To't.   45

OTHER Mass, I cannot tell.

Enter HAMLET *and* HORATIO *afar off*

CLOWN Cudgel thy brains no more about it, for your dull ass will not
mend his pace with beating; and when you are asked this question
next, say a grave-maker. The houses he makes lasts till doomsday.
Go, get thee to Yaughan, fetch me a stoup of liquor.   50

                                       [Exit Second Clown]

        In youth when I did love, did love,   *Song*

           Methought it was very sweet

        To contract-o the time for-a my behove,

           Oh methought there-a was nothing-a meet.

HAMLET Has this fellow no feeling of his business? A sings in   55
grave-making.

HORATIO Custom hath made it in him a property of easiness.

HAMLET 'Tis e'en so, the hand of little employment hath the daintier
sense.

CLOWN   But age with his stealing steps   *Song*   60

           Hath clawed me in his clutch,

        And hath shipped me intil the land,

           As if I had never been such.

        [Throws up a skull]

HAMLET That skull had a tongue in it, and could sing once. How the
knave jowls it to th' ground, as if 'twere Cain's jawbone, that did   65
the first murder. This might be the pate of a politician which this
ass now o'erreaches, one that would circumvent God, might it not?

HORATIO It might my lord.

The two skulls thrown out by the gravedigger provoke Hamlet to muse on mortality. He reflects that in spite of all a lawyer's legal documents entitling him to land, death is the only end.

1 Brooding on mortality

The gravedigger's casual throwing out of skulls prompts Hamlet to meditate upon death. The flattering courtier (lines 69–72) for all his breeding, finishes up with his bones used as mere skittles (line 77). A lawyer, for all his legal skills and documents, ends up in the grave. Hamlet uses many legal expressions in lines 83–94; most relate to legal documents (deeds) about buying land:

'quiddities/quillets' = small distinctions of meaning

'tenures' = renting property or land

'action of battery' = suing for assault

'statutes' = legal documents acknowledging debts

'recognizances' = kinds of statutes

'fines' = legal documents for freehold of land

'vouchers' = persons who warranted (vouched for) titles to land

'recoveries' = legal process of holding fines

'indentures' = joint agreements (each person kept half the document)

'conveyances' = deeds of land purchase.

Why does Hamlet use so much legal language? It may be to make the point that for all the complicated disputes about the ownership of land, all anyone finishes up with is the six feet of a grave. What do you think?

2 Hamlet's puns

The sentence in lines 89–90 contains four puns on the word 'fine'. Work out the meaning of each.

---

my Lady Worm's dead (belonging to worms)
chopless without jaws
mazard head
revolution change of fortune
breeding bringing up

loggets skittles (in the Elizabethan game, sticks were thrown at a post)
shrowding sheet funeral shroud
sconce head
They are sheep . . . in that people who believe in legal documents are stupid

HAMLET Or of a courtier, which could say 'Good morrow sweet lord,
　　　how dost thou sweet lord?' This might be my Lord Such-a-one,　　70
　　　that praised my Lord Such-a-one's horse when a meant to beg it,
　　　might it not?
HORATIO Ay my lord.
HAMLET Why, e'en so, and now my Lady Worm's, chopless, and
　　　knocked about the mazard with a sexton's spade. Here's fine　　75
　　　revolution, and we had the trick to see't. Did these bones cost no
　　　more the breeding but to play at loggets with 'em? Mine ache to
　　　think on't.
CLOWN　　　　　　A pickaxe and a spade, a spade,　　　　　　*Song*
　　　　　　　　　For and a shrowding sheet,　　　　　　　　　80
　　　　　　　　Oh a pit of clay for to be made,
　　　　　　　　　For such a guest is meet.
　　　　　　　　　[Throws up another skull]
HAMLET There's another. Why may not that be the skull of a lawyer?
　　　Where be his quiddities now, his quillets, his cases, his tenures, and
　　　his tricks? Why does he suffer this rude knave now to knock him　　85
　　　about the sconce with a dirty shovel, and will not tell him of his
　　　action of battery? Hum, this fellow might be in's time a great buyer
　　　of land, with his statutes, his recognizances, his fines, his double
　　　vouchers, his recoveries. Is this the fine of his fines and the recovery
　　　of his recoveries, to have his fine pate full of fine dirt? Will his　　90
　　　vouchers vouch him no more of his purchases, and double ones too,
　　　than the length and breadth of a pair of indentures? The very
　　　conveyances of his lands will scarcely lie in this box, and must
　　　th'inheritor himself have no more, ha?
HORATIO Not a jot more my lord.　　　　　　　　　　　　　　95
HAMLET Is not parchment made of sheepskins?
HORATIO Ay my lord, and of calves' skins too.
HAMLET They are sheep and calves which seek out assurance in that.
　　　I will speak to this fellow. Whose grave's this sirrah?
CLOWN Mine sir.　　　　　　　　　　　　　　　　　　　　100
　　　　　　　　　　(Sings)
　　　　　　　Oh a pit of clay for to be made
　　　　　　　　For such a guest is meet.
HAMLET I think it be thine indeed, for thou liest in't.
CLOWN You lie out on't sir, and therefore 'tis not yours. For my part,
　　　I do not lie in't, yet it is mine.　　　　　　　　　　　　105

The gravedigger's punning and playing with language prompt Hamlet to reflect on the way peasants imitate courtiers. The gravedigger reveals Hamlet is thirty years old.

1 Contemporary references? (in small groups)

Every writer reflects something of the age in which he or she lives. Shakespeare is no exception. His plays contain much evidence of the contemporary preoccupations of Elizabethan and Jacobean England. Several lines opposite would perhaps have been recognised by Shakespeare's audiences as wry comments on their own society.

lines 116–18 peasants are more and more ('this three years') imitating courtiers in language and behaviour

lines 123–31 all Englishmen are mad

lines 140–2 the sexually transmitted disease syphilis was an increasing feature of English life. Many were killed by the pox ('pocky corses').

Talk together about whether each of the three contemporary references above could amuse a modern audience today. Also discuss whether you think each represents a different type of humour, aimed at different social class sections of the audience.

2 Hamlet's age

Identify the two lines spoken by the gravedigger that establish Hamlet's age as thirty. Then consider whether you think of Hamlet as that age – or older or younger. How old do you think the following are: Gertrude? Claudius? Horatio? (See also pages 250–1.)

---

quick living
absolute precise, literal
by the card accurately (like a sailor with a compass card)
equivocation deliberate ambiguity, double meaning
picked over-refined

galls his kibe scuffs his chilblain (treads on his heels)
sexton gravedigger
laying in burial
tanner workman who turns animal skins to leather

HAMLET Thou dost lie in't, to be in't and say 'tis thine. 'Tis for the dead, not for the quick, therefore thou liest.

CLOWN 'Tis a quick lie sir, 'twill away again from me to you.

HAMLET What man dost thou dig it for?

CLOWN For no man sir.   110

HAMLET What woman then?

CLOWN For none neither.

HAMLET Who is to be buried in't?

CLOWN One that was a woman sir, but rest her soul she's dead.

HAMLET How absolute the knave is! We must speak by the card, or   115
equivocation will undo us. By the lord, Horatio, this three years
I have took note of it: the age is grown so picked, that the toe of
the peasant comes so near the heel of the courtier, he galls his kibe.
How long hast thou been grave-maker?

CLOWN Of all the days i'th'year, I came to't that day that our last King   120
Hamlet o'ercame Fortinbras.

HAMLET How long is that since?

CLOWN Cannot you tell that? Every fool can tell that. It was the very
day that young Hamlet was born, he that is mad and sent into
England.   125

HAMLET Ay marry, why was he sent into England?

CLOWN Why, because a was mad. A shall recover his wits there, or if
a do not, 'tis no great matter there.

HAMLET Why?

CLOWN 'Twill not be seen in him there. There the men are as mad as   130
he.

HAMLET How came he mad?

CLOWN Very strangely they say.

HAMLET How, strangely?

CLOWN Faith, e'en with losing his wits.   135

HAMLET Upon what ground?

CLOWN Why, here in Denmark. I have been sexton here man and boy
thirty years.

HAMLET How long will a man lie i'th'earth ere he rot?

CLOWN Faith, if a be not rotten before a die, as we have many pocky   140
corses nowadays that will scarce hold the laying in, a will last you
some eight year, or nine year. A tanner will last you nine year.

HAMLET Why he more than another?

Hamlet expresses disgust at the thought that Yorick, once so full of tricks and laughter, is now merely a skull. The physical corruption brings his mother (or women in general) to his mind.

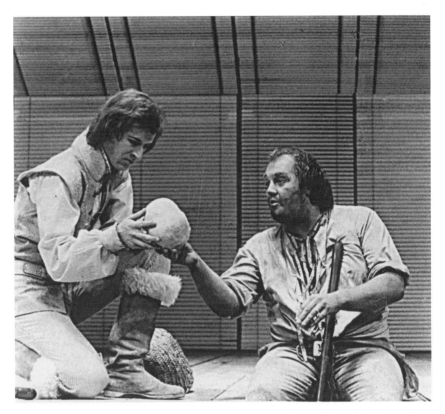

'Alas poor Yorick!' Lines 156–65 are the culmination of Hamlet's brooding on death and corruption. He holds in his hand the skull of his childhood companion, the jester Yorick, who was once so full of life.

hide skin
whoreson poxy (expressing contemptuous familiarity)
lien you lain
Rhenish Rhine wine
My gorge rises I am sickened
gibes jokes
were wont . . . roar made every-one at dinner laugh uproariously

chop-fallen miserable (down in the mouth)
favour appearance
Alexander Alexander the Great, conqueror who ruled a massive Empire (356–323 BC)
too curiously over-complicatedly

CLOWN Why sir, his hide is so tanned with his trade, that a will keep
out water a great while, and your water is a sore decayer of your   145
whoreson dead body. Here's a skull now: this skull hath lien you
i'th'earth three and twenty years.

HAMLET Whose was it?

CLOWN A whoreson mad fellow's it was. Whose do you think it was?

HAMLET Nay I know not.   150

CLOWN A pestilence on him for a mad rogue, a poured a flagon of
Rhenish on my head once. This same skull sir, was Yorick's skull,
the king's jester.

HAMLET This?

CLOWN E'en that.   155

HAMLET Let me see. [*Takes the skull.*] Alas poor Yorick! I knew him
Horatio, a fellow of infinite jest, of most excellent fancy, he hath
borne me on his back a thousand times – and now how abhorred
in my imagination it is! My gorge rises at it. Here hung those lips
that I have kissed I know not how oft. Where be your gibes now?   160
your gambols, your songs, your flashes of merriment that were wont
to set the table on a roar? Not one now, to mock your own grinning?
Quite chop-fallen? Now get you to my lady's chamber, and tell her,
let her paint an inch thick, to this favour she must come. Make her
laugh at that. – Prithee Horatio, tell me one thing.   165

HORATIO What's that my lord?

HAMLET Dost thou think Alexander looked o' this fashion i'th'earth?

HORATIO E'en so.

HAMLET And smelt so? Pah!   [*Puts down the skull*]

HORATIO E'en so my lord.   170

HAMLET To what base uses we may return, Horatio! Why may not
imagination trace the noble dust of Alexander, till a find it stopping
a bunghole?

HORATIO 'Twere to consider too curiously to consider so.

Hamlet reasons that death transforms great kings into trivial objects. A priest tells Laertes that Claudius's command has granted Ophelia a Christian funeral. As a suicide, the church would deny her burial.

1 Glory comes to dust

Write another four-line verse for Hamlet that expresses the sentiments of lines 175–83 ('with modesty enough' = without exaggeration; 'loam' = mortar; 't'expel' = to keep out; 'flaw' = wind).

2 Funeral procession (individually or in large groups)

How would you stage the entry of the funeral procession? Work out how each of the characters express their feelings. Page 267 shows how Ophelia's funeral was presented in film and stage versions of *Hamlet*.

3 The priest: harsh or sympathetic?

This is the priest's one appearance, and he has only thirteen lines. Imagine the actor asks you for advice. Take him carefully through his lines, explaining why he replies as he does to Laertes's angrily repeated question about why Ophelia is not receiving a full Christian burial.

For example, you could say whether you think the priest firmly believes in the Church's view of suicides (that they were damned to suffer eternally in hell). People taking their own lives were therefore not allowed to be buried on consecrated ground, and were denied the ritual of the Christian burial service. Consider whether you think the priest might try to soften that harsh ruling, and speak comfortingly to Laertes.

The actor is concerned that how he acts 'must be in full accord with the themes of the play'. How do you help him? You will find pages 258–9 will give you valuable background information.

---

maimèd rites incomplete ritual
Fordo destroy
estate high rank
Couch Hide
obsequies funeral rites
warranty authority
ground unsanctified
 unconsecrated ground

last trumpet doomsday
Shards pottery fragments
crants wreaths of flowers, garlands
strewments flowers strewn on the
 grave
sage requiem solemn music for
 the dead

HAMLET No faith, not a jot, but to follow him thither with modesty 175
enough, and likelihood to lead it, as thus: Alexander died, Alexander
was buried, Alexander returneth to dust, the dust is earth, of earth
we make loam, and why of that loam whereto he was converted
might they not stop a beer-barrel?

               Imperious Caesar, dead and turned to clay, 180
               Might stop a hole, to keep the wind away.
               Oh that that earth which kept the world in awe
               Should patch a wall t'expel the winter's flaw!
But soft, but soft! Aside – here comes the king,
The queen, the courtiers.

Enter CLAUDIUS, GERTRUDE, LAERTES, *and a coffin,* [*with* PRIEST]
              and LORDS *attendant*

                            Who is this they follow? 185
And with such maimèd rites? This doth betoken
The corse they follow did with desperate hand
Fordo it own life. 'Twas of some estate.
Couch we awhile and mark.   [*Retiring with Horatio*]
LAERTES What ceremony else? 190
HAMLET That is Laertes, a very noble youth. Mark.
LAERTES What ceremony else?
PRIEST Her obsequies have been as far enlarged
    As we have warranty. Her death was doubtful,
    And but that great command o'ersways the order, 195
    She should in ground unsanctified have lodged
    Till the last trumpet. For charitable prayers,
    Shards, flints, and pebbles should be thrown on her.
    Yet here she is allowed her virgin crants,
    Her maiden strewments, and the bringing home 200
    Of bell and burial.
LAERTES Must there no more be done?
PRIEST   No more be done.
    We should profane the service of the dead
    To sing sage requiem and such rest to her
    As to peace-parted souls.

Laertes insults the priest. Gertrude mourns Ophelia. Laertes curses Hamlet and leaps into the grave. Hamlet comes forward, and Laertes tries to strangle him. The attendants stop the fight.

1 Gertrude's wish (in pairs)

Talk together about how lines 210–13 add to your knowledge of Gertrude. Begin by telling each other whether her wish for Hamlet and Ophelia to marry came as a surprise to you.

2 In or out of the grave?

In some productions, Hamlet leaps into the grave and Laertes struggles with him there. The directors of these productions argue that the fight in the grave is highly symbolic. But other directors feel strongly that the stage direction '*Laertes climbs out of the grave*' must be obeyed.

Imagine you are directing the play. Decide whether Hamlet is to leap into the grave, where Laertes will fight him. Argue your case using evidence in the script and your view of Hamlet's character.

3 Brotherly love

Consider in turn each of the six sentences Laertes speaks opposite. For each, write two words expressing the emotional tone of the sentence (the first might be 'tender, loving').

4 Hamlet the Dane

'The Dane' usually means 'King of Denmark'. Hamlet therefore seems to be claiming the throne of Denmark. Suggest how he speaks line 225 and how each main character (Claudius, Gertrude, Laertes, Horatio) should react.

---

churlish ignorant
liest howling suffer in hell
decked decorated
most ingenious sense life
 (essential feeling)
quick living

Pelion/Olympus mountains in
 Greece
Conjures the wandering stars
 bewitches the planets
splenitive hot-tempered

LAERTES   Lay her i'th'earth,   205
    And from her fair and unpolluted flesh
    May violets spring. I tell thee, churlish priest,
    A ministering angel shall my sister be
    When thou liest howling.
HAMLET   What, the fair Ophelia!
GERTRUDE Sweets to the sweet, farewell.   [*Scattering flowers*]   210
    I hoped thou shouldst have been my Hamlet's wife.
    I thought thy bride-bed to have decked, sweet maid,
    And not t'have strewed thy grave.
LAERTES   Oh treble woe
    Fall ten times treble on that cursèd head
    Whose wicked deed thy most ingenious sense   215
    Deprived thee of. Hold off the earth awhile
    Till I have caught her once more in mine arms.
                    Leaps in the grave
    Now pile your dust upon the quick and dead
    Till of this flat a mountain you have made
    T'o'ertop old Pelion or the skyish head   220
    Of blue Olympus.
HAMLET [*Advancing*]   What is he whose grief
    Bears such an emphasis? whose phrase of sorrow
    Conjures the wandering stars, and makes them stand
    Like wonder-wounded hearers? This is I,
    Hamlet the Dane.
            [*Laertes climbs out of the grave*]
LAERTES   The devil take thy soul. [*Grappling with him*]   225
HAMLET Thou pray'st not well.
    I prithee take thy fingers from my throat,
    For though I am not splenitive and rash,
    Yet have I in me something dangerous
    Which let thy wisdom fear. Hold off thy hand.   230
CLAUDIUS Pluck them asunder.
GERTRUDE   Hamlet, Hamlet!
ALL   Gentlemen!
HORATIO Good my lord, be quiet.
                [*The Attendants part them*].
HAMLET Why, I will fight with him upon this theme
    Until my eyelids will no longer wag.

> *Hamlet rants that his love for Ophelia was infinitely greater than Laertes's, and that he can match any action, however improbable. He leaves with an enigmatic remark. Claudius takes control.*

1 'I'll rant as well as thou' (in pairs)

Why, in lines 236–51, does Hamlet rant so furiously against Laertes's love for his sister? Speak the lines to each other several times in an exaggerated way, using gestures. Then talk together about possible reasons for Hamlet's extravagant language. Also consider what his final two lines (lines 258–9) might mean.

2 Gertrude's doves

In lines 253–5, Gertrude says that Hamlet will become as meek as a dove whose yellow-feathered chicks have just hatched ('golden couplets are disclosed'). Do you think her lines are in character? Why do you think she uses this image rather than another?

3 What is in Claudius's mind? (in pairs)

Claudius has five sentences in lines 260–6. One partner speaks each sentence, pausing after each. In the pauses, the other partner voices Claudius's reasons for each sentence.

4 '*Exeunt*' – everyone leaves the stage (in small groups)

Invent a piece of stage business (an action) for each of the characters as they exit. Perhaps some actions take place over Ophelia's grave. Each character's wordless action expresses his or her feelings about what has happened in the scene. Make sure you include the gravedigger and the priest.

---

forbear him leave him alone
'Swounds by God's wounds
Woo't would you (wilt thou)
eisel vinegar
outface outdo
prate rant, bluster

our ground . . . zone the earth
  under our feet touches the sun
Ossa mountain in Greece
Hercules Greek god with huge
  strength and boastful manner
the present push immediate action
living lasting

GERTRUDE O my son, what theme?   235
HAMLET I loved Ophelia; forty thousand brothers
       Could not with all their quantity of love
       Make up my sum. What wilt thou do for her?
CLAUDIUS Oh he is mad Laertes.
GERTRUDE For love of God forbear him.   240
HAMLET 'Swounds, show me what thou't do.
       Woo't weep, woo't fight, woo't fast, woo't tear thyself?
       Woo't drink up eisel, eat a crocodile?
       I'll do't. Dost thou come here to whine,
       To outface me with leaping in her grave?   245
       Be buried quick with her, and so will I.
       And if thou prate of mountains, let them throw
       Millions of acres on us, till our ground,
       Singeing his pate against the burning zone,
       Make Ossa like a wart. Nay, and thou'lt mouth,   250
       I'll rant as well as thou.
GERTRUDE   This is mere madness,
       And thus awhile the fit will work on him;
       Anon, as patient as the female dove
       When that her golden couplets are disclosed,
       His silence will sit drooping.
HAMLET   Hear you sir,   255
       What is the reason that you use me thus?
       I loved you ever – but it is no matter.
       Let Hercules himself do what he may,
       The cat will mew, and dog will have his day.   *Exit*
CLAUDIUS I pray thee good Horatio wait upon him.   260
                           Exit Horatio

       (*To Laertes*) Strengthen your patience in our last night's
          speech;
       We'll put the matter to the present push. –
       Good Gertrude, set some watch over your son. –
       This grave shall have a living monument.
       An hour of quiet shortly shall we see,   265
       Till then in patience our proceeding be.
                             Exeunt

Hamlet tells Horatio how he could not sleep on the ship. He searched in Rosencrantz and Guildenstern's cabin for the letter from Claudius. It ordered that he should be executed immediately on arrival in England.

1 What have they just been talking about? (in pairs)

The scene begins with: 'So much for this sir, now shall you see the other . . .'. Discuss what you think Hamlet and Horatio have been talking about, then improvise an exchange lasting about one minute which leads into line 1.

2 'There's a divinity that shapes our ends . . .'
(in small groups)

'Divinity' may be the will of God, a kind of Christian fate that determines the direction of people's lives. Hamlet says that what happens to everyone in the end is decided by a divine force, however much a human may try to plan. An individual has very little real power over what he or she will become. Keep lines 10–11 in mind and discuss:

a whether Hamlet's fate in the play is shaped by a 'divinity', or whether he is in control of his own destiny

b whether you believe that 'there's a divinity that shapes our ends, rough-hew them how we will'. (Do you think that in spite of all your own planning and action, what will happen to you is already determined?)

c whether the two lines mark a development in Hamlet's character (that of Christian patience) that has not been evident before.

3 'Here's the commission'

Write the letter from Claudius ordering the immediate execution of Hamlet. Use lines 19–25 as your inspiration.

---

mutines in the bilboes mutineers in their chains
indiscretion instinct, intuition
pall go stale
Rough-hew roughly shape or plan
Fingered their packet stole their documents

in fine in conclusion
Larded decorated
Importing concerning
bugs and goblins . . . life horrors that would follow if I lived
supervise first reading
no leisure bated no time spared

ACT 5   SCENE 2
The Great Hall of Elsinore Castle

Enter HAMLET *and* HORATIO

HAMLET So much for this sir, now shall you see the other.
       You do remember all the circumstance?
HORATIO Remember it my lord!
HAMLET Sir, in my heart there was a kind of fighting
       That would not let me sleep. Methought I lay   5
       Worse than the mutines in the bilboes. Rashly,
       And praised be rashness for it – let us know,
       Our indiscretion sometime serves us well
       When our deep plots do pall, and that should learn us
       There's a divinity that shapes our ends,   10
       Rough-hew them how we will –
HORATIO   That is most certain.
HAMLET Up from my cabin,
       My sea-gown scarfed about me, in the dark
       Groped I to find out them, had my desire,
       Fingered their packet, and in fine withdrew   15
       To mine own room again, making so bold,
       My fears forgetting manners, to unseal
       Their grand commission; where I found, Horatio –
       O royal knavery! – an exact command,
       Larded with many several sorts of reasons,   20
       Importing Denmark's health, and England's too,
       With ho! such bugs and goblins in my life,
       That on the supervise, no leisure bated,
       No, not to stay the grinding of the axe,
       My head should be struck off.
HORATIO   Is't possible?   25
HAMLET Here's the commission, read it at more leisure.
       But wilt thou hear now how I did proceed?
HORATIO I beseech you.

Hamlet tells how he wrote a substitute letter commanding the execution of Rosencrantz and Guildenstern. He feels no remorse for their death.

---

1 Write Hamlet's letter

Hamlet describes the letter he wrote to send Rosencrantz and Guildenstern to their death. It contained an earnest 'conjuration' (entreaty) from Claudius to England as his faithful subject nation ('tributary'). Write the letter, 'fair' (in neat handwriting) using lines 31–47 as your guide. Seal it with wax and the imprint of a ring, or design your own seal ('palm' (line 40) refers to the palm tree whose leaves symbolise peace; 'a comma 'tween their amities' suggests that there is only a short break in the friendship of Denmark and England).

2 'They are not near my conscience' (in groups of three)

Hamlet sends Rosencrantz and Guildenstern to their death without a qualm of conscience. Talk together about whether Rosencrantz and Guildenstern deserve their fate. What does the decision to send his two 'friends' to their death and yet feel no remorse suggest to you about Hamlet's character?

3 Enact Hamlet's escape (in groups of four)

Tom Stoppard's play, *Rosencrantz and Guildenstern are Dead*, acts out lines 4–55 in which Hamlet describes how he engineered his escape from the ship, and how Rosencrantz and Guildenstern now head towards England in his place. The 1991 Zeffirelli film also shows the sequence (and the beheading of the two courtiers in England).

Take parts as narrator, Hamlet, Rosencrantz and Guildenstern. Create your own narrated mime to show the action described.

---

benetted round trapped and surrounded
Or . . . to my brains before I could alert my mind
statists politicians
yeoman's a loyal attendant's
debatement consideration
shriving time opportunity to confess their sins

ordinant directing, ordaining
Subscribed signed
gave . . . impression sealed it
insinuation devious intervention
pass thrust
fell incensèd points deadly sword points

HAMLET Being thus benetted round with villainies,
　　　　Or I could make a prologue to my brains,　　　　　　　　　30
　　　　They had begun the play. I sat me down,
　　　　Devised a new commission, wrote it fair.
　　　　I once did hold it, as our statists do,
　　　　A baseness to write fair, and laboured much
　　　　How to forget that learning; but sir, now　　　　　　　　35
　　　　It did me yeoman's service. Wilt thou know
　　　　Th'effect of what I wrote?
HORATIO　　　　　　　　　　　　Ay good my lord.
HAMLET An earnest conjuration from the king,
　　　　As England was his faithful tributary,
　　　　As love between them like the palm might flourish,　　　40
　　　　As peace should still her wheaten garland wear,
　　　　And stand a comma 'tween their amities,
　　　　And many suchlike as-es of great charge,
　　　　That on the view and knowing of these contents,
　　　　Without debatement further, more, or less,　　　　　　　45
　　　　He should those bearers put to sudden death,
　　　　Not shriving time allowed.
HORATIO　　　　　　　　　　　　How was this sealed?
HAMLET Why, even in that was heaven ordinant.
　　　　I had my father's signet in my purse,
　　　　Which was the model of that Danish seal;　　　　　　　50
　　　　Folded the writ up in the form of th'other,
　　　　Subscribed it, gave't th'impression, placed it safely,
　　　　The changeling never known. Now, the next day
　　　　Was our sea-fight, and what to this was sequent
　　　　Thou know'st already.　　　　　　　　　　　　　　　　55
HORATIO So Guildenstern and Rosencrantz go to't.
HAMLET Why man, they did make love to this employment.
　　　　They are not near my conscience. Their defeat
　　　　Does by their own insinuation grow.
　　　　'Tis dangerous when the baser nature comes　　　　　60
　　　　Between the pass and fell incensèd points
　　　　Of mighty opposites.
HORATIO　　　　　　　　　　　Why, what a king is this!

Hamlet argues that he is well justified in killing Claudius. He regrets his behaviour towards Laertes, seeing him as a fellow-revenger. Hamlet comments dismissively on Osric, and mocks him. Osric tells of a wager.

1 Reasons for revenge (in pairs)

Hamlet lists four reasons for revenge in lines 63–6: that Claudius has killed his father ('my king'), slept with his mother, pushed in front of Hamlet's own claim to the throne ('between th'election and my hopes'), and is plotting Hamlet's death.

Put the four reasons in order of importance to Hamlet, then discuss your own thoughts about their relative importance.

2 What is behind Horatio's words?

Does Horatio seem guarded in his reply at lines 71–2 to Hamlet's question about killing Claudius? Decide which of the following you think is most likely to explain Horatio's words:

a he doesn't agree with Hamlet's intention to kill Claudius

b he agrees with Hamlet, but is warning him of the risks

c some other motive – what?

3 Osric, 'this water-fly'

In lines 81–98, Shakespeare creates Osric's character by what is said about him, to him and by him. For example, 'let a beast . . . king's mess' suggests that however unworthy a man is, if he has wealth, he will be given a place ('a crib') at the king's banqueting table ('mess'). Consider each sentence in lines 81–98, and suggest the tone of voice in which you think each is said. Also decide on any suitable accompanying action to each sentence.

Does it . . . stand me now upon don't you think I now must
th'election the choosing of the king
angle fishing hook
cozenage deceit, trickery

canker of our nature disease of humanity
come/In further evil grow in more villainy
issue outcome
to say 'one' a brief moment
chough jackdaw

HAMLET Does it not, think thee, stand me now upon –
         He that hath killed my king, and whored my mother,
         Popped in between th'election and my hopes,   65
         Thrown out his angle for my proper life,
         And with such cozenage – is't not perfect conscience
         To quit him with this arm? And is't not to be damned
         To let this canker of our nature come
         In further evil?   70
HORATIO It must be shortly known to him from England
         What is the issue of the business there.
HAMLET It will be short. The interim's mine,
         And a man's life's no more than to say 'one'.
         But I am very sorry, good Horatio,   75
         That to Laertes I forgot myself,
         For by the image of my cause, I see
         The portraiture of his. I'll court his favours.
         But sure the bravery of his grief did put me
         Into a towering passion.
HORATIO   Peace, who comes here?   80

Enter young OSRIC

OSRIC Your lordship is right welcome back to Denmark.
HAMLET I humbly thank you sir. – Dost know this water-fly?
HORATIO No my good lord.
HAMLET Thy state is the more gracious, for 'tis a vice to know him.
         He hath much land and fertile; let a beast be lord of beasts, and   85
         his crib shall stand at the king's mess. 'Tis a chough, but as I say,
         spacious in the possession of dirt.
OSRIC Sweet lord, if your lordship were at leisure, I should impart a
         thing to you from his majesty.
HAMLET I will receive it sir with all diligence of spirit. Put your bonnet   90
         to his right use, 'tis for the head.
OSRIC I thank your lordship, it is very hot.
HAMLET No believe me, 'tis very cold, the wind is northerly.
OSRIC It is indifferent cold my lord, indeed.
HAMLET But yet methinks it is very sultry and hot for my complexion.   95
OSRIC Exceedingly my lord, it is very sultry, as 'twere – I cannot tell
         how. But my lord, his majesty bade me signify to you that a has
         laid a great wager on your head. Sir, this is the matter –

Osric praises Laertes as an outstanding model of a gentleman. He uses such affected language that Hamlet makes fun of him by responding in a style that is even more elaborate and obscure.

1 Without drawing breath

Hamlet clearly despises Osric's affected manner and language. In lines 106–12, Hamlet makes up words ('definement' = definition, 'inventorially' = as an inventory/list), uses pompous phrases ('the verity of extolment' = the truth of praising) and repeats himself ('a soul of great article' = the list of his attributes is long).

In the 1993 Royal Shakespeare Company production, Kenneth Branagh as Hamlet spoke the lines very quickly and utterly clearly, in a single breath. Try it yourself!

Osric, Royal Shakespeare Company, 1984.

excellent differences gifted accomplishments
soft society good manners
card or calendar guide or handbook
the continent . . . would see every attribute a gentleman seeks
perdition loss
yaw zig-zag
infusion qualities
dearth uniqueness
semblable only likeness
umbrage shadow
meed merit, achievements

HAMLET I beseech you remember.

[*Hamlet moves him to put on his hat*]

OSRIC Nay good my lord, for my ease in good faith. Sir, [here is newly   100
come to court Laertes; believe me an absolute gentleman, full of
most excellent differences, of very soft society and great showing.
Indeed, to speak feelingly of him, he is the card or calendar of
gentry, for you shall find in him the continent of what part a
gentleman would see.   105

HAMLET Sir, his definement suffers no perdition in you, though I know
to divide him inventorially would dozy th'arithmetic of memory,
and yet but yaw neither in respect of his quick sail. But in the verity
of extolment, I take him to be a soul of great article, and his infusion
of such dearth and rareness as, to make true diction of him, his   110
semblable is his mirror, and who else would trace him, his umbrage,
nothing more.

OSRIC Your lordship speaks most infallibly of him.

HAMLET The concernancy, sir? Why do we wrap the gentleman in our
more rawer breath?   115

OSRIC Sir?

HORATIO Is't not possible to understand in another tongue? You will
to't sir, really.

HAMLET What imports the nomination of this gentleman?

OSRIC Of Laertes?   120

HORATIO His purse is empty already, all's golden words are spent.

HAMLET Of him sir.

OSRIC I know you are not ignorant –

HAMLET I would you did sir, yet in faith if you did, it would not much
approve me. Well sir?]   125

OSRIC You are not ignorant of what excellence Laertes is.

[HAMLET I dare not confess that, lest I should compare with him in
excellence, but to know a man well were to know himself.

OSRIC I mean sir for his weapon; but in the imputation laid on him
by them, in his meed he's unfellowed.]   130

HAMLET What's his weapon?

OSRIC Rapier and dagger.

HAMLET That's two of his weapons, but well.

Osric tells of Claudius's wager: in a twelve-bout duel between Hamlet and Laertes, Laertes will not win three more bouts than Hamlet. Osric leaves, and Hamlet and Horatio exchange amused comments about him.

1 'How if I answer no?'

Experiment with different ways of speaking line 151: 'How if I answer no?'. For example, try it as if Hamlet does not want to fight the duel, or as if Hamlet doesn't care what happens, or with defiance. Try leaving a long pause between 'answer' and 'no' to experience the effect it makes.

Decide which style of speaking you think is most appropriate.

2 Osric's character

Horatio sees Osric as a precocious (very forward) juvenile: 'This lapwing runs away with the shell on his head'. A lapwing chick leaves its nest very shortly after hatching, often with parts of its shell still sticking to its head.

Hamlet suggests that no one else is likely to praise Osric ('there are no tongues else for's turn') so he does well 'to commend it (his duty) himself'. He compares him to a baby that 'did comply with his dug' (made a deal with his mother's breast). Hamlet goes on to say that Osric is typical of the flock ('bevy') of frothy, superficial people fashionable in these frivolous ('drossy') times. They burst like bubbles when they face some real test. The 'fanned and winnowed opinions' are the wise, carefully considered opinions that people like Osric simply ignore.

List Osric's character traits, finding lines to support your ideas. Try to think of someone in public life today who is like Osric.

Barbary Arab
impawned wagered
six French rapiers . . . and so
  equipment wagered by Laertes
liberal conceit fanciful decoration
edified by the margent
  enlightened by an explanation (as
  in the margin of a book)

germane relevant
hangers straps to hold swords to
  belts
vouchsafe the answer accept the
  challenge
the breathing exercise
yesty collection yeasty (frothy)
  brew, trivial people

OSRIC The king sir hath wagered with him six Barbary horses, against
the which he has impawned, as I take it, six French rapiers and   135
poniards, with their assigns, as girdle, hangers, and so. Three of
the carriages in faith are very dear to fancy, very responsive to the
hilts, most delicate carriages, and of very liberal conceit.

HAMLET What call you the carriages?

HORATIO I knew you must be edified by the margent ere you had done.   140

OSRIC The carriages sir are the hangers.

HAMLET The phrase would be more germane to the matter if we could
carry a cannon by our sides; I would it might be hangers till then.
But on, six Barbary horses against six French swords, their assigns,
and three liberal-conceited carriages – that's the French bet against   145
the Danish. Why is this impawned, as you call it?

OSRIC The king sir, hath laid sir, that in a dozen passes between yourself
and him, he shall not exceed you three hits. He hath laid on twelve
for nine. And it would come to immediate trial, if your lordship
would vouchsafe the answer.   150

HAMLET How if I answer no?

OSRIC I mean my lord, the opposition of your person in trial.

HAMLET Sir, I will walk here in the hall. If it please his majesty, it is
the breathing time of day with me. Let the foils be brought, the
gentleman willing, and the king hold his purpose, I will win for   155
him and I can. If not, I will gain nothing but my shame and the
odd hits.

OSRIC Shall I redeliver you e'en so?

HAMLET To this effect sir, after what flourish your nature will.

OSRIC I commend my duty to your lordship.   160

HAMLET Yours, yours.

[Exit Osric]

He does well to commend it himself, there are no tongues else for's
turn.

HORATIO This lapwing runs away with the shell on his head.

HAMLET A did comply with his dug before a sucked it. Thus has he,   165
and many more of the same bevy that I know the drossy age dotes
on, only got the tune of the time and outward habit of encounter,
a kind of yesty collection, which carries them through and through
the most fanned and winnowed opinions; and do but blow them
to their trial, the bubbles are out.   170

[Enter a LORD

225

A lord asks will Hamlet duel with Laertes now or later? Hamlet is ready. Horatio warns that he will lose, and offers to give his apologies, but Hamlet feels the time is ripe. He asks Laertes to pardon him.

1 Before the duel (in pairs)

Hamlet does not think he will lose the duel, but feels a kind of foreboding ('how ill all's here about my heart'). He is resolute, however, and sees 'special providence in the fall of a sparrow' (see Saint Matthew's Gospel). 'Providence' can mean 'foresight' or 'timeliness' or 'divine intention and care of God'. Hamlet seems ready to accept whatever fate has in store for him. Whether death comes sooner or later, it will come. What matters is the frame of mind to meet death: 'the readiness is all'. Since no one really knows the meaning of life, what does it matter to die early ('betimes')?

Talk together about Hamlet's mood(s) at this point in the play, then prepare a reading of lines 183–96. Experiment with ways of speaking. Is he level in tone and calm; determined and reflective; excited, changeable and foolhardy; uneasy but resolute? Or does he show a combination of these and other qualities?

2 What do you think? (in pairs or small groups)

Work through Hamlet's lines 192–6 a sentence at a time to see how far you agree with the point of view expressed in each sentence. You will find help in Activity 1 above.

3 Stage direction

Write notes and draw diagrams to show how you would perform the stage direction between lines 196–7.

---

commended him sent his compliments
attend await
play swordfence
In happy time just at the right time
gentle entertainment courteous greetings

at the odds according to the wager
gaingiving misgiving (gainsaying)
repair hither coming here
augury predictions of the future
betimes early
This presence everybody here
exception grievance, wish for revenge

LORD My lord, his majesty commended him to you by young Osric,
who brings back to him that you attend him in the hall. He sends
to know if your pleasure hold to play with Laertes, or that you will
take longer time.

HAMLET I am constant to my purposes, they follow the king's pleasure. 175
If his fitness speaks, mine is ready; now or whensoever, provided
I be so able as now.

LORD The king and queen, and all, are coming down.

HAMLET In happy time.

LORD The queen desires you to use some gentle entertainment to 180
Laertes, before you fall to play.

HAMLET She well instructs me.]

[Exit Lord]

HORATIO You will lose, my lord.

HAMLET I do not think so. Since he went into France, I have been in
continual practice; I shall win at the odds. But thou wouldst not 185
think how ill all's here about my heart – but it is no matter.

HORATIO Nay good my lord –

HAMLET It is but foolery, but it is such a kind of gaingiving as would
perhaps trouble a woman.

HORATIO If your mind dislike anything, obey it. I will forestall their 190
repair hither, and say you are not fit.

HAMLET Not a whit, we defy augury. There is special providence in
the fall of a sparrow. If it be now, 'tis not to come; if it be not to
come, it will be now; if it be not now, yet it will come – the
readiness is all. Since no man of aught he leaves knows, what is't 195
to leave betimes? Let be.

A table prepared, with flagons of wine on it. Trumpets, Drums and Officers
with cushions. Enter CLAUDIUS, GERTRUDE, LAERTES *and* LORDS, *with*
other Attendants with foils, daggers and gauntlets

CLAUDIUS Come Hamlet, come and take this hand from me.

[Hamlet takes Laertes by the hand]

HAMLET Give me your pardon sir, I've done you wrong;
But pardon't as you are a gentleman.
This presence knows, 200
And you must needs have heard, how I am punished
With a sore distraction. What I have done,
That might your nature, honour and exception
Roughly awake, I here proclaim was madness.

Hamlet claims that his madness, rather than he himself, was to blame for the death of Polonius. Laertes, with reservations, accepts Hamlet's apology. Hamlet praises Laertes's fencing skills. They choose rapiers.

1 Hamlet's apology (in groups of three or four)

Hamlet fulfils his mother's request to 'use some gentle entertainment to Laertes' (line 180) before the duel. Talk together about your views on each of the following statements:

a Hamlet's apology to Laertes is genuine and sincere

b Hamlet's explanation for his killing of Polonius ('madness') is false

c his claim that he has suffered from a 'sore distraction' (line 202) is untrue

d he seems to have forgotten the death of Ophelia

e he claims that chance and accident are to blame.

2 Laertes's reply: sincere or deceitful? (in pairs)

Laertes intends, secretly and treacherously, to kill Hamlet. But in lines 216–24, he says he is satisfied as far as natural feelings go ('in nature') but must obey a higher moral code (that of vengeance, his 'terms of honour') to keep his reputation pure ('name ungored'). He promises not to wrong Hamlet's love.

One person reads lines 216–24, pausing at each punctuation mark. In each pause, the other partner, as Laertes, says either 'true' or 'false', and explains what his secret thoughts really are at that moment.

3 The choosing of foils (in groups of four)

Write notes for the actors based on lines 231–8, to make the choosing of the foils as dramatically effective as possible. Remember that Laertes knows that one is poison-tipped. How will he make sure he gets the right rapier? Is Osric in on the plot to kill Hamlet?

---

tane taken
faction party
That I have shot . . . brother
  I have hurt you accidentally
some elder . . . honour qualified
  experts

voice . . . peace judgement in
  favour of reconciliation
Stick fiery off stand out brilliantly
bettered improved
likes me pleases me
all a length all the same length

Was't Hamlet wronged Laertes? Never Hamlet.   205
If Hamlet from himself be tane away,
And when he's not himself does wrong Laertes,
Then Hamlet does it not, Hamlet denies it.
Who does it then? His madness. If't be so,
Hamlet is of the faction that is wronged,   210
His madness is poor Hamlet's enemy.
Sir, in this audience,
Let my disclaiming from a purposed evil
Free me so far in your most generous thoughts,
That I have shot my arrow o'er the house   215
And hurt my brother.
LAERTES   I am satisfied in nature,
Whose motive in this case should stir me most
To my revenge; but in my terms of honour
I stand aloof, and will no reconcilement
Till by some elder masters of known honour   220
I have a voice and precedent of peace
To keep my name ungored. But till that time
I do receive your offered love like love,
And will not wrong it.
HAMLET   I embrace it freely,
And will this brother's wager frankly play.   225
Give us the foils, come on.
LAERTES   Come, one for me.
HAMLET I'll be your foil Laertes. In mine ignorance
Your skill shall like a star i'th'darkest night
Stick fiery off indeed.
LAERTES   You mock me sir.
HAMLET No, by this hand.   230
CLAUDIUS Give them the foils, young Osric. Cousin Hamlet,
You know the wager?
HAMLET   Very well my lord.
Your grace has laid the odds a'th'weaker side.
CLAUDIUS I do not fear it, I have seen you both.
But since he is bettered, we have therefore odds.   235
LAERTES This is too heavy, let me see another.
HAMLET This likes me well. These foils have all a length?

*Claudius orders wine and celebrations if Hamlet is successful. He will
drink a toast if Hamlet wins, and put a pearl in the wine. Hamlet makes
two hits. Claudius offers the poisoned cup but Hamlet declines to drink.*

1 The poisoned cup

Imagine you are directing a rehearsal of the play. You are asked two
questions by the actors: (i) Is Hamlet suspicious about the drink at line
260? (ii) How should Claudius say 'Gertrude, do not drink!' at line
268? Make your replies.

The duel. Choose a line from pages 231 or 233 as a suitable
caption for this moment.

stoups flagons, large jars (see stage direction, line 196)	**wary** watchful
quit win	**palpable** tangible, definite
ordnance cannons	**Stay** wait
union pearl	**fat** unfit, sweaty (or is Gertrude joking?)
kettle kettledrum	**carouses** drinks
without outside	

OSRIC Ay my good lord.

Prepare to play

CLAUDIUS Set me the stoups of wine upon that table.
If Hamlet give the first or second hit, 240
Or quit in answer of the third exchange,
Let all the battlements their ordnance fire.
The king shall drink to Hamlet's better breath,
And in the cup an union shall he throw
Richer than that which four successive kings 245
In Denmark's crown have worn. Give me the cups,
And let the kettle to the trumpet speak,
The trumpet to the cannoneer without,
The cannons to the heavens, the heaven to earth,
'Now the king drinks to Hamlet!' Come, begin, 250
And you the judges bear a wary eye.

Trumpets the while

HAMLET Come on sir.

LAERTES Come my lord.

They play

HAMLET One.

LAERTES No. 255

HAMLET Judgement.

OSRIC A hit, a very palpable hit.

LAERTES Well, again.

CLAUDIUS Stay, give me drink. Hamlet, this pearl is thine.
Here's to thy health.

Drum, trumpets sound, and shot goes off

Give him the cup. 260

HAMLET I'll play this bout first, set it by awhile.
Come.

[*They play*]

Another hit. What say you?

LAERTES A touch, a touch, I do confess't.

CLAUDIUS Our son shall win.

GERTRUDE   He's fat and scant of breath.
Here Hamlet, take my napkin, rub thy brows. 265
The queen carouses to thy fortune, Hamlet.

HAMLET Good madam.

CLAUDIUS Gertrude, do not drink!

Gertrude drinks from the poisoned cup. Laertes wounds Hamlet. In a scuffle, they exchange rapiers and Hamlet wounds Laertes. The queen falls and dies. Laertes reveals the treacherous plot.

1 Mortal wounds on Hamlet and Laertes (in pairs)

In many productions (at line 280) Laertes wounds Hamlet deceitfully, at a point in the duel that Hamlet thinks is an interval. Decide whether in your production you would have Laertes acting so dishonourably. Then, to make your decision clear to the audience, work out how you would stage the wounding of Hamlet by Laertes and the subsequent scuffle and wounding of Laertes by Hamlet.

2 The death of Gertrude: accident or suicide? (in pairs)

The queen dies by drinking from the poisoned cup that Claudius intended for her son. Every actor playing Gertrude thinks hard about whether she knows the cup is poisoned and whether her death is an accident or suicide (see line 269). One partner argues for Gertrude committing suicide. The other argues for Gertrude not knowing the drink is poisoned.

3 How does Claudius react?

Both Laertes and Gertrude reveal that treachery is at work. Gertrude says that she has been poisoned. Laertes says he has wounded Hamlet with a poisoned rapier and that the king is to blame. As the fingers of accusation point to Claudius, how will he react? Advise the actor on what he should do during lines 288–310.

---

pass thrust
make a wanton of me treat me as a spoilt child
incensed inflamed, mad, out of control

as a woodcock to mine own springe like a foolish bird, caught in my own trap
sounds swoons
Unbated and envenomed sharp and poisonous

GERTRUDE I will my lord, I pray you pardon me.
> [*Drinks*]

CLAUDIUS [*Aside*] It is the poisoned cup. It is too late. 270

HAMLET I dare not drink yet madam, by and by.

GERTRUDE Come, let me wipe thy face.

LAERTES My lord, I'll hit him now.

CLAUDIUS   I do not think't.

LAERTES And yet it is almost against my conscience.

HAMLET Come, for the third, Laertes. You do but dally. 275
> I pray you pass with your best violence.
> I am afeard you make a wanton of me.

LAERTES Say you so? Come on.
> *Play*

OSRIC Nothing neither way.

LAERTES Have at you now!   [*Wounds Hamlet*] 280
> *In scuffling they change rapiers*

CLAUDIUS Part them. They are incensed.

HAMLET Nay, come again.   [*Wounds Laertes*]
> [*Gertrude falls*]

OSRIC Look to the queen there, ho!

HORATIO They bleed on both sides. How is it my lord?

OSRIC How is't Laertes? 285

LAERTES Why, as a woodcock to mine own springe, Osric.
> I am justly killed with mine own treachery.

HAMLET How does the queen?

CLAUDIUS   She sounds to see them bleed.

GERTRUDE No, no, the drink, the drink – O my dear Hamlet –
> The drink, the drink – I am poisoned.   [*Dies*] 290

HAMLET Oh villainy! – Ho, let the door be locked!
> Treachery! Seek it out!
> [*Laertes falls*]

LAERTES It is here Hamlet. Hamlet, thou art slain,
> No medicine in the world can do thee good,
> In thee there is not half an hour of life – 295
> The treacherous instrument is in thy hand,
> Unbated and envenomed. The foul practice
> Hath turned itself on me; lo, here I lie,
> Never to rise again. Thy mother's poisoned –
> I can no more – the king, the king's to blame. 300

Hamlet wounds Claudius and forces him to drink from the poisoned cup. Claudius dies. Laertes forgives Hamlet, then dies. Hamlet prevents Horatio from suicide, and asks him to report his (Hamlet's) story.

---

1 'Treason, treason!'

In the BBC film, as Hamlet stabbed the king, Claudius spoke 'Treason, treason!'. The court remained silent, even though the script suggests that everyone on stage speaks the words (line 302). If you were directing the play, who would you have speaking the line? Remember, if you follow the script, even Horatio shouts 'treason'. Is that likely?

2 Images of death

Hamlet's line 315 refers to death as 'this fell sergeant' who is 'strict in his arrest'. Try to conjure up the image in your mind. Compare your image with that imagined by another student.

3 'A wounded name'

Hamlet forbids Horatio to take the poison and commit suicide. Rather, he wants Horatio to 'report me and my cause aright/To the unsatisfied' (those who do not know the full story). He wants to ensure that his 'name' (reputation) is favourably remembered.

Think of three reasons why Hamlet seems so concerned about his reputation. Choose four to six words that you think Hamlet would wish to be included in any description of him after his death. Then choose four to six words of your own to describe how you see Hamlet. Do the two lists of words match each other?

---

union precious pearl
is justly served gets his just deserts
tempered mixed
chance mischance
mutes silent watchers
fell cruel

antique Roman ancient Roman (who would commit suicide rather than live dishonestly)
ha't have it
Absent thee from felicity leave behind happiness

HAMLET The point envenomed too! Then, venom, to thy work!

Hurts the king

ALL Treason, treason!

CLAUDIUS Oh yet defend me friends, I am but hurt.

HAMLET Here, thou incestuous, murderous, damnèd Dane,
    Drink off this potion. Is thy union here?   305
    Follow my mother.   *King dies*

LAERTES   He is justly served,
    It is a poison tempered by himself.
    Exchange forgiveness with me, noble Hamlet.
    Mine and my father's death come not upon thee,
    Nor thine on me.   *Dies* 310

HAMLET Heaven make thee free of it! I follow thee.
    I am dead, Horatio. Wretched queen adieu.
    You that look pale, and tremble at this chance,
    That are but mutes or audience to this act,
    Had I but time, as this fell sergeant death   315
    Is strict in his arrest, oh I could tell you –
    But let it be. Horatio, I am dead,
    Thou livest; report me and my cause aright
    To the unsatisfied.

HORATIO   Never believe it.
    I am more an antique Roman than a Dane.   320
    Here's yet some liquor left.

HAMLET   As th'art a man,
    Give me the cup. Let go, by heaven I'll ha't.
    O God, Horatio, what a wounded name,
    Things standing thus unknown, shall live behind me!
    If thou didst ever hold me in thy heart,   325
    Absent thee from felicity awhile,
    And in this harsh world draw thy breath in pain
    To tell my story.

March afar off, and shot within
    What warlike noise is this?

Before dying, Hamlet declares Fortinbras is his choice as King of Denmark. Fortinbras wonders at the sight of so many dead bodies. The English ambassador tells that Rosencrantz and Guildenstern are dead.

In the 1991 Zeffirelli film, Hamlet dies beside his mother.
How would you stage Hamlet's death?

1 The sequence of deaths (in pairs)

The sequence of deaths is: Gertrude, Claudius, Laertes, Hamlet. Consider the dramatic effect if the sequence had been different. For example, imagine Shakespeare's fellow actors trying to persuade him to have Gertrude dying last of all. What might he reply?

---

warlike volley gunfire salute
o'ercrows triumphs over
prophesy . . . Fortinbras predict
 Fortinbras will be chosen as king
voice vote
occurrents more and less all the
 events

solicited brought about (my vote);
 Hamlet does not complete his
 sentence
aught anything
quarry heap of dead bodies
cries on suggests
toward being prepared
senseless without sense or feeling

OSRIC Young Fortinbras, with conquest come from Poland,
       To the ambassadors of England gives   330
       This warlike volley.
HAMLET   Oh I die, Horatio,
       The potent poison quite o'ercrows my spirit.
       I cannot live to hear the news from England.
       But I do prophesy th'election lights
       On Fortinbras; he has my dying voice.   335
       So tell him, with th'occurrents more and less
       Which have solicited – the rest is silence.   *Dies*
HORATIO Now cracks a noble heart. Good night sweet prince,
       And flights of angels sing thee to thy rest. –
       Why does the drum come hither?   340

Enter FORTINBRAS *and* ENGLISH AMBASSADORS, *with drum, colours
and Attendants*

FORTINBRAS Where is this sight?
HORATIO   What is it you would see?
       If aught of woe or wonder, cease your search.
FORTINBRAS This quarry cries on havoc. O proud death,
       What feast is toward in thine eternal cell
       That thou so many princes at a shot   345
       So bloodily hast struck?
I AMBASSADOR   The sight is dismal,
       And our affairs from England come too late.
       The ears are senseless that should give us hearing,
       To tell him his commandment is fulfilled,
       That Rosencrantz and Guildenstern are dead.   350
       Where should we have our thanks?

Horatio asks for the bodies to be placed on view, and says he will tell how the carnage came about. Fortinbras claims the throne of Denmark. He commands that Hamlet be carried with due ceremony to the platform.

1 'Carnal, bloody, and unnatural acts' (in small groups)

Either: Enact each incident (there are at least seven) in lines 359–64. Try each one in two ways: first, closely tied to the actual events in the play; second, freely, letting your imagination run.

Or: Write the outline of the story Horatio intends to tell, suggesting how he is likely to portray Hamlet, Claudius and Gertrude.

2 Denmark under Fortinbras

One production of *Hamlet* ended with the final line as an instruction for Horatio to be taken off and shot. Fortinbras was obviously going to rule Denmark as a tyrant. Work out how Fortinbras speaks his final nine lines to show what kind of king you think he will be.

3 Claudius or Hamlet? (in small groups)

In the Royal Skakespeare Company's 1993 production, Horatio pointed to Hamlet as he spoke 'He' in line 353. Talk together about why you think he chose to do this (rather than the conventional stage practice of pointing to Claudius). What does pointing at Hamlet rather than Claudius suggest about Horatio's character?

4 A fitting end?

Argue for and against ending the play at line 337 ('the rest is silence').

5 A final image (individually or in groups)

What is the final image an audience would see at the end of your production of *Hamlet*? Either make your own sketch or notes, or create a tableau of the last image the audience sees as the lights fade.

so jump upon at the very moment of	**vantage** good fortune
	presently immediately
judgements punishments	**wild** disturbed, uncertain
put on (line 362) brought about	**put on** (line 376) made king
forced cause distorted truths	**passage** funeral march
rights of memory (see 1.1.86–9, 102–4)	**rite** rituals
	peal of ordnance gun salute

HORATIO   Not from his mouth,
             Had it th'ability of life to thank you;
             He never gave commandment for their death.
             But since, so jump upon this bloody question,
             You from the Polack wars, and you from England,   355
             Are here arrived, give order that these bodies
             High on a stage be placèd to the view,
             And let me speak to th'yet unknowing world
             How these things came about. So shall you hear
             Of carnal, bloody, and unnatural acts,   360
             Of accidental judgements, casual slaughters,
             Of deaths put on by cunning and forced cause,
             And in this upshot, purposes mistook
             Fallen on th'inventors' heads. All this can I
             Truly deliver.
FORTINBRAS   Let us haste to hear it,   365
             And call the noblest to the audience.
             For me, with sorrow I embrace my fortune.
             I have some rights of memory in this kingdom,
             Which now to claim my vantage doth invite me.
HORATIO Of that I shall have also cause to speak,   370
             And from his mouth whose voice will draw on more.
             But let this same be presently performed,
             Even while men's minds are wild, lest more mischance
             On plots and errors happen.
FORTINBRAS   Let four captains
             Bear Hamlet like a soldier to the stage,   375
             For he was likely, had he been put on,
             To have proved most royal; and for his passage,
             The soldier's music and the rite of war
             Speak loudly for him.
             Take up the bodies. Such a sight as this   380
             Becomes the field, but here shows much amiss.
             Go bid the soldiers shoot.
             Exeunt marching, after the which a peal of ordnance are shot off

Looking back at the play
Activities for groups or individuals

1 What caused the tragedy?

Consider each of the following in turn and discuss how each contributes
to the tragedy of *Hamlet*:

a fate: the inevitable working out of destiny
b the supernatural: ghostly intervention
c the personality of Claudius
d the personality of Hamlet
e Denmark: is a corrupt society the major cause of the tragedy?
f the mischance of being captured by pirates.

2 Obituaries

The floor is littered with corpses at the end of the play – and others
have died earlier. Write the obituary of one dead character.

3 Point of view

Tell the last moments of the play from the point of view of either
Fortinbras, Horatio or Osric.

4 Fortinbras's first action

What will be Fortinbras's first political action as king? Make your
choice, then compare it with other students' choices. Can you agree on
his most probable action?

5 Casting the play

One of the most important tasks in any production is casting the play:
choosing actors for each part. First, make a list of the qualities you
think each of the major characters possesses. Second, cast the play
(from actors, fellow students or other people you know). Choose a role
that you yourself would you like to play. Why?

6 Newspaper report

As a newspaper reporter write the story of what has happened at
Elsinore in Act 5 Scene 2. Your readers want an exciting read. Your
editor wants an accurate, truthful account. You have thirty minutes to
produce your copy.

7 The most interesting question

What is the question you would most like to ask each of the following: Hamlet, Claudius, Gertrude, Shakespeare, the gravedigger? Write a separate question for each. Then pool all your questions in the class. Decide which are most interesting. Answer them in role!

8 Time-scale

Draw a 'time-line' plotting the sequence of events in the play

9 How have they changed?

Follow one character through the play. Draw a chart or diagram showing in detail how they change in the course of the action.

10 Most . . . to least

Make several lists of the names of all the characters in the play so that they range from 'most' to 'least' along a number of scales. Remember that often there is no right answer, but some answers can be more firmly justified in the script than others. Analyse your lists to find what connections you feel exist between them. Here are some 'scales', but invent your own.

youngest .... oldest

most likeable .... least likeable

most moral ('good') .... least moral ('bad')

person with whom I most identify ... least identify with

most decisive .... least decisive

most reliable .... least reliable

11 Survey your class

Design a short questionnaire to find out what your fellow students think about certain aspects of *Hamlet*. You could investigate their attitudes to characters, involvement with the story, identification of 'most liked'/'least liked' scenes, and so on. Feed back the results of your survey to the class as a whole.

12 Modern relevance

Make a list of all the things you would say to include in an argument that *Hamlet* is relevant to today's world.

The world of Elsinore

Millions of words in thousands of books and articles have been written on *Hamlet*. They stand in ironic contrast to Hamlet's final words 'The rest is silence'. The character of Hamlet himself has attracted most critical commentary. In the nineteenth century he appealed to the romantic melancholic mood and was constructed as the noble doomed hero. In the second half of the twentieth century more attention has been given to his contradictions and unpleasantness: a man who can speak great poetry yet revile a young woman, stab her father in a sudden violent moment, and send two old friends to their death without a twinge of conscience.

There is something sponge-like about *Hamlet*. It absorbs the interests and anxieties of any culture and any age. When 'squeezed out' in performance and criticism it renders back those interests and preoccupations as abstracts and brief chronicles of the time. Just as Hamlet described the purpose of playing as to show 'the very age and body of the time his form and pressure', so every society reproduces *Hamlet* to mirror itself. Thus a Rumanian production in the late 1980s portrayed Denmark as a totalitarian police state in Eastern Europe. A German production in the 1970s presented Ophelia as a Bader-Meinhof terrorist. And in the 1960s the Royal Shakespeare Company's Hamlet was a contemporary student, complete with long college scarf.

Because of the infinite variety of *Hamlet*, it is a battlefield of conflicting interpretations. Each claims its own view of the play is 'right', but each one is filtered through the ideologies of the times. Those ideologies may be political, religious, literary or aesthetic. The greatness of *Hamlet* is that it bears and outlives every interpretation, offering itself for fresh interpretations in each generation.

The next three pages give just **one** interpretation ('reading') of the play against which you can test your own reading. It is a 'committed interpretation' that focuses mainly on the world of *Hamlet*: the society in which the characters are set. Work through the 'committed interpretation' that follows. Argue with it sentence by sentence. Find out how much you agree or disagree with it, using evidence from the script to support your own interpretation. Remember: the next three pages give only one point of view!

'Denmark's a prison': one point of view

The play is set in a politically and culturally interconnected Europe: Denmark, Norway, Poland, France, Germany, England. Elsinore is not a remote backwater, but a vital strategic place in European political and social life. Its young aristocrats are educated at Wittenberg University, and it claims England as one of its dependent states, subdued by bloody combat (Act 4 Scene 3, lines 54–60).

But Claudius's Denmark is insecure. When the play opens it is a country feverishly preparing for war. The nervous anxiety of that preparation is evident in the very first words spoken: 'Who's there?'. Barnardo, the relieving sentry, mistakenly challenges Francisco, when military discipline requires Francisco to challenge the newcomer. When the Ghost appears, it may be a visitor from the supernatural world, but its meaning is political: 'It bodes some strange eruption to our state' (Act 1 Scene 1, line 69).

There are echoes of an older, feudal world of the dead fathers (old Hamlet and old Fortinbras) who settled disputes by personal combat guided by a chivalric code ('law and heraldry'). But that older society of honour is giving way to the new world of Claudius. He is a smooth negotiator, an efficient unscrupulous schemer who prepares for war but settles territorial quarrels by dispatch of ambassadors and formal treaties. He is truly a 'politician' of the type Hamlet reviles in the graveyard: 'one that would circumvent (outwit) God' (Act 5 Scene 1, line 67).

The people of Denmark barely appear in the play, but Claudius increasingly sees them as a threat to his rule. They are 'the distracted multitude', 'the rabble', 'false Danish dogs' who favour Hamlet, or who call for Laertes to be king. All such unreliable people must be closely watched, even more so those like Hamlet, who are a direct threat to Claudius's rule. It would be dangerous to allow Hamlet to return to Wittenberg, so Claudius refuses permission. He keeps Hamlet under surveillance at home, with the devious words: 'Here, in the cheer and comfort of our eye' (Act 1 Scene 2, line 116). That comforting eye will shortly employ two of Hamlet's close friends to spy on him. When Hamlet tells Rosencrantz and Guildenstern 'Denmark's a prison' (Act 2 Scene 2, line 234), he is not simply speaking metaphorically.

The chief minister of state, Polonius, is a willing instrument of Claudius's desire to keep his subjects under surveillance. In the England of Queen Elizabeth I, Polonius's equivalent was Lord Burghley who also believed in close surveillance to maintain order.

Just as Burghley maintained an extensive network of spies, so Polonius is infected by the same desire to overhear in secret, to keep all potential dissidents under surveillance. He spies on Hamlet, using his own daughter as bait. Even his own family must be watched. Though Polonius utters conventional decencies to Laertes ('these few precepts'), he sets a spy on his own son. It is hardly surprising that rumours circulate in Denmark. After the death of Polonius there is no shortage of 'buzzers' (rumour-mongers) to infect Laertes's ears.

For all the ordered formalities of Claudius's court and the seemingly close domesticity of Polonius's family, a sense of corruption grows throughout the play. 'Something is rotten in the state of Denmark' says Marcellus (Act 1 Scene 4, line 90), and the stench of decay at the heart of personal and social life increasingly infects the language. The madness that Hamlet assumes and into which Ophelia descends is the individual symptom of a deeper social malaise. Hamlet projects his disgust onto a variety of targets: Claudius, his mother's or Ophelia's sexuality, death itself. But his words mirror the deeper social corruption that pervades Denmark: 'foul deeds', 'maggots', 'carrion', 'offal', 'rank corruption mining all within', 'the ulcerous place', 'an unweeded garden'. However civilised are outward appearances, the routine oppressions of a police state prevent truly human growth.

The two women in the play are little more than pawns in a patriarchal world of sexual exploitation. Gertrude has been 'taken to wife' by Claudius. Just as he has seized Denmark, so too he appropriates her body. His description of her as 'Th'imperial jointress to this warlike state' (Act 1 Scene 2, line 9) merely acts as a further legitimation of his claim to Denmark's throne. She has no real power, but is a possession to be fought over by king and prince, husband and son. Ophelia is even more of an object manipulated by men. Her brother lectures her, seeking to control her sexuality. Her father uses her as bait in a spy trap, like a farmyard animal: 'I'll loose my daughter to him' (Act 2 Scene 2, line 160). Hamlet takes out on her all his misogyny (hatred of women). The masculine brutalities of Denmark quite literally drive her mad.

Hamlet's Denmark is like the England of Shakespeare's own time. It is a transitional society between an older world of feudalism and an emerging new world of bourgeois capitalism. The historical England and the fictional Denmark stand between the unquestioned loyalties of a hierarchical chivalric code and the unfettered individualism that seeks to maximise both profits and desires. Hamlet, with his reflective self-questioning, is as much a modern man as a Renaissance prince. His preoccupation with notions of sin and salvation shows he is the product of a feudal world where religion is used as an instrument of control. But his style of thought marks him out as a true individual. He is trapped in this changing world and subject to its contradictions. Hamlet can both reflect 'What a piece of work is a man!' (Act 2 Scene 2, line 286) and casually dismiss Rosencrantz and Guildenstern to their deaths.

His personal vendetta against Claudius is in reality a struggle for political power, just as Claudius's murder of old Hamlet was a political assassination. Such political struggles mirrored the anxieties of Shakespeare's England. Elizabeth's reign might have seemed on the surface to be stable and secure, but it was always subject to dangerous threats of overthrow by a powerful faction of the nobility. Like every writer, Shakespeare reflects the social conditions of his own times.

At the end of the play, Fortinbras and his army take over. This is not the harmonious end of a domestic tragedy, with order restored by a benevolent ruler. Rather, it is the brutal *realpolitik* of a society that, at base, rests on the dominance of a state by a small but militarily powerful minority. The voice of the people will be as stifled under Fortinbras as it was under Claudius.

The 'quietus' (peace) that Hamlet finally achieves in death might represent private fulfilment, but it is politically empty and futile. Such a way of coming to terms with death is an ideological mystification that masks the harsh realities of political and social life in Hamlet's Denmark.

A warning

The interpretation offered on pages 243–5 comes with a warning. Although it does express a view of the play that some people hold, it is not the only view, nor is it the single 'right' view. It is unlike everything else in this edition of the play because it neglects other viewpoints in claiming its particular reading of *Hamlet* is true. So treat it with great caution, criticise it, argue with it, and sort out how much or how little you agree with it. You will be able to work out your own view by arguing with it. It will also help you to form your own opinion of the social and political world of the play by making up and answering questions of all types. For example: does Gertrude make any political decisions? What will be Fortinbras's first action as king? Is Fortinbras right when he says: 'For he was likely, had he been put on, To have proved most royal' (Act 5 Scene 2, lines 376–7) – would Hamlet have made a good king?

The character of Hamlet

'You would pluck out the heart of my mystery.' Hamlet's words to Guildenstern describe what thousands of books and articles have tried to do since *Hamlet* was first performed. But his character remains elusive. Hamlet plays many roles throughout the play: alienated outsider, potential suicide, actor, swordsman, joker, friend of Horatio, angry son, blood-thirsty revenger, lacerating self-critic. His mood swings from depression to elation, from extreme self-loathing to quiet acceptance of his fate in 'the readiness is all'. Hamlet's complex character continues to fascinate, because it is impossible to pin down its infinite variety.

Hamlet has been seen as an ironic commentator on mortality and sin; a man with acute sexual problems; a genuine madman; a clever impersonator of madness; a man tortured by irreconcilable moral dilemmas; an unhappy adolescent; a puritanical fundamentalist; a dreamer; a philosopher; a truly noble prince.

Copy and complete the spider diagram, using as many words and phrases as you can think of to describe the character of Hamlet. Afterwards group the qualities according to common or related elements. Are there dominant character traits?

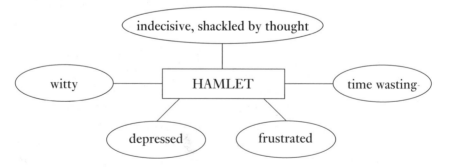

Hamlet's delay?

Hamlet is a son sworn to avenge his father's murder. Yet not until the final moments of the play does he finally kill Claudius. Is he, as Laurence Olivier's film presented him, 'a man who could not make up his mind' – a procrastinator? Some reasons for Hamlet's procrastination may be: he does not believe in vengeance and is held back by Christian conscience; he is genuinely unbalanced and cannot bring himself to act; he gets caught up in playing a madman, and that 'antic disposition' takes him over; he is a prey to melancholy. But perhaps he does not delay at all; he carries out the revenge of his father's death as soon as is reasonably possible, and even at the moment of killing Claudius, he faces the accusation of treason from everyone else on stage.

Talk together about whether you think Hamlet really does procrastinate when it comes to his revenge. Give reasons for your view.

Four portrayals of Hamlet. Which comes closest to your own image of him?

Hamlet's sexual identity

What is Hamlet's attitude towards the two women in the play? Some productions have suggested that Hamlet is sexually obsessed by his mother. Other productions imply that he truly loved Ophelia. Almost every possibility about Hamlet's sexuality has been explored on stage, on film and in print, as the following views suggest:

An Oedipus complex? Hamlet is in love with his mother, and is violently jealous of Claudius, his stepfather. This 'Oedipus complex' makes him unable to have a loving relationship with Ophelia, whom he treats badly. His hatred for Claudius is based on sexual jealousy, since Claudius has not only usurped his father's crown, but also his mother's bed.

A puritan? Hamlet is severely puritanical about love and love-making. He is appalled by what he sees as the lust that drives the relationship between Claudius and Gertrude. His disgust at his mother's sexuality makes him despise all women. Ophelia is a victim of this loathing as Hamlet subjects her to virulent verbal abuse full of sexual innuendo.

A true lover? Hamlet genuinely loves Ophelia. He urges her to go to a nunnery to escape the torturous, prison-like nature of love in the world that Denmark represents. His harsh words cover his deep love for her, and he is being 'cruel only to be kind'.

An immature boy? Hamlet is unready for love. His sexual bantering with Polonius, Rosencrantz and Guildenstern is immature male behaviour. He is unable to understand his mother's sexual life or to appreciate Ophelia's innocent and more mature affection for him.

A split personality? Hamlet both loves and hates Ophelia, and simultaneously admires and abhors his mother. His sexual feelings for Ophelia and his mother fight against his other feelings. His reason attempts to reconcile these sexual and emotional tensions, but thought itself makes him unable to act.

Private love versus public office? Hamlet's sexual confusion arises not from his personality but from his position as prince of Denmark. He may not 'choose for himself' in marriage but must think first of his responsibility to the country.

Find two or more quotations from the script to support each of the above viewpoints. Arrange the six interpretations in order of reasonableness to you, using the evidence in the play.

Hamlet: a tragic hero?

'Tragedy' is the conventional description of a play that portrays human suffering and the decline and death of a hero or heroine. Traditionally the hero (or heroine) was of high status, and the fall from grace immense. But some modern tragedies, like Arthur Miller's *Death of a Salesman,* have an ordinary person as their 'tragic hero'. To help your thinking about Hamlet's character, consider the following interpretations of Hamlet as a tragic hero:

Tragic flaw? The hero's downfall is caused by a 'tragic flaw' or blemish in character. Hamlet's weakness may be that he 'thinks too much' and cannot make up his mind. The resulting inaction leads to his death. But Hamlet's 'tragic flaw' ('vicious mole in nature' Act 1 Scene 4, line 24) may be some other feature in his character responsible for his downfall.

A tragedy of fate? The hero has no real control over his destiny. Once the spring of Hamlet's tragic narrative is released, it unwinds inevitably towards its conclusion: the death of Hamlet. His fate is predetermined. As Hamlet says, 'There's a divinity that shapes our ends . . . '

A tragedy of chance? Accident and bad luck determine the fate of the hero. The unplanned chance encounter with the pirate ship, for example, brings Hamlet back to Denmark. Hamlet accidentally kills Polonius. The tragic hero is the victim of random uncertainty.

Irreconcilable opposites? The hero's character comprises irreconcilable sets of forces. Hamlet's mind and feelings are filled with such tensions: reason battles with passion; love is contrasted with lust; action is inhibited by thought. Hamlet struggles with a wish to die and an urge to live. *Hamlet* can be read as the tragedy of a man trapped between such contraries.

Hero as paragon? The tragic hero has an excess of virtues. This nineteenth century Romantic view of Hamlet as a Renaissance prince suggests that he is more noble and refined than ordinary people, and that his nobility and purity carry the seeds of their own destruction. Hamlet cannot live in the world because he is too 'good' for it. His sensitivity and noble qualities lead to his downfall.

Find evidence (quotations or actions in the play) to support each of the above viewpoints. Decide which interpretation you favour most. Then write your own view of Hamlet as a tragic hero.

Young Hamlet?

The very first mention of Hamlet in the play is as 'young Hamlet'. A number of features create the impression of a youthful Hamlet. He seems faced with familiar problems of adolescence: relations with the opposite sex, coming to terms with responsibility, finding one's own personality. He has problems with his mother and stepfather, and with coming to terms with the death of his own father. In Shakespeare's day, university students like Hamlet were much younger than today's undergraduates.

On stage Hamlet has often been played by youthful-looking actors. The tradition is to portray him as being in his late twenties or thirties. Richard Burbage, the first actor ever to play Hamlet (in 1601) was thirty-four when he created the role. But some actors have played the part when they were well past forty. Sarah Bernhardt, a French actress, played him when she was fifty-six. In the eighteenth century, Thomas Betterton played the part when he was over seventy.

It is not necessary to be bound by 'factual' evidence in the script that strongly suggests he is thirty (see Act 5 Scene 1, lines 120–38). A director can choose which age to present Hamlet (and other characters) according to his or her interpretation of the play. Decide what age you would choose to present Hamlet if you were directing the play. Give reasons for your decision, remembering how it will affect the age of other characters.

A play for young people?

Some hints are given above why *Hamlet* is relevant to young people today. Other reasons for contemporary appeal can be suggested:

- Hamlet's rebellious, 'misunderstood' nature
- his struggle against adult vices and deceptions
- his awareness of the need for honour and propriety
- he feels he is surrounded by 'these tedious old fools'
- he desperately seeks some outlet for his feelings
- his constant self-questioning, seeking his own identity and the meaning of what he sees and experiences
- he is not sure who to trust and feels some of his friends betray him
- he suspects he is constantly being watched by his elders.

Either : Imagine you are seeking funds to mount a production of *Hamlet* that will tour schools and youth centres. You have found a potential sponsor who has assured you she will give you the money you need provided you can convince her that *Hamlet* is relevant to young people today. Argue your case.

Or: Write an idea for a script in which some of the themes in *Hamlet* are embodied in a scene or play for people of your age. Rehearse and perform it, either live or on tape.

Sarah Bernhardt, 1899.

Master Betty, a thirteen-year-old actor who was a famously successful Hamlet in 1804–05.

Mark Rylance, 1988.

Phil Bowen, 1978

Revenge Tragedy

Revenge Tragedy was hugely popular when Shakespeare began his play-writing career. The central feature of each Revenge play was a hero (or villain) who sought to avenge a wrong. Largely influenced by the Roman dramatist Seneca, Elizabethan playwrights served up a rich diet of madness, melancholy and revenge. In the ten years before *Hamlet* was performed, enthusiastic crowds flocked to see Thomas Kyd's *The Spanish Tragedy*, Marlowe's *Jew of Malta*, and Shakespeare's *Titus Andronicus*.

Elizabethan Revenge Tragedy contained typical ingredients: a melancholy hero/avenger; a hesitating avenger (without hesitation the play would be over too quickly); a villain who was to be killed in revenge; complex plotting; murders (usually from sexual motives) and other physical horrors; a play-within-a-play; sexual obsession and lust related to the passion for revenge; a ghost who calls for revenge; real or feigned madness; the death of the revenger. The plays were usually set in Italy or Spain, but the Elizabethans seemed able to relate the wider themes of each play to their own world.

The typical structure of a Revenge Tragedy had five parts:

- *exposition* usually by a ghost (providing motivation for revenge)
- *anticipation* in which detailed planning of the revenge takes place
- *confrontation* between avenger and intended victim
- *delay* as the revenger hesitates to perform the killing
- *completion* of the revenge (often with the death of the revenger)

Hamlet has four revenge plots. Hamlet vows to revenge his father's death at the hands of Claudius. Laertes swears to avenge **his** father's death at the hands of Hamlet. Fortinbras seeks to avenge **his** father's death at the hands of King Hamlet. Another son seeking revenge is Pyrrhus: he slaughters Priam, whose son had killed Pyrrhus's father.

Hamlet has many elements of Elizabethan Revenge Tragedy. Merely telling the story makes it sound very sensational: eight deaths, a mad woman, a fight in a grave, and so on. But *Hamlet* has outlived most other revenge plays and is still immensely popular. Why? Use the information given above to identify in what ways *Hamlet* can be regarded as an Elizabethan Revenge Tragedy. Then suggest reasons why *Hamlet* continues to hold great appeal, after almost 400 years.

The morality of revenge

Today, many people consider revenge immoral because it takes the law into its own hands. It is seen as a profoundly unsocial act. But it seems to be a very human impulse: to exact retribution from someone who has done wrong to you or your family. Revenge follows the Old Testament maxim 'an eye for an eye, a tooth for a tooth'. Revenge is still central to some criminal 'codes of honour' (for example, the 'vendetta' among the Sicilian mafia).

In Shakespeare's time, revenge was a crime in law, and was also an irreligious act. For the Church of the late sixteenth century, revenge was considered a sin. The revenger's soul was damned, condemned to suffer everlasting torment in hell. That thought preoccupies Hamlet for much of the play.

Talk together about your views on the following statements:

- revenge is always wrong
- *Hamlet* is not so much a revenge play as a play about revenge
- the play suggests that revenge does not pay
- *Hamlet* is more a tragedy than a revenge play: its focus is on the fall of a hero rather than on the execution of a pledge to revenge
- the revenge plot of *Hamlet* is one of the least important elements in the play.

Francis Bacon on revenge

Francis Bacon, a contemporary of Shakespeare, called revenge 'a kind of wild justice'. In an essay on revenge in 1625 he wrote:

> The most tolerable sort of revenge is for those wrongs which there is no law to remedy, but then let a man take heed the revenge be such as there is no law to punish; else a man's enemy is still beforehand, and it is two for one. Some, when they take revenge, are desirous the party should know whence it cometh. This is the more generous. For the delight seemeth to be not so much in doing the hurt as in making the party repent ... This is certain, that a man that studieth revenge keeps his own wounds green, which otherwise would heal and do well. Public revenges are for the most part fortunate, as that for the death of Caesar. But in private revenges it is not so. Nay rather, vindictive persons live the life of witches, who, as they are mischievous, so end they infortunate.

Write a reply to Bacon. Begin 'In Hamlet's case . . . ', and argue the points Bacon makes in his essay. Alternatively, write a reply that argues with Bacon's position from your own point of view.

An earlier version of *Hamlet*

Shakespeare may have based *Hamlet* on a twelfth-century revenge story about an early Prince of Denmark: Amleth. The tale appears in an early sixteenth-century book that Shakespeare probably knew, Saxo Grammaticus's *Historiae Danicae*:

> Amleth's father defeats the King of Norway in a duel, but is murdered by his own brother Feng, who marries his brother's widow, Gerutha. Amleth plans revenge, but to divert suspicion from his plan to kill Feng. Amleth starts behaving as a madman, but his language is such a mixture of cleverness and craziness that he is tested in various ways. In the first test, 'a fair woman' is sent to him, with the purpose of finding out if he will behave normally towards her. He reveals to her that he is really sane, but he makes her swear she will not reveal his secret. Next, one of Feng's friends hides in Amleth's mother's bedroom in order to overhear what Amleth says to his mother. Amleth senses he is being spied upon, kills the spy, and feeds his body to the pigs, piece by piece. Amleth strongly condemns his mother for not being faithful to her first husband's memory, but so swiftly marrying Feng after being widowed. Feng becomes even more suspicious of Amleth and plots to kill him by sending him to England with two servants. The servants bear a secret instruction from Feng to the King of England ordering Amleth's immediate death. Amleth steals the messengers' document and re-writes it, ordering their deaths. He also adds a request that the daughter of the English king should marry Amleth. Eventually Amleth returns to Denmark – to discover his own funeral is taking place! He battles successfully with members of Feng's court, destroys the palace by fire, finds Feng in bed – and kills him. Afterwards, Amleth hides, uncertain how the people of Denmark will view his deeds. At last, Amleth comes out of hiding and makes a public speech to defend and justify what he has done. The people are delighted, feeling that Amleth has freed them from tyranny. They declare Amleth as king. Amleth has a long and victorious reign, ending only when he is killed in battle.

Identify some of the major changes and additions Shakespeare made to Saxo's story in writing *Hamlet*. Try to suggest reasons for these changes. For example, do some of Shakespeare's changes make for greater dramatic effect?

Revenge: novel, film or television

Many modern novels, films or television plays are based on the theme of revenge: for example, some cowboy westerns, mafia or gangster movies. Write a brief outline of a modern revenge story or play, using a number of elements from *Hamlet*. Then write in full the opening chapter of the story, or the first scene of the play.

Hamlet the revenger. Alan Howard in the Royal Shakespeare Company's 1970 production.

Madness and melancholia

Madness is a major theme of the play. The following activities will help your understanding of the major questions that are often raised about madness in *Hamlet*.

1 Why does Hamlet 'put an antic disposition on'? Talk together about the following possible reasons why Hamlet decides to act strangely:

- to observe Claudius more easily behind the mask of madness
- to speak more freely and critically as a 'madman' or 'fool'
- because others will speak more openly to him as a madman
- because only by pretending madness can he achieve revenge
- because Shakespeare is re-telling an old story (see page 254)
- because that is the only way he can cope with his emotions
- some other reason.

2 Do you think Hamlet really is mad at any point during the play or just pretends madness throughout?

3 Consider in turn: Claudius, Gertrude, Polonius, Ophelia, Horatio, Rosencrantz and Guildenstern. Write a paragraph for each character giving their answer with reasons to the question 'Is Hamlet mad?'. Then write Hamlet's own answer to that question.

4 Today, doctors and psychiatrists rarely use the words 'mad' or 'lunacy'. Instead, they use such expressions as 'manic–depression' (violent mood swings), 'schizophrenia' (deranged perceptions and emotions), 'suffering from a nervous breakdown', 'psychotic' (suffering from delusions, dangerously out of contact with reality), 'emotionally disturbed', 'mentally ill'. Choose one of these modern descriptions and write a report on Hamlet under that heading.

5 'Though this be madness, yet there is method in't' says Polonius about Hamlet's language (Act 2 Scene 2, line 200), meaning there is a kind of sense in what Hamlet says. Could his words apply equally to Ophelia's distracted language? Read through all that Ophelia says in Act 4 Scene 5 and suggest why she speaks as she

does. Afterwards, talk together about why you think she has been driven into actual madness.

6 The language of madness? Find four examples of where you think Hamlet speaks 'madly'. Say why you think Hamlet uses each. For example, if you think 'Get thee to a nunnery' (Act 3 Scene 1, line 119) is an example, what might he mean?

Albrecht Dürer's engraving of 'Melancholia' (1514). Dürer's engraving has often been used in programmes for stage productions of *Hamlet*. Discuss why you think it is frequently chosen as a powerful picture to illustrate the play.

7 An Elizabethan medical text described the symptoms of melancholy: 'sad and fearful . . . distrust, doubt, diffidence or despair, sometimes furious, and sometimes merry . . . sardonian (sardonic), and false laughter . . . every serious thing for a time, is turned into a jest, and tragedies into comedies' (Timothy Bright, *Treatise on Melancholy*, 1586). How accurately does this describe Hamlet?

Sin and salvation

In Shakespeare's day the threat of hell and eternal damnation was much more sharply felt than it is today. Many Elizabethans were obsessed by what would happen to them after death. They believed that one of three possibilities awaited them. If they died in a state of grace, with all their sins confessed, they would go to heaven and enjoy eternal peace. If none of their sins was confessed and forgiven they would go to hell and endure eternal suffering. The third possibility was purgatory, where those who had not made full confession would go. There they suffered until their unconfessed sins were burnt away (purged). Suicides were bound for hell in whatever state they died.

Hamlet explores this obsession with the afterlife. In his first soliloquy Hamlet longs for the peace of death ('O that this too too solid flesh would melt'), but recognises that suicide is forbidden by God ('Or that the Everlasting had not fixed his canon gainst self-slaughter'). In his 'To be, or not to be' soliloquy, he broods on the uncertainty of knowing what will happen after death. It is 'the dread of something after death' that makes us endure the oppressions of life (Act 3 Scene 1, lines 56–82).

Later in the play, Ophelia is denied the full rites of Christian burial because it is thought she has taken her own life ('Her death was doubtful'). The priest at her funeral says that only Claudius's command prevented what she should properly receive as a suicide: not 'charitable prayers', but 'shards, flints and pebbles should be thrown on her'. Such was the pronouncement of the church on suicides.

The Ghost tells how he suffers in purgatory: 'confined to fast in fires, till the foul crimes done in my days of nature are burnt and purged away' (Act 1 Scene 5, lines 11–13). Because he died without having a chance to confess his sins, he must undergo torment before he can earn a place in heaven, reconciled to God. But Hamlet cannot be sure whether the Ghost is good or bad: 'Be thou a spirit of health, or goblin damned' (Act 1 Scene 4, line 40).

The question of whether the Ghost is to be trusted or not haunts Hamlet for much of the play. It reflects the Elizabethan view that some ghosts were benign, others evil, tempting humans to behave badly and so damn themselves to an afterlife of torment in hell. Hamlet fears what he has seen may be 'a devil' who 'Abuses me to damn me'.

To test whether it is a 'damned ghost' sent to lure his own soul to eternal damnation, Hamlet contrives the play in which he hopes to 'catch the conscience of the king'. When Claudius reveals his guilt by his reaction to the mousetrap play, Hamlet is convinced the Ghost has spoken true: 'I'll take the ghost's word for a thousand pound' (Act 3 Scene 2, line 260).

Hamlet's delay in avenging his father's murder can be partly explained by his beliefs about sin and salvation. Shortly after the play scene, Hamlet finds Claudius at prayer. The fact that Claudius is praying stops Hamlet from instantly killing the king. Hamlet's own father suffers after death because Claudius killed him at a moment when he was unprepared for heaven, not having confessed his sins. Now Hamlet wishes Claudius to experience the same horrible suffering after death. He therefore sheaths his sword and decides to wait, to catch Claudius at a moment 'That has no relish of salvation in't'. That moment will be when Claudius is committing a sin: 'drunk asleep, or in his rage, Or in th'incestuous pleasure of his bed, At game a-swearing' (Act 3 Scene 3, lines 89–91). Killing him at such a moment, when he has no thoughts of heaven in his mind, will surely send Claudius to hell, to eternal damnation. Ironically, as Claudius reveals , the king has not been successfully praying at all: 'My words fly up, my thoughts remain below. Words without thoughts never to heaven go' (Act 3 Scene 3, lines 97–8).

Dr Johnson, an eighteenth-century essayist, poet and Shakespeare critic, believed Hamlet's thoughts when he found Claudius at prayer 'too terrible to be read or uttered'. Johnson's view influenced productions for over a hundred years. Hamlet's speech (Act 3 Scene 3, lines 73–96) was either cut in performance or was interpreted as not expressing Hamlet's real intentions, but simply an excuse to procrastinate, to delay the action.

What do you think?

1 Talk together about what you think of Dr Johnson's view in the preceding paragraph.

2 Consider in turn each of the following: Polonius, Rosencrantz and Guildenstern, Ophelia, Laertes, Gertrude, Claudius. Imagine you are Hamlet and write a paragraph about each of the characters saying whether you feel responsible for his or her death, whether each one deserved his or her death, and what you think will happen to each character after death.

The language of *Hamlet*

1 Soliloquies

Hamlet is famous for his soliloquies. A soliloquy is a kind of internal debate spoken by a character who is alone on stage (or believes himself or herself to be alone). Soliloquies reveal the character's true thoughts and feelings. Hamlet's soliloquies give the impression of a man discovering what he thinks as he speaks.

a Consider each of Hamlet's soliloquies in turn (pages 23, 49, 95, 105, 133, 139 and 169). Find different 'voices' for Hamlet as he engages in a conversation with himself as:

- a bloodthirsty revenger
- a reflective philosopher, trying to reason unemotionally
- a self-critical actor, commenting on his own performance
- an ironical observer
- an observer disgusted with the human condition
- someone who desperately wishes to take a decision.

b Select one of Hamlet's soliloquies and work out a dramatic presentation of it. You could share the lines around your group, and have several persons echoing key lines or phrases in unison. Try speaking it as a conversation, or to the audience, or to a portrait of another character, or to a stage property. Experiment with possible styles of delivery, for example, as a radio broadcast complete with sound effects, or a dialogue of inner voices.

2 Questions

Hamlet is a play full of questions. Barnardo's opening challenge 'Who's there?' symbolises the questioning tone that characterises the whole play. Virtually everyone in the play wishes to find something out. On almost every page questions are asked. Hamlet himself is insistently self-questioning.

Choose any page at random. Identify the questions on that page, and check how many are answered. Repeat the activity for several more pages. Decide which questions can be easily answered, and which cannot. Then make up a few questions of your own about the play. Try to answer them in a small group. Put any you cannot answer to the class as a whole.

3 Doubling language: a cause of delay?

Hamlet is the longest of Shakespeare's plays. One way of explaining the length is that Hamlet procrastinates (puts off the killing of Claudius). The theme of procrastination is embodied in the language:

a Repetition of words or phrases: for example 'tush, tush', 'Speak, speak', 'too too solid flesh'.

b The use of 'and' to achieve a doubling effect. For example, in Horatio's explanation of Denmark's war preparations (Act 1 Scene 1, lines 80–107) he uses 'law and heraldry', 'comart and carriage', 'hot and full', 'here and there', 'food and diet', 'strong hands and terms compulsatory', 'post-haste and romage'.

Search through the play for examples of these two 'doubling' devices. Talk together about their dramatic effect and how they provide insights into character and situation.

4 Hamlet: the listener

Hamlet is a great listener. He listens intently to what is said to him and often seizes on a word or phrase to construct his own reply. His very first words: 'A little more than kin, and less than kind' (Act 1 Scene 2, line 65), imply that Claudius is too presumptuous in calling him 'son' (kin), and that his nature (kind) is unlike Claudius's. His next line 'I am too much i'the sun' puns on Claudius's 'son'. His following two replies to Gertrude pun ironically on her use of 'common' and 'seems'. Hamlet revels in how the slipperiness of language gives potential for bitter or comic puns or ironic retorts. He uses puns to great effect, picking up a speaker's words and giving them back with a different meaning. The Gravedigger is the only other character in the play to use this style of 'deliberate misunderstanding'. He gives Hamlet a taste of his own medicine.

a Identify examples of this linguistic technique of Hamlet's. Against which characters does he use it most frequently?

b Hamlet not only listens carefully to others. He listens intently to himself and comments on his own thoughts. Find the soliloquies in which he comments on his own thoughts and feelings (for example, with self-disgust or reproof).

5 Imagery: 'the dawn in russet mantle clad'

Hamlet abounds in imagery: vivid words and phrases that conjure up emotionally-charged mental pictures in the imagination ('He would drown the stage with tears'). They carry powerful significance, far deeper than their surface meanings. They enrich both particular moments ('the slings and arrows of outrageous fortune . . . a sea of troubles') and the themes of the play such as appearance and reality, madness, revenge, delay, sin and salvation, friendship and faithlessness. An image cluster that appears very frequently throughout the play illuminates the related themes of corruption and disease, pain and suffering, death, and disorder in nature. Here, the imagery expresses that 'something is rotten in the state of Denmark', usually either as a simile: 'These words like daggers enter in my ears', or as a metaphor: 'Denmark's a prison'.

Choose one of Hamlet's soliloquies and pick out the imagery it uses. Find a powerful way of displaying your findings (perhaps as a set of drawings, a collage, or a poem or story of your own).

6 'Thee' and 'you'

In Shakespeare, as a general rule, 'thou/thee' tend to be used by family members to each other, to indicate warmth of affection, or to social inferiors. 'You' tends to be a rather cold and distant way of addressing someone. Trace through Act 3 Scene 4 to see how Gertrude and Hamlet use the words as an indication of their feelings towards each other. But remember Shakespeare never sticks slavishly to a rule!

7 Verse and prose

A rough rule of thumb in Shakespeare is that low-status and comic characters speak prose and aristocrats speak verse. But in *Hamlet* there are plenty of exceptions to that questionable rule. Context is more important. Thus the players (low-status) speak verse in the Gonzago play (to emphasise they are playing aristocratic characters). Hamlet and Ophelia (high-status) express madness in prose. Another consideration is that verse is more suitable than prose to moments of high dramatic or emotional intensity. So 'serious' scenes are likely to be in verse, 'comic' episodes in prose.

But Shakespeare was never afraid to break a rule or convention. Hamlet's 'What a piece of work is a man' (Act 2 Scene 2, lines 286–91) is in prose, but it has all the qualities claimed for poetry.

Find several examples of where characters speak in prose in the play. Put forward arguments about why you think Shakespeare gave them prose at those moments.

8 'A' = 'he'

You will find throughout the play that characters often use 'a' for 'he'. The first example is in Act 1 Scene 1 when Barnardo says of the Ghost 'Looks a not like the king?' (line 43). Most editions of the play substitute 'he' throughout, but in this edition we keep 'a' because we think it represents the commonly used informal slurred pronunciation of Shakespeare's time (and, to some extent, of our own time). Do you think it would be advisable to change 'a' to 'he' throughout? Why?

9 What did Shakespeare write?

Shakespeare probably wrote *Hamlet* around 1601. But for two reasons there is a problem of knowing exactly what he wrote (let alone what he intended). First, he was a playwright, and undoubtedly had second thoughts as he worked with his fellow-actors rehearsing and performing the play. Second, there are three versions of the play, from which all later editors make their choices as they prepare their own edition for publication.

The First Quarto (Q1: the 'bad quarto'), published in 1603 and thought to be a pirated (unauthorised) version, put together by some actors and sold for a quick profit. It has 2,154 lines.

The Second Quarto (Q2: the 'good quarto'), published in 1604 and thought to be Shakespeare's response to the 'bad quarto', in order to establish the 'correct' version. It has 3,674 lines.

The First Folio (F1), published in 1623. This is thought to be Shakespeare's version of the play to make it even more suitable for the stage. But remember that Shakespeare died in 1616, and the First Folio was compiled seven years later by two of his fellow actors (see page 268). It has 3,535 lines (including 83 that do not appear in Q2).

Some lines of the script are in square brackets [ ]. These are the lines in Q2 that were cut out of F1. It is generally believed that Shakespeare cut these lines to make a more actable version of the play. Find several of the sections in square brackets (for example pages 39–40, 153 and 193). Discuss what might have been Shakespeare's reasons for cutting them. But remember – no one can be certain that Shakespeare himself in fact did so! Would you cut the lines in performance? Give reasons for your decision.

Theatre and acting in *Hamlet*

'The play's the thing … '. *Hamlet* richly displays Shakespeare's interest in his own profession as actor and playwright, and the London theatres at the end of the reign of Queen Elizabeth I. *Hamlet* is an intensely theatrical play, with many references to playing and acting. Play acting is concerned with a puzzle that obsesses Hamlet: the difference between appearance and reality, truth and falsehood. Hamlet uses a company of travelling players to perform a stage murder. The performance traps Claudius into revealing his guilty conscience: a fiction has discovered the truth of the Ghost's story (which is, of course, itself a fiction).

The play resonates with the language of theatre: 'play', 'act', 'show', 'perform', 'applaud', 'prologue', 'shape' (costume), and 'part'. Hamlet's soliloquies are like an actor reflecting on the part he has to play. He sees the players as 'the abstract and brief chronicles of the time', and the purpose of acting as holding 'the mirror up to nature'. For Hamlet, the function of drama is to portray the nature of society: 'to show virtue her own feature, scorn her own image, and the very age and body of the time his form and pressure'.

Shakespeare seized every opportunity to exploit the potential of theatrical performance. The play is filled with highly dramatic scenes: the Ghost's five appearances; Hamlet's raging at Ophelia and Gertrude; the dumb-show; the fight in the grave. The final scene has abundant theatrical opportunities and references: the duel between Hamlet and Laertes; the many deaths, witnessed by çmutes or audience to this act'; the entry of Fortinbras (preceded by '*March afar off, and shot within*'); Horatio's 'give order that these bodies high on a stage be placed to the view'; Fortinbras's order that 'four captains bear Hamlet like a soldier to the stage'; and the final stage direction: '*Exeunt marching, after the which a peal of ordnance are shot off*'.

a Identify moments or scenes that provide opportunities to create striking theatrical effects. Select one and work out how you would stage it for maximum dramatic impact. Then stage it!

b Collect words in the play about actors, acting or the theatre. Use them to write an essay (or dialogue in question and answer form) on '*Hamlet* is a tragedy dominated by the idea of the play'.

'The tragedians of the city'

On several occasions, Shakespeare's own company of players was forced to tour when plague closed the London theatres. The players' appearance at Elsinore echoes the experience of troupes of London actors as they toured the English provinces or continental Europe. On tour they performed in the great halls of country houses or on makeshift stages in inn-yards or town squares.

Around the time Shakespeare wrote *Hamlet*, an acting company of boy players was enjoying great success in London. For a short time these 'little eyases' (unfledged hawks) threatened the livelihood of some adult professional acting companies. The adult players were forced to tour because they could not attract London audiences. Hamlet's exchanges with Rosencrantz and Guildenstern in Act 2 Scene 2, lines 295–333, are thought to be about these boy players and the 'war of the theatres' (see page 84). For a short time, there was intense rivalry between adult companies as their resident playwrights mocked each other in their plays ('much throwing about of brains').

The members of Shakespeare's acting company (The King's Men, originally The Lord Chamberlain's Men) worked together closely for over twenty years. They knew each other very well and may have contributed to Shakespeare's script. Because of his fascination with acting, Shakespeare may have put into *Hamlet* private jokes and theatrical references that would have amused his fellow players at the Globe on London's Bankside:

1.5.152 'You hear this fellow in the cellarage' (the space under the Globe stage?)

1.5.97 'this distracted globe' (the Globe Theatre? Hamlet's head? the world?)

3.2.91 'I did enact Julius Caesar' (the actor who played Polonius may well have created the role of Julius Caesar written by Shakespeare shortly before *Hamlet*)

2.2 .284–5 'this majestical roof fretted with golden fire' (the sky, or the painted 'heavens' of the Globe's stage?)

2.2.386–91 'thy face is valanced (bearded) since I saw thee last'; 'Pray God your voice . . . be not cracked' (Was Shakespeare joking at his fellow actor's changed appearance, and the thought that the boy actor who played the female parts would all too soon grow up?).

A mirror up to nature

One of the reasons that *Hamlet* has fascinated people for nearly 400 years is that it has relevance in every age. It reveals not only important aspects of Hamlet's Denmark or Shakespeare's England, but also today's society. *Hamlet* affords opportunities to appraise the nature of society in our own time as well as in Shakespeare's.

Identify several ways in which *Hamlet* portrays significant features of each of the following: Hamlet's Denmark; Shakespeare's England; your own society today. Then discuss whether you think Shakespeare was a moralist: a playwright who believed he had a moral duty to write about important issues ('necessary questions') of the day.

Hamlet's advice to the players

Remind yourself of Hamlet's advice to the players on pages 111–13. Then try one or more of the following:

a 'Suit the action to the word.' Take any line at random from the play and act it out in accordance with Hamlet's advice. Are some actions more suitable than others?

b Hamlet suggests there are in any audience 'the judicious' (educated, knowledgeable people), and 'the unskilful' and 'barren' (ignorant, merely fun-loving). He says that actors should always play to 'the judicious' and not play to the gallery by making the 'unskilful' and 'barren' laugh. What do you think this view suggests about Hamlet's (or Shakespeare's) character? Do you think it is good advice to actors?

The players vanish

The players disappear after performing their play in Act 3. They are never again seen in *Hamlet*. What happens to them? Write the memoirs of either the player king or the player queen as they look back at that night in Elsinore and what happened in the months following.

'And all for Hecuba': the power of theatre

Hamlet is fascinated by the player's tears as he speaks about Hecuba (see pages 92–5). Here is an actor weeping for a fictitious character in a play! Talk together about why you think the 'make-believe' of theatre can affect some people so powerfully. You might begin by asking: 'Why do people pay money to go to see a play that can make them weep?'.

Hamlet on film and on stage. Two representations of the funeral of Ophelia. Talk together about the differences between Shakespeare on film and Shakespeare in the theatre. Then work out how you would present Ophelia's funeral (or another scene of your choice) on film and on stage.

William Shakespeare 1564–1616

1564 Born Stratford-upon-Avon, eldest son of John and Mary Shakespeare.

1582 Marries Anne Hathaway of Shottery, near Stratford.

1583 Daughter, Susanna, born.

1585 Twins, son and daughter, Hamnet and Judith, born.

1592 First mention of Shakespeare in London. Robert Greene, another playwright, described Shakespeare as 'an upstart crow beautified with our feathers …'. Greene seems to have been jealous of Shakespeare. He mocked Shakespeare's name, calling him 'the only Shake-scene in the country' (presumably because Shakespeare was writing successful plays).

1595 A shareholder in 'The Lord Chamberlain's Men', an acting company that became extremely popular.

1596 Son Hamnet dies, aged eleven.
Father, John, granted arms (acknowledged as a gentleman).

1597 Bought New Place, the grandest house in Stratford.

1598 Acted in Ben Jonson's *Every Man in His Humour*.

1599 Globe Theatre opens on Bankside. Performances in the open air.

1601 Father, John, dies.

1603 James I grants Shakespeare's company a royal patent: 'The Lord Chamberlain's Men' became 'The King's Men' and played about twelve performances each year at court.

1607 Daughter, Susanna, marries Dr John Hall.

1608 Mother, Mary, dies.

1609 'The King's Men' begin performing indoors at Blackfriars Theatre.

1610 Probably returned from London to live in Stratford.

1616 Daughter, Judith, marries Thomas Quiney.
Died. Buried in Holy Trinity Church, Stratford-upon-Avon.

The plays and poems
(no one knows exactly when he wrote each play)

1589–1595 *The Two Gentlemen of Verona, The Taming of the Shrew, First, Second and Third Parts of King Henry VI, Titus Andronicus, King Richard III, The Comedy of Errors, Love's Labour's Lost, A Midsummer Night's Dream, Romeo and Juliet, King Richard II* (and the long poems *Venus and Adonis* and *The Rape of Lucrece*).

1596–1599 *King John, The Merchant of Venice, First and Second Parts of King Henry IV, The Merry Wives of Windsor, Much Ado About Nothing, King Henry V, Julius Caesar* (and probably the *Sonnets*).

1600–1605 *As You Like It, Hamlet, Twelfth Night, Troilus and Cressida, Measure for Measure, Othello, All's Well That Ends Well, Timon of Athens, King Lear.*

1606–1611 *Macbeth, Antony and Cleopatra, Pericles, Coriolanus, The Winter's Tale, Cymbeline, The Tempest.*

1613 *King Henry VIII, The Two Noble Kinsmen* (both probably with John Fletcher).

1623 Shakespeare's plays published as a collection (now called the First Folio).